DISCARD

DATE DUE

Table of Contents

Introduction

by Harold D. Lasswell

American political science is becoming less narrowly centered on North America and Europe, and more global and systematic in scope. Stephens' analysis of Peru impressively exemplifies both tendencies.

The author turns the spotlight directly on the land-based power elite of Peru, and contrary to many analysts of the situation, concludes that the fundamental fact is a continuing class bipolarity in which the landed class has retained its dominant position. Stephens has accepted the challenge that must be met by all ruling class analyses and has tested this interpretation by examining the history of land reform down to 1968.

The most distinctive feature of the treatment of Peruvian politics is an "operational code" designed to summarize the characteristic strategies by which the elite has succeeded in retaining its authority and control. He does not mince words in describing deeds. Rule No. 16, for instance, is "Direct use of force to protect elite interests is often easier and more effective than attempting quieter exercise of power." Or Rule No. 17: "Reject the 'idea of Peru,' for the Peruvian nation exists only marginally to the interests of the Clan which are first and foremost economic and financial."

In many ways the most vivid material about the perspectives of the power elite comes from the papers and proceedings of seminars conducted by Dr. Stephens for over a hundred Peruvians who were briefly in the United States, and who opened many avenues of observation and experience to the author. I, for one, wish that it were feasible to reprint more direct quotations. They are rich in detail reflecting the standard socialization of the upper class person, and the psychic wrench involved in shaking loose from the symbolic and the material swords of church and state. It becomes much easier to understand why, in the biting rhetoric of the agitator, the state is still the violence department of the church, and the church is the fraud department of the state.

Although the symbolic material is less systematically gathered than it might have been, the author is justified in using it as he does. It harmonizes with the data obtained from other sources, such as the testimony of Latin American literature and the monographic treatments of particular communities.

Several important hints about the future of Peru emerge from this judicious and configurative investigation. Effective demands to build a modern nation state are gaining strength among young engineers and other professional formations. To some extent these emerging elements come from dissenting elements in the power elite. In some measure they originate in the nuclear families of the middle groups in Peruvian society. In any case they are likely to be technically minded utopians or reformers who operate within the traditional framework of an authoritarian ideology that finds little place for effective power sharing, and is notably impatient with the "sham democracy" exhibited by "imported" legislatures and mass political parties. The inference would appear to be that an oligarchy of "engineers" or "professionally trained officers," for example, may substitute for an older oligarchy without passing directly to a democratic system of public order.

Whatever inferences are drawn from this forthright volume we are indebted to Stephens for a book that counts.

Preface

One of the guiding spirits of modern political analysis, Harold D. Lasswell, has urged the systematic examination of the context and configuration in which political phenomena occur. What you are about to read is an exploration of the context of a political system where a landed elite retains a preponderant share of political power. The country is Peru. No revolutionary breakthrough of the peasant majority of the country, alone or in combination with urban population, has yet occurred. This is so despite half a century of agitation by the Aprista Party, spokesman of the oppressed Indian masses. Instead, the political order remains firmly in the hands of the traditional ruling class, combining Church and military elements, a landed elite and a wealthy commercial sector. This study concentrates on but one of these, the landed elite, not in isolation but in relation to the other segments of Peruvian society. A number of facets are dealt with in examining the social configuration in which Peru's political system functions. One is the political role played by the propertied upper class. A second is the socio-political role of the latifundio or large estate. Another facet consists of the landed elite's political behavior patterns, expressed in a series of hypotheses called "rules of the game." Most important, the prevailing values and attitudes of this social group come in for treatment. Ways in which attitudes and political habits are inculcated in the youthful elite member receive prime attention.

Besides Harold D. Lasswell's strong influence on the work, indebtedness is owed also to Nathan Leites, Edward C. Banfield, Seymour Lipset and Barrington Moore, Jr., among the newer generation of political scientists, historians and sociologists. All share a preoccupation with elites and, particularly, with the mental world and behavior of actors in the political drama. Each shares the common aim of understanding the social milieu in which an elite group functions. The work owes much to an extensive review of the literature dealing both with elites and with Latin American politics generally. I have drawn also upon notes and observations made during a three year series of short, intensive seminars exploring institutional aspects of the Andean environment. These were attended by some 115 young Latin American professionals, a majority of whom were Peruvians.

Following the introductory chapter, initial attention centers on socio-politico phenomena of a region that is rarely treated in the literature, the mountainous interior zone of Peru. Critical concern centers in this chapter on the hacendado as a social type and on the latifundio as an institution having deep roots and wide socio-economic and political ramifications. A chapter then deals with a prime political type evident among the landed elite, the "cacique" or rural boss, intimately allied with the central government in Lima. This chapter is followed by an examination of the all important Catholic Church's role in shaping the value system and attitudes of the upper class Peruvian. The chapter also dwells on the Church function in the interior in serving as a link with the Indian masses who make up sixty percent of Peru's population. Chapter V looks at the upper class family whose common bond is most often a rural property that remains in the family for generations.

Continuing the analysis of the landed elite, Chapter VI turns to the coastal plantations that, despite their occasional modernity, share a similar political role to those of the Sierra. This chapter examines the idea of a Peruvian "oligarchy" by tracing inter-relationships between large landholdings and Cabinet appointments. It serves as a bridge to the next chapter dwelling on elite political maneuverings regarding pressures for reform of the outmoded latifundio system of land tenure. Here, I discuss the "counter-elite," considering this to be largely composed of technician-type upper middle class representatives who desire a drastically changed Peru, beginning with successful agrarian reform. Returning to Lasswell "constructs," the concluding chapter seeks to draw the many strands together into some general conclusions. Generalizations as to certain political tendencies at work in Peru appear also, given the limitations imposed by the nature of this study. Research tasks for the future are outlined. There is a high degree of awareness among scholars and practitioners alike regarding the Latin American landed elite's being perhaps the main stumbling block to progress and reform in this hemisphere. Considerable attention has, therefore, been given to the policy implications of this research effort. These are presented in the final chapter. Perhaps the main finding in the volume, which becomes its central thesis, is that the landed elite's political predominance is traced to its hold on the principal source of wealth in the country, but even more to its value system and to its skill in playing the political game in Peru. As a contribution to knowledge, the conclusion presented suggests the elimination of alternative "explanations" for the extraordinary survival capacity shown by this elite.

For the most part, this work explores "terra incognita." Little has been written about the values and political practices of this or other ruling groups because the landed elite role has been traditionally hidden from view. The reader's indulgence is asked for the byways explored and the absence of a straight route to a certain destination. If I have served to draw attention to the importance of the subject, hoping to stimulate other students and perhaps return myself to more fruitful exploration of a difficult subject area, I am content.

Grateful acknowledgment is made to Dr. John Plank of the Brookings Institution for guiding this study as it approached its final stages. Responsibility for errors, of factual or interpretative nature, lies with me.

Richard H. Stephens

MAN FOLLOWS AN EVER-ENLARGING SET OF RULES

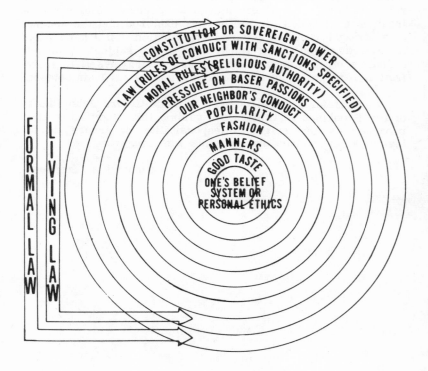

Figure 1. Distinction between Living Law
(or Living Culture) and Formal Law (see p. 5)

Author's Introduction

Prevailing life styles in that barren zone dominated by the forbidding Andes Mountains, even to the casual observer, call to mind an antique, bygone world. Half a decade of personal conversations with some 115 younger members of the region's upper class, a ruling group that has shown a unique survival capacity, cast clear light on the dynamic, explosive character of the political process. In the following pages, you will read the tentative judgments of these elite individuals, each seeking to apply (during a series of six seminars from 1964 to 1969) Harold D. Lasswell's "configurative principle," the act of perceiving and naming a social pattern. Added to my own review of specialized literature on the politics of particular countries, their views bear out the peculiar features of the Peruvian polity described in this work.

Aside from the political system's being a holdover from a bygone age (for where else has a landed aristocracy managed to rule successfully well into the last half of the 20th century?), what salient judgments emerge about Peru's politics? My desire has been to throw light on intra-cultural, informal political behavior rather than concentrate on historical events, formal procedures and the surface aspects of local institutions. Presented as a series of generalizations are a number of the "rules of the game" of a system of elite politics. Perceptions of the growing up process in Peru appear in these pages, as do the ways in which the youthful participants in the seminars revealed their own inner lives and "identity," in the sense of how the inner order of a person gradually gains intelligibility. The "identity" assumed by most was that of defender of the upper class position vis-à-vis that of the mass of the population. Our search for regularities in political behavior as revealed in "rules" had a certain predictive value. The reassertion of primacy by the Peruvian Armed Forces in the 1968 coup d'etat was clearly foreshadowed in the descriptions of the system during the dialogues.

1

Point of Departure

A concrete point of departure marked the whole effort
reported in this volume. The rigid standpoint adopted was
the idea of "lived law" as distinct from formal, written law.
The notion of lived law, also called "living culture" or the
"background of culture, " justifies a preliminary word. Focus-
ing on one's own or another people's hidden ways of thinking
and feeling and acting does not come easy. Lived law exists
in the "do's and don'ts" passed on from mother to child. It
exists in proverbs and folk wisdom. It is expressed in the
phrase "the ways of the world. " Lived law or "living
culture" is rarely written down. To do so is unsafe because
one is dealing with something regarded as unseemly or to be
hidden from view. Yet, "living culture" determines how
things happen in practice. Above all, lived law exists in
rules. These may be expressed both in rules of the game
and in personal codes of conduct. Rules are to be found in
every aspect of life. They exist in the ideas that guide
morals, philosophy, religion, ethics and ideological systems.
In rural Latin America, essentially a non-literate culture,
the rules that make up lived law are transmitted by tradition.
Tales, poems, songs and oral teaching are the vehicles.
Rules are transmitted also by art.

A people's lived law is always coherent with their
fundamental beliefs. Lived law encompasses many elements
which are but silent memories. Values, beliefs and rules
together form lived law. These are passed on from generation to generation in the Andes region as elsewhere. Usually
this happens without awareness on the part of either the
parent or the child.

One example of the "living culture" of the Andean
Zone is the tradition of reaching agreement by a show of
power. Political groups may appeal to university students
to take action. Demonstrations occur. The motive is to give
national political leaders a basis for recommending and carrying out policies. Ability to arouse action is power.

It is part of the very texture of the Andean societies
for an individual to be expected to use authority, in whatever
form it is available to him, to achieve his immediate ends.
Coercion is the rule. One may look at the way Presidents
and Prefects on down firmly believe that social benefits flow
from the top down. The channel is from the patrón in the

form of the landlord or the central government to the campesino.
If the benefits do not flow, the subordinate official or campesino simply waits.   A Prefect once praised the headman of
a village of fifty families for refusing to try to raise thirty
pesos (about $2.50) to buy a log to improve a bridge.   "It
is the Ministry of Works responsibility.   They will take care
of it," he told them.   But the bridge was never repaired.

One can also see lived law in the avidity with which
upper class persons seek the post of catedrático.   The term
refers to the holder of a university catedra or chair.   Besides the renown and prestige it brings, the catedrático's
position is very powerful.   He is the "big boss," but is badly
paid.   His powerful position in the community and his great
distance from the students are compensations for his low
economic status.   Outside their university duties, most
catedráticos are lawyers, physicians, politicians or high officials.   Barring an ouster due to a change of political regime, a man, once appointed, usually manages to hold the
position for life.   He is the absolute head of a Facultad, one
of the autonomous schools that make up the typical university.
Attempts to change the archaic catedra system occur.   Some
success has been achieved, notably in Colombia.   But most
such efforts are doomed to failure due to lived law.   Those
who must vote changes are Senators and Deputies who are
among those enjoying personal advantages under the present
system.   These men are often holders of catedras themselves
or have a close relative who is a catedrático.   These legislators form part of the problem on which they are asked to
legislate.   It is not likely that changes will be converted into
law--not, at least, if they can help it.   Reform of the system
faces the same obstacles as proposals in the United States
for changes in a system of price supports for well-to-do
farmers when Congressmen and officials are prime beneficiaries.

In rural South America, "living culture" is seen in the
intensely personal relationship of the large landholder or
gamonal with his followers.   It is a tie mixed with sentiments of loyalty and the expectation of favors on the peasants' part.   What is given in return is unquestioning obedience to the boss, especially at election time.   What political
intermediaries in rural regions (called caciques) seek is a
similar relationship with a local Municipal Councillor or a
Deputy with ties to the national government.   In return for
the cacique's loyalty, favors and concessions can be obtained.

Lived Law as Inner Order

One can understand the behavior treated in this work by taking the two extremes: law as we know it, which is a rigid, explicit rule of behavior formulated by a sovereign power, coercively imposed for general observance; and lived law, "living culture," which is, by contrast, formulated, enforced and absorbed in a clandestine way. We live rules, under this latter law, much as we breathe air, without awareness on the part of ourselves or any persons involved. Artists, writers, religious leaders, philosophers regulate society by setting down the rules we obey. They do so in a clandestine manner. They do not respond to immediate, articulated demands the way legislators do. They respond to the human need for rules, for guidance in one's daily behavior. Lived law presides over external rapports and responds to the human need for inner order. Each person conforms in a uniform way. He integrates himself and finds his path through life in a subjective way.

The need for lived laws, for rules in harmony with a community's deepest beliefs, springs from human nature. We all need guidance. We need to act in harmony with our fellow men. Many examples of lived law and rules of the game will be presented in these pages. All are instances, in the highest sense, of man's intimate need for discipline and guidance.

Rules making up "living culture" do not die out. Lived laws keep on living long after those who formulated them have passed away. Lived law persists even when the times, language, culture and beliefs of the rule-makers have vanished.

The task of fixing or recording this vital part of a total social order is fraught with difficulty. The phenomenon that I set out to examine is usually hidden under a welter of personal observations, one's own and the other person's. Often, it is considered in too sketchy a manner, with isolated examples cropping up in a novel, a conversation, a debate. Because it is something unseen or unknown, it is not to be considered non-existent. I emphasize the nature of "living culture" to make up for inadequate analysis by scholars of this phenomenon. The difficulty also is one of inadequate conceptuality, for anthropologists and political scientists are only now coming to grips with this aspect of reality.

Lived law, rules or "living culture" are similar to the concept of culture, but the latter is more inclusive. All are abstractions. It is impossible to think about human behavior without these particular abstractions. Abstractions help in sensing a particular problem, such as how to be "at home" or at ease in a given environment. The terms are necessary devices of understanding. In an effort to "integrate" one notion with another, we often simply enlarge abstractions so that we get further and further from reality. The danger exists with the idea of lived law. What is generally called "culture" is a much vaguer concept than we are willing to admit. Both it and the "background of culture" are something far removed from the rigid, well-defined absolute which anthropologists often insist upon.

Upper Class Makes the Rules

Discernible in the "living culture" of the Andean region is a strictly hierarchical society. A dominant upper class exists at the top in each of the several countries, including Peru. Such persons are an elite consisting mainly of a number of well known families, persons who identify each other as elite. This upper class comprises many functional elites impossible to define with any precision, other than that they share common sets of values. One group does stand out--the holders of large tracts of land. One cannot think of the region's politics without reckoning with the landholding class. One cannot assess the values and patterns of "living culture" without being aware of the difference in power and wealth that landownership brings in its train.

In following chapters, I shall examine upper class prerogatives, especially as they manifest themselves in the political sphere. Differences between the dominant upper class and subjected lower class are very marked in law and custom. They exist also in subtle or invisible expressions. The latter are part and parcel of the "living culture" we shall be studying. All countries in the region, for example, illustrate the principle that, no matter what the political regime, the people in power tend to be the same. They do this with such consistency that most of the rest of the population are effectively excluded from power. The wealth that flows from possession of power is equally denied them. No matter which country in the Andean Zone we consider, a few of the populace lead and the others follow.

This work represents a modest attempt to examine
systematically the ruling, land-based upper class of Peru, a
country where patterns unfamiliar to most Americans brought
up in the democratic tradition persist without serious challenge.   The results of these researches lead to novel insights about political formulas, folklore and myths which go
far toward determining Peru's internal and external policies.
The concept that a few rule the many is basic in contempo-
rary thought.   Much of what follows is based on it.

Significance of Upper Class Family

To understand the major assumptions underlying this
volume, let us turn to one important way in which Andean
culture is organized.   This is the fact that, wherever one
turns in political matters, the upper class family is always
present.   Rules, as we have seen, form part of a man's development from birth onwards.   It is the family, along with
religion, that constitutes the prime source of the rules of
life which govern the member of the upper class.   It is within the bosom of the family that the elite men and women of
the region acquire the rules or measures which they are to
employ to gauge another's behavior.   It is through the socialization process--growing up within the culture, a matter
which will be treated in some detail--that one learns the
great differences between the ideal and the actual, between
what people say and how they really behave.   A young boy
who lived in the upper class section of an interior town was
praised by his father for making some trowels.   But when
the upper class lad took them to the market to sell them, he
was stopped on the way and severely beaten by his father for
"putting the family's name to shame. "

Unless one is among a sheltered few within the upper
class, he soon learns everybody should find his protection
in the warp and woof of one's family or the larger upper
class society.   Without such protections, man in these societies is alone in the world, waiting to be devoured by one
sharper or better connected than oneself.   Most Peruvians
for example, obey a double standard.   There is one code
valid within the family circle, with relatives and honorary
relatives (compadres), intimate friends and close associates.
There is another code regulating life outside.   Witl.in, they
assiduously demonstrate all the better qualities: they are
relatively reliable, obedient, generous, brave, and capable
of self-sacrifices.   The Peruvians' family loyalty is their

true patriotism. In the outside world, amidst the chaos and
the disorder of society, they often feel compelled to employ
the wiles of skilled in-fighters. All official and legal authority is considered hostile until proved friendly or harmless.
If government cannot be ignored, it should be captured, neu-
tralized or deceived for the family's benefit. A man may be
saddled or endowed by this culture with a number of ties he
cannot escape. For instance, family ties are so strong that
the elevation of a person to a place of power means power
for the whole family. The same phenomenon occurs elsewhere in Latin America and the Mediterranean world. A
brother who would refuse to associate his brothers with his
success would be deemed an unworthy person.

Fundamental Spanish-Latin Characteristics

Besides the strict hierarchical and family-oriented
character of society, Andean culture possesses other inher-
itances from Latin Europe. Among these is the stress on
spiritual, non-material values. In settling the New World,
the Spaniards had a monopoly of their own race. Spain did
not leave the Middle Ages behind when it came to America.
Instead, Spain transplanted a tendency to cling to past forms,
giving the region an "immutability." Latin culture resists
the pull of universal evolution toward industrialization, equality and rapid change. The Spaniard's feeling for the land
rests deep in the Andean's Latin American soul. Spain be-
queathed a dense network of personalist, private ties, which
protect those who are already strong, the upper class representatives, and thereby further prop up the existing order.
All these traits have served as strong pulls toward "order"
in the region.

In the following pages, you will discern these order-
serving patterns: A strong reverence for the past; hard efforts to reproduce in the New World the atmosphere of the
Old, notably in architecture; a general lassitude upset by
occasional exertions (brought on by the belief that only per-
fection deserves the effort of attainment); a deep-rooted Catholicism that embraces the ideal of man's relation to Maker,
and the belief that the Church's influence should be exerted
constantly in favor of the existing regime; the Andean dwel-
ler's belief that his culture forms a coherent whole and is
not defective in his eyes.

But Spain gave to the Andean countries also "personal

freedom serving" traits.   Spaniards, in their spirit of indi-
viduality, feel deeply that moral and juridical forms "conflict with our nature. "   Each person seems to care for himself or his family alone, refusing submission, denying any
social goal outside his family, clan or friends.   There is the
Spanish-Latin's deep longing for freedom, a highly personal
kind of liberty marked by, for example, intense longings and
feelings for one's own locality.   In politics, this freedom appears in the delight governments take in reversing all the
acts of one's predecessor in high office.

        The typical upper class Latin American enjoys a
greater amount of personal freedom than does the average
person living in the U. S.   Local liberty is no less prized
than individual liberty.   Local authorities are accustomed to
freedom from control from central governments.   One finds
examples of this spirit of freedom in the mobile peasantry.
Culturally conservative, this element is most instrumental in
unsettling the present social order.   The educated peasants
are more inclined to be revolutionary for they have seen the
possibilities that life in the capital cities offers.   Localism
is seen, too, in the fact that frontier areas often show a
tendency to rebel against central authorities.   The rebellions,
often as not, are led by peasants returned from the large
cities.   Colombia's rural unrest in recent decades is a typical case.

Value Placed on Individualism

        Other values are desired besides localism and person-
al freedom and order.   Andean dwellers are notable for reliance on religious myths, legends and tales.   Most of these
were derived from Spain.   Others, rooted in the Inca pre-
conquest culture, afford simple explanations of complex natural phenomena.   Not only are these myths reality but they
are the only reality known about man and nature.   They are
not fiction or fancy but the only science that Andean man has
known.   Catholicism, as we shall see, presents a wide range
of myths.   The upper class bases its rule, its continued
power, on Church-taught tradition.   The Church responds to
man's need to belong, to be identified with more than a
merely static, transitory, almost illusory situation.   It identifies the inhabitants with something which knows no beginning, no end.   The Catholic religion, the body of beliefs by
which Hispanic-Andean culture locates itself in the world and
in nature, expresses for the bulk of the inhabitants the fur-

thest and highest goals of human living.

Individualism, as we have noted, is a key value. It springs from the struggle of subjective, personal desires, e.g., for growth. These run up against a society organized on a strict hierarchal basis in disregard of human nature. The middle and lower class individual finds himself in the world ruled by power. Those with power to act as individuals are the upper class and that power is universally desired. In West Coast South America, power is most clearly demonstrated by the landholding class. On one typical hacienda, absolute control over the lives of the colonos or peasants rested with a thin faced man in his thirties, the patrón. He only seemed to like two things: to ride furiously and to beat his colonos. One of the peasants recounted his hard life: "Even when we worked an extra day a week for him, he beat us." One day, a colono's six year old son lost one of the hacienda's sheep in the hills. A fox, he said, had eaten it. When the patrón learned of this, he flew into a rage. He grabbed a knife and cut off the boy's ear and put it in his pouch. The patrón threw the peasant, his son and wife and other child off the property, because he thought the peasant had gone to the authorities to complain.

The episode shows the dependency relationship of the bulk of the population. Only a few persons at the top of the social scale can afford to be individuals. The spirit of individualism must combat not only guidance prescribed by local mores or law; it must take account of unseen, almost undetectable factors transmitted from parent to child, from one generation to another. This aspect of the culture, the individualism that resists control, signifies a proud and sensitive people. I shall turn to this in the chapters that follow. The "living culture" of a people is something far more complex than what we see at first glance. What we want to know about it is far more boundless than we can hope to know, at least in our present state of scientific knowledge.

Principal Social Patterns

Before placing this work in the literature dealing with Peru, let us look briefly at the life-style of the landed upper class, its shared common situation, interests and prerogatives. In Peru, the thought processes and life style of this class are rooted in a bygone age. A member of that class invited me to spend the day on his hacienda, one of the larg-

est in the country.   The buildings were unchanged from the
17th century when they were built.   The gardens, redone by
his father, were laid out in the style of a French chateau.
The main house was comfortable inside, but one had the feeling of being thrust back into a style of life of that earlier
century.   In the nearby town, this young member of the aristocracy was greeted in a respectful manner on all sides.
The hacienda owner pointed to a knot of Indians in ragged
dress and said: "See, how these people smile at me.   They
do not hate me.   These people are content with their lot and
ask for nothing more. "

     The baroque, in an artistic, spiritual and architectural
sense, still pervades the region.   The 400 year Colonial era
lingers on, 150 years after its nominal demise.   As they
were in that era, titles are much sought after today.   During
the long Colonial period, the upper class lived cut off from
responsibilities.   It inevitably became overbearing, while the
populace was kept ignorant, poor, superstitious, harassed by
tax-collectors and religious authorities.   At times, the Indian
population broke out in bloody but short-lived riots.   Most of
the time, the people were kept happy by the distribution of
alms and the splendid performance of public spectacles.   The
show was all important in Colonial times.   In Peru, the
Baroque age is still unsurpassed in the breathtaking beauty
of public buildings, churches, parks and old residences.

     The antique world that lives on in cathedrals exists,
too, in the lived law of the inhabitants.   Colonial life utilized
fully many of the people's latent talents, tastes and inclina-
tions.   As elements of Spanish life, oppression, tedium and
revolt were stronger in Peru than elsewhere in the American
colonies.   Centralization sought to submit all to a common
purpose and the supremacy of the King.   Society became
formed of two main layers: at the top, a wealthy few; at the
bottom, the vast ragged, picturesque and powerless crowds.
This contrast remains to the present day.

The Study in the General Literature

     Two currents of political science literature converge
in the pages that follow.   One concerns elites; the other
deals with Latin American politics.   My method called for an
examination of numerous writings to see what was said about
the prevalent theory of life of the Latin American elite, whose
power is intimately tied with ownership of land.   What is the

composition, the attitudes and the role of the people who occupy upper class positions? Who make up the "political
elite," in the sense of the real power holders in society?
On these vital points the literature is very scanty.   One of
the few to deal with these themes is Frank Tannenbaum.   He
points to a curious anomaly in writings on Latin America,
both from within and outside the region.[1] He singles out the
continuing political, social and economic importance of the
institution of the hacienda, or large landed estate, in country
after country.   Nevertheless, educated Latin Americans rarely write or speak of the institution or subject it to critical
analysis.   "Except for an occasional novel, it is never written about or seriously studied," writes Tannenbaum.   "The
intellectuals who were mostly children of the hacienda were
not conscious of its existence--like the air we breathe."   He
points to the lack of a "principle of legitimacy" (once the
Spanish Crown disappeared from the scene in the early 19th
century) as a prime cause of political instability in the region.   He observed that government was "personal, intimate,
a matter among friends, a family affair."   Elected government at the national center was important, but at the local
level "he who governs has always governed."   Elections are
unnecessary at this level as "everyone recognizes who the
real governor is . . . the true government of the district is
the caudillo, locally known and accepted whose power and influence has lodged in him 'naturally'."   The central government's authority extended only so far as this caudillo (other
terms for this leading personage are hacendado, patrón, cacique or gamonal) permitted.   His power rested ultimately on
control of large tracts of land.   Collectively, these personages and their many kin by blood or obligation throughout the
land constitute the landed elite.

          Here is a central phenomenon that urgently needs fur-
ther exploration.   Why the importance of rural zones in a
country like Peru?   Because, Tannenbaum says, this is where
the bulk of the people are.   In this peasant culture, the rural area is where the dominant values abide.   Not only in
Peru but in most countries in the region, the mass of the
population lives on or under the shadow of large estates.
Tannenbaum, echoing native writers, declares that centuries
of oral tradition have been handed down in the unchanging
life of the hacienda.   The entities usually consist of a large
self-contained estate plus dependent villages and often a rural
town.   The institution still dominates the lives of rural people in these countries politically and economically.   Part of
its influence derives from the values and style of life of the

landowning class. By emulation, these largely determine the
behavior of the middle and lower classes. The masses of
rural mestizos and Indians retain their beliefs and customs
even in migrating to the slums surrounding the cities. A
recent study declares that rural Latin America holds the key
to the region's future. [2]

Other Writers Stressing Importance
of Landowning Elite

Throughout the literature on Latin America, one finds
little evidence of the kind of uneasiness on the part of the
upper class about the existing order that might lead them to
change it. This is particularly true with regard to the out-
dated system of local-central government relations. Martin
Needler, among others, traces Latin American political instability largely to the constant tug-of-war between central
governments and the rural zones. [3] The history of these
countries is one of coups d'état, barracks rebellions, palace
revolts, a type of institutionalized political change popularly
called "revolutions. " Clearly, we are dealing with political
behavior of a unique kind that encourages such instability at
the center.

In effect, these changes have been a circulation of
persons and factions within a ruling elite. Charles W. Anderson identifies not instability per se as the prime problem
of Latin American politics but "the discrepancy between formal intention and concrete realization, between the enactment
and the implementation. "[4] This is due to "the commitment
of individuals and groups to social institutions other than the
state, government and the nation. " As we shall see, the
former include the extended family and the landed estate,
among others. Governments are weak, unstable and inef-
fectual, Anderson says, because this "is in the interest of a
small elite which controls all the major institutions of the
society. " Most Latin American development thought holds
that the elite lies at the crux of the matter of growth and
change in the region. The problem is to get the state to
"effectively fulfill the commitments to economy and society
that characterize virtually all Western nations. " But the
dominant landed elite, exercising a control of the rural masses, with an antiquated value system and outlook, will not
allow this to happen.

Claudio Veliz dwells on Latin America's "feudal structure with a capitalist facade. "[5] He stresses that the upper class in a country like Peru has shown a unique survival capacity whereas elsewhere in the world the aristocracy has, with few exceptions, disappeared. Merle Kling dwells on the chronic, limited violence character of revolutions in the area. These changes produce no basic shifts in economic, social or political policies. [6] George Blanksten observes that "if the term is used precisely, true revolution--a basic change in the political system, a recasting of the social or-der--is surprisingly infrequent in Latin America. "[7] Some countries, of course, have undergone true revolutions, Me-xico, Bolivia and Cuba being the chief examples. The Bo-livian National Revolution of April, 1952 saw the incorpora-tion of the Indians into full citizenship status, giving them the right to vote, own land and keep arms. Land was re-distributed on a large scale. [8] Silvert says that rotating the executive of a country by revolution may be a sign of stabil-ity--"events are marching along as they always have. "[9] Ad-dressing himself specifically to the pattern in Peru, James Payne says in the same vein: "To treat violence and mili-tary coups as aberrations places one in the awkward position of insisting that practically all significant political events in the past half century are deviations. "[10] A vital point arises here. Do these revolutionary disturbances indicate a pattern of conduct rather than instability? Have resorts to military intervention, for example, become institutionalized as part of the "rules of the game" for an elite-dominated society? One senses that the critical factor is the views and methods of politics that have become habitual to the political elite, and other principal political factors.

Robert Scott speaks of the prevailing situation in Peru as one where the traditional powers, namely, the landowners, the Army and the Church, no longer agree among themselves regarding the proper political process. The newer interests, such as industry, labor and the technicians, are either co-opted by the traditional ruling group or remain in competition with one another. [11] As representatives of the middle class, they are basically non-revolutionary and non-ideological, be-ing more interested in improving their immediate economic situation. A thoroughgoing structural change in the society is demanded only by leftists and by a few intellectuals.

Influence on Political Life of
Family and Education

Among U.S. political scientists and historians writing

on Peru, William Stokes points to the importance in these
phenomena of the nature of Hispanic cultural heritages. [12]
This is an archaic culture, he holds. The scheme of education shapes an intellectual attitude that prizes Hispanic vir-
tues rather than those of the modern, technological order.
Peru's leading writers have said the same about the underlying realities of their society. Writing in the older tradition
of the descriptive essay, these thinkers single out the type
of character produced by educational and socializing influences
as the central political problem of the region. Mariano H.
Cornejo, a Peruvian statesman of the early 20th century,
said that Peru's lack of progress stemmed from the fact that
Peruvians had "inherited a timidity of character from the
aboriginal race" as well as a past characterized by supersti-
tion and fanaticism. [13] Javier Prado found Peru's "soil filled
with wealth, in contrast to the poverty of Peru's inhabitants. "
This was so because its people had not developed industry,
commerce and capital. The educator Manuel Vicente Villerán
said that predilection for bureaucratic jobs was the evil.
"Bureaucracy competes with and overwhelms all the industries . . . it is but one form of the expression of the aver-
sion to work inherited from class distinction. " These Peruvian thinkers join critics in other Latin American countries
in declaring that it is necessary for their compatriots "to
change intellectually and socially, " to develop "a practical
sense of life and a capacity for material work. "

    The prevailing theory of life emphasized status, an
attitude of mastery on the part of the elite and subservience
on the part of all other classes. Daniel Cosío Villegas puts
his finger on "the abominable indifference that separates our
low from our high classes. " [14] Joining Tannenbaum and
others, Cosío Villegas signalizes the characteristic feature of
the Latin American political and social scene: "the closed
cloister" as the common geographic unit. "A spot of humanity here, another there, and between them emptiness. "
Many travelers to Latin America experience this feeling of
"an empty continent. " It leads to the low degree or total
lack of social relationship between one hacienda or interior
town and the next. The coastal zones are characterized by
similar cloisters, the largest of which, the capital, seeks to
use its power and authority for its own benefit. The result
is that "the country or nation is an entity in good part fictitious. "

Dearth of Contemporary Literature on Ruling Groups

The method of study adopted here seeks to get at the ethos of a ruling class, however unpalatable the idea of a "ruling class" is to Americans.   Norton Long has written that the existence of a ruling class is a feature of all societies. [15]   The Greek philosopher Aristotle held that the upper class and the effective constitution were one and the same, since the upper class members often personified the constitution.   In the centuries since Aristotle, a considerable literature has been built up on aristocracies and oligarchies. [16] Montesquieu's "Spirit of the Laws" carries on the search of the Greek thinker for the ethical principle embodied in a constitution which permits a few to rule over the many. Machiavelli foreshadowed 19th and 20th century interest in the actual political behavior of individual rulers.   Roberto Michels' classic study of political parties sums up as "the iron law of oligarchy" that rule by a few men is characteristic of all organizations.   When the few are not responsible to the many, then it is oligarchy, according to R. M. McIver in his Web of Government.

Latin America's aristocratic establishment, the oldest and largest in the Western World, receives little attention in the writings on elites.   Research on this governing class which, in Claudio Veliz' words, has "managed to hold onto most of its land, a considerable part of its power and all of its social prestige, " is notably absent. [17]   Recommended techniques for elite studies place chief reliance on biographic data on individuals, such as Cabinet ministers, parliamentarians, company directors and political leaders. [18]   Lasswell suggests, besides biographic information, such methods as the scrutiny of elite tactics (for example, in manipulating votes of client groups) and elite utterances in speeches, conversation and published, especially autobiographical, works. Valuable evidence flows from study of interlocking positions, such as those in government, banks, company directorships, diplomatic posts, political party executives and certain well-known families.   He directs special attention to principles and maxims that may be articulated among the elite.   Their mode of conduct in typical situations, such as elections, cabinet formation and civil disturbances, reveals much about elite perspectives, identifications and expectations.

Of the many things that might be known about a gov-

erning class within a society, special significance attaches
to their value orientations.   Distinctive elite practices represent another useful focus.   Actions are in large measure
conditioned by attitudes.   Knowing a person's (or a social
class') belief system gives some foreknowledge of how he or
they will act.   The belief and value system of the upper
class is mirrored in the conduct of lower classes, especially
in Latin America.   A prime objective of this inquiry has been
to get at the "code" or "rules of the game" of the Latin
American elite.   Looking at their fundamental conceptions
and values, their basic ways of thinking and feeling, as they
reveal them to one another, has been the principal method of
investigation designed to achieve this objective.

Because Peru's landed elite is the top power class,
other Peruvians fear them.   The capacity of the country's
ruling class to impose deprivations, to take away one's job,
to send one into exile, to ostracize one in the press, is frequently demonstrated.   Indirect study seemed to me necessary
because of the veto that political elites wield over serious
study of their methods and power sources.   Peruvian intellectuals, with the few exceptions noted below range themselves on the side of the conservative class, if only because
of their own upper class origins.   Currying favor rather than
castigating a country's rulers or exposing their practices to
public gaze is a traditional stance of intellectuals in Peru.
The aristocratic prejudice against learning, typical of Peru
no less than other countries, has meant that little theorizing
is done by defenders of the existing state of affairs.   Peruvian literature on elite behavior is limited to modest efforts
to identify which individuals or families constitute the landholding elite.   Nor is this lack remedied by recent works by
foreigners.   Seymour Lipset's recent work cited above deals
with cultural, labor, business and university elites but omits
mention of the most important of all, the landowning upper
class.   The book contains few detailed analyses of specific
processes.   It does not deal with politics in specific countries, which need to be treated in limited and controlled
ways.   One looks through this book and other literature on
Latin America in vain for something akin to Edward Banfield's
study of an Italian village or Lucien Pye's work on political
processes in Burma. [19]

Utilization of Elite Studies

What guidelines from past studies of elites have been

followed in this research? The elite has been defined as
"those positions in society which are at the summits of key
social structures, i.e., the higher positions in the economy,
government, military, politics, religion, mass organizations,
education and the professions." Following Harold D. Lasswell who says the elite are those with greatest access to and
control of values, I have sought to establish what values are
deemed to be politically relevant by an elite or class that
bases itself in ownership of large tracts of land. Peru's
particular landed elite plays a major role in determining the
likelihood for economic growth and political stability. This
proposition constitutes an underlying assumption of this study.
Gaetano Mosca's Ruling Class declares that members of a
ruling minority have some attribute that is highly esteemed
and very influential in the society in which they live. [20] In
Peru, that attribute is land. Mosca advises one to seek out
the constant traits a particular ruling class possesses. Much
of this inquiry aims at isolating these variables insofar as
they affect the working of the political order. They are herein called "rules of the game." They derive from the prevailing values. As a founder of the modern study of elites,
Mosca ascribed great importance to problems relating to the
persistence, composition or organization of a country's ruling
class. The belief system of such a group especially merits
study as well as their ways of renewing themselves, for example, by admitting capable newcomers from the lower strata of society.

        Pareto is another writer on elites making noteworthy
contributions to my research design. [21] He advises against
looking at "derivations" about elites. These are the easy
explanations, the associations of ideas and non-logical arguments found with great frequency in the literature. Most
Latin American intellectuals write almost exclusively about
these mere associations of ideas rather than dealing in knowledge empirically derived. The "residues," on the other
hand, of an elite class are of greatest importance. Residues
are concerned with what men actually do. Pareto points to
the things that most assure the survival of a social class as
sure clues of the existence of one or more particularly important residues. Formalism in life is one of these, e.g.,
formal religious observances, or formality in the presence
of the patriarchal head of the family. A sense of loyalty to
one's clan, a feeling for the value of certain customs or
rites, a sense of personal integrity and identity, a desire to
promote one's family interests--these are examples of residues that we shall meet on the following pages.

Finally, in the brief survey of elite writings bearing
on this study, mention should be made of Max Weber's
"ideal types" inasmuch as the object of my study, the values,
attitudes, belief system and behavior patterns of the landowning upper class, will be approached by applying "ideal type"
analysis to the elite.   Weber's valuable analytical tool was
developed to sharpen awareness of the unique characteristics
of a phenomenon.   I shall dwell on several "types" within the
Peruvian upper class: the "gamonal, " the "cacique, " the
"conservative politician, " the "Church politician" and the
"reform-minded aristocrat. "   These are dealt with always in
relation to the landed elite.   The various chapters treat theoretically the "pure" ideal of each one of these types, as
they cropped up in the seminars and other research activity.
In a few instances, examples in the form of anecdotes or
"eye witness accounts" have been included in Appendix II to
make more concrete this "pure type. "   The purpose of such
analysis is to show the internal consistency of the landed
elite's value structure and outlook.   The potent cultural mo-
tivations behind the behavior of representative individuals
within this elite should also stand in bold relief through the
device of "ideal types. "

Notes

1. Frank Tannenbaum, "Toward an Appreciation of Latin
    America. "   The United States and Latin America (Co-
    lumbia University, New York: The American Assembly,
    1956), pp. 29-38.

2. Andrew Pearse, "Agrarian Change Trends in Latin Amer-
    ica, " Latin American Research Review, Vol. 1, No. 3
    (1966), pp. 45-69.

3. Martin C. Needler, "Putting Latin American Politics in
    Perspective, " Inter-American Economic Affairs, Vol.
    XVI, No. 2 (Autumn, 1962).

4. Charles W. Anderson, "Political Factors in Latin American
    Economic Development, " Journal of International Affairs,
    Vol. 20 (1966), pp. 245-247.

5. Claudio Veliz, "Obstacles to Reform in Latin America, "
    The World Today, Royal Institute of International Af-
    fairs (January, 1963), pp. 23-26.

6. Merle Kling, "Toward a Theory of Power and Political Instability in Latin America," Western Political Quarterly, Vol. 9 (March, 1966), p. 49.

7. George I. Blanksten, "The Politics of Latin America," in The Politics of Developing Areas, edited by Gabriel Almond and James Coleman (Princeton: Princeton University Press, 1960), p. 497.

8. Robert J. Alexander, The Bolivian National Revolution (New Brunswick, New Jersey: Rutgers University Press, 1958), p. 58.

9. Kalman Silvert, The Conflict Society: Reaction and Revolution in Latin America (New Orleans: The Hauser Press, 1961), p. 20.

10. James Payne, "Peru: The Politics of Structured Violence," Journal of Politics, Vol. 27 (May, 1965), p. 369.

11. Robert E. Scott, "Political Elites and Political Modernization," Elites in Latin America, edited by Seymour M. Lipset and Aldo Solari (London: Oxford University Press, 1967), pp. 135-142.

12. William S. Stokes, "Violence as a Power Factor in Latin American Politics," Western Political Quarterly (September, 1952), p. 445.

13. These quotes from Javier Prado Cornejo and Manuel Vicente Villarán are cited in Leopoldo Zea, The Latin American Mind, translated by James H. Abbott and Lowell Dunham (Norman: University of Oklahoma Press, 1963), pp. 187-191 and 194-197.

14. Daniel Cosío Villegas, American Extremes (Austin, Texas: University of Texas Press, 1964), p. 75.

15. Norton Long, "Aristotle and Local Government," Social Research, Vol. 24 (Autumn, 1957), pp. 290-295.

16. The sources cited here (Montesquieu, Machiavelli, Michels, McIver) stress the importance of studying aristocracies and oligarchies. Formidable conceptual problems exist, however, in dealing with the term "oligarchy," which is often used to name Peru's ruling

element. Preston James' Latin America, 3d ed. (New
York: Odyssey Press, 1959), p. 202 says: "In Peru,
the politics have long been under the control of the landowning and commercial aristocracy, supported by the
officers of the Army. " How to identify its members?
How to determine the extent to which the group actually
"rules"? I have generally avoided the term in favor of
an identifiable landowning element in the country called
herein a "landed elite. " (See Appendix I.) To determine its relative power position, I have been guided by
Robert A. Dahl ("A Critique of the Ruling Elite Model, "
American Political Science Quarterly, Vol. 52 (June,
1958), pp. 463-469). Dahl's "test of who rules" is the
examination of a series of concrete decisions. Such decisions are taken up in Chapter VI (decisions as to who
becomes a Cabinet Minister in Peru) and Chapter VII
(decisions on agrarian reform legislation and its implementation, the most notable "key issue" in Peruvian
politics during the past decade and a half).

17. Claudio Veliz (ed.), Obstacles to Change in Latin Amer-
     ica (London: Oxford University Press, 1965); also his
     The Politics of Conformity in Latin America (London:
     Oxford University Press, 1967).

18. Harold D. Lasswell, D. Lerner and C. E. Rothwell,
     The Comparative Study of Elites (Stanford, Calif. : Stan-
     ford University Press, 1952) pp. 25-27.

19. Edward C. Banfield, The Moral Basis of a Backward
     Society (Glencoe, Illinois: The Free Press, 1958) and
     Lucian W. Pye, Politics, Personality and Nation Build-
     ing: Burma's Search for Identity (New Haven: Yale
     University Press, 1962). Banfield's central hypothesis,
     set forth on page 85, is that "the inhabitants act accord-
     ing to this rule, maximize the material and short run
     advantages of the nuclear family, and assume all others
     will do likewise. " This approach served to stimulate
     some of the tentative formulations offered in this dis-
     sertation about "rules of the game" of Peruvian politics.

20. Gaetano Mosca, The Ruling Class, edited and revised by
     Arthur Livingston (New York: McGraw Hill, 1939) pp.
     164-166.

21. Vilfredo Pareto, The Mind and Society, edited by Arthur
     Livingston, translated by A. Bongiorno and A. Living-
     ston (London: J. Cape, 1935), Vol 3, pp. 423-424.

national politics in Peru. The mass of the population, instead of being citizens of a nation, are subjects living under the local authority of a lord or patrón. Even the Indian and mestizo owners of minifundios, tiny plots of land from twelve to twenty-five acres usually, are subject to the social and political authority of the large estate. They need the large estate's community services and means of transportation. They need day-to-day employment to add to their income. Lacking the protections afforded by the estate, the minifundio owners often as not flee to the capital in search of livelihood.

Latifundios differ in some respects from large, modern coastal plantations. The former exist mainly in remote fastnesses of the Andes Mountains, hidden in an archaic, backward society that most Peruvians would rather shun. The plantations, in contrast, concentrate on a single crop for export--either cotton or sugar. These farms pay wages, however low, and use lands economically. Latifundios of the Sierra waste land and avoid money payments, generally conceding the workers small plots for sharecropping or in exchange for services. Despite the modern farm sector, Peruvian (and Latin American) agriculture is still dominated by the archaic latifundios. The majority of the country's population is indirectly affected by the political and economic authority of their owners. It is worth ascertaining why this is so.

Traveling to interior towns and adjacent farms, one sees the trenchant contrast between an excessively poor low class and a disproportionately powerful and rich high class. Daniel Cosío Villegas writes that "perhaps the only thing that these two classes have in common is their dense ignorance. For the rest, they could not be more different or more distant."[4] The peasant masses live at the subsistence level. A tremendous demographic pressure is everywhere visible. The 1961 census shows the population of the interior as 5.9 million persons, although it is placed as high as seven million, or sixty percent of the country's total. Ethnically, Peru's population is fifty percent Indian, ten percent white and forty percent mestizo. An estimated five million of the rural inhabitants are Aymara and Quechua Indians. They live for the most part in rural zones, since cities are few. The six interior towns which had a population of over 25,000 in 1961 together had a combined population of only 241,183 inhabitants, almost all whites and mestizos.

Owing to the scarcity of towns and the system of
large landholdings, the masses of Indians live either on the
latifundios or in their own villages ("comunidades indígenas").
Indian concentrations are greatest in the departments of
Apurimac and Puno in the extreme south and Cajamarca in
the north.   As of June, 1961, the Government of Peru had
legally recognized 1,586 "comunidades" with a total of
1,367,000 inhabitants.   Some 3,000 other "comunidades" are
believed to exist which have not been legally recognized.
The remaining Indians, numbering upwards of two million (a
1950 estimate showed one million Indians living on 1,200 haciendas), constitute the all-important labor force dwelling on
the haciendas. [5]   Recurring "invasions," strikes and pitched
battles in these departments, especially in the period 1961-
63, reveal the quantity of explosive material, in the number
and state of mind of these Indian masses in Peru's interior.

Four features stand out in the agrarian system that
has developed: (1) The existence side by side of Indian Communities clinging to ancient beliefs and traditions and the
great estates enjoying the available power and wealth.
(2) The bare subsistence of life: in the search for cash
crops, increasingly commercial, wage-paying plantations
take the place of the traditional hacienda.   (3) Demand for
labor plus demographic pressure gives rise to periodic mi-
grations: the peasants flow to and from coastal agricultural
enterprises, the mines or roadbuilding projects and to the
capital, Lima.   (4) A developing system of markets opens to
the peasants opportunities to exchange small quantities of
goods through barter.   This, coupled with the growing importance of unions and syndicates among the Indian and mestizo peasants, points to an awakened rural mass.   Markets
have a vital role in determining the future of the populations,
since unionizing efforts can be traced to these communal
markets. [6]

The density of the population since Colonial times has
been the source of richness in this desolate and barely accessible wilderness.   Rigid master-slave arrangements carried over from the Inca regime enabled a handful of whites
to exploit a fabulous native labor force.   Together with land
and mineral riches, the Indians constituted the objects of
conquest as well as the basis of wealth in the region.   With
the passage of time, a hierarchical social order became
deeply implanted.   A powerful group of white Spaniards and
criollos dominated the native masses through mestizo administrators.   The 16th century system of encomiendas (grants of

Indian populations with the land they occupied by the Spanish
Crown to the conquistadores) gradually became the system of
haciendas.   Historically, the tendency of the landholders has
been to constantly expand their rural properties.   This has
usually been at the expense of the neighboring Indian communities.   Here, in brief, is the origin of the land tenure
system and the rigidly stratified social relations that have
led to prevailing value structures and sharpening conflicts
in the Sierra of Peru.

Social Conditions and World View of the Peruvian Peasant

Peruvian First Vice President Edgardo Seoane has
provided a graphic picture of the conditions in which the Indians and mestizo masses live (excerpted from remarks to an
Andean Seminar held at Brookings Institution in January-Feb-
ruary, 1964):

> Unfortunately, there exists in the Sierra of Peru
> the traditional hacienda where the Indian is a ver-
> itable slave, where they pay exceedingly low wages
> and where housing and nourishment are very defi-
> cient.   I have seen in the heights of the Depart-
> ment of Ancash Indians carrying enormous blocks
> of ice with the sole protection of a piece of leather
> on their backs, taking them to the region of the
> Callejon de Huaylas to prepare a refreshment that
> in Peru is called 'raspadilla. '   One can imagine
> what, in economic compensation, this extraordinary
> effort to transport these blocks of ice from the
> heights to the lower valleys means, to the end of
> selling a drink whose price is less than two cents.
>
> I have seen in the same part of the country Indians
> carrying bundles of flax to gathering points 4 or 5
> kilometers distant for daily wages of 70 or 80
> centavos of a sol (about 3 cents).   Even though it
> seems incredible, I have seen, in the same region,
> Indians collecting fruit peelings thrown away by
> residents of the Hotel at Chancos to use them for
> food.
>
> In the region of Apurimac, the wife of a hacendado
> told me of the meager output of the Indian popula-
> tion in terms of their work.   She said that they
> were a lazy race, made into brutes by alcohol and

coca.   I asked her about the food that they received from the hacienda.   She replied that every-
day they were given a barley cake, a portion of
salt and a handful of coca.   It took much work for
me to explain to her, an educated woman, about
calories and proteins as well as about the protective foods that a man needs in order to produce.
I told her that as a tractor needs gasoline and lu-
bricants, so a human being needs certain quantities
of food in order to be able to work.   The extraordinary thing is that these people, who get food
that is barely subsistence, can work at all.

Elite Values Understandable by Reference to Peasants' Situation

It is vital to explore the reality touched upon by
Seoane if one is to understand Peru's landed elite.   The typical characteristics of the campesino situation (the term includes both Indians and mixed bloods or mestizos) are these:
He has been denied the benefits of education.   Illiteracy
among female Indians has been estimated at ninety-five percent and among males seventy-five to eighty-five percent,
taking those seventeen years and older.   Well over fifty percent of rural children of school age do not attend school and
then only the lowest elementary grades (in Peru as a whole
forty percent of the children do not receive any schooling).
The educational task is not easy since one third of all the
country's inhabitants speak Quechua or Aymara.   As noted
above by Vice President Seoane, campesinos suffer from
malnutrition, cutting their work capacity by more than half.
A CIDA study classified eighty-five percent of peasants'
houses in the Sierra (sixty-five percent on the coast) as very
bad.   These mud huts form the "rancherías" of the haciendas,
without water, ventilation or sewage disposal.   Clothing,
which is the main means of distinguishing mestizos from Indians (including the mixture of the two known as the "cholo"),
reflects a somewhat better state of affairs.   The Sierra
peasant, who is principally a herder, has alpaca wool for
weaving.   His sources of livelihood are among the lowest in
the world.   Depending on his relationship with the land and
a patrón, a campesino's income varies from the scraps and
castoffs cited by Edgardo Seoane to the eighteen soles (sixty-
five cents) daily paid by coastal haciendas.   In between, one
finds the infinite variety of arrangements.   Hacendados will
grant the use of small strips of land in return for twenty to

fifty percent of the crop, plus usually three days of unpaid
work a week by the campesino and his family. Yanaconas,
peones relatively high on the peasant social scale, who get
on well with the hacendado may receive the right to farm
without the hated unpaid labor services. As noted below,
the command the hacendado enjoys over the yanacona's vote
is an important source of the former's political power.

Much has been written on the psychology of the peasant. In the Peruvian Andes, anomie, cultural disorientation,
a sense of despair giving way to desperation and a spirit of
rebellion seem to be the characteristics noted by many observers. The rancheria on a large estate or the autonomous
comunidad indigena with its members acting as freeholders
of tiny strips of land (sometimes allocated by furrows, not
by parts of acres) still remains the largest social unit recognized by the peasants. They vigorously identify themselves
with their community and hold themselves apart from other
Indian communities. The members are intensely conservative. Lacking adequate resources in land, water, technical
knowledge and contacts with the outside world, the majority
are unable to produce marketable commodities. Their inability to speak Spanish isolates them from the channels of
communication between community and nation. They cling to
the traditional "rejection pattern" of their ancestors. The
production of sufficient corn, barley or other subsistence
crop remains their major goal in life. The main factor
working for change is migration. Inheritance problems reduce available land in many communities to one and one-
quarter acre per family.[7] Some one million peasants mi-
grated to the country's seventeen cities (more than one-half
million to Lima alone) in the years 1940-1961. These mi-
grations, with many persons returning to the Sierra, constitute a powerful acculturation force. Migration is changing
many activities of the Indians and destroying some of the
conservative spirit of the rural peasants. Returning Indians
have discovered the existence of alternatives to what they
have been accustomed to receive at the hands of the landowning class. Work for wages, purchase of land, small scale
commerce and industry and, perhaps most significant, membership in peasant syndicates and unions open new perspectives to them.

Peasant Values vis-à-vis Upper Class

To the lower strata in Peruvian society comprising

Indians, mestizos and cholos, "Peru" as a concept lies beyond their ken.   The Peruvian "nation" they identify as the
highly centralized administration located in Lima.   Strong
local feelings, toward one's region, hacienda or extended
family, replace the sentiment of being a "Peruvian." There
is a well-founded belief that the benefits flowing from the
state are reserved for Limeños, or for the wealthy class.
"Serranos" support willingly only those political movements
that seem to aim at arresting centralizing tendencies in the
structure of the state.   Solidarity toward the local group
takes the place of larger loyalties.   In all classes, one
notes passivity and subordination of the individual to those
higher in the social scale as outstanding characteristics.
Adult years, particularly, are noted for utter passivity and
conformity.   Experience has shown this is the best way to
"hold onto one's place" in the Peruvian social hierarchy. [8]

     Prospects of bettering one's place, for members of
the lower classes, are virtually nil.   "Keeping distances" is
an outstanding trait of the social system.   This is accomplished by a quick rebuff and indication of displeasure at any
attempt at upward mobility.   The Catholic religion plays an
important part in maintaining respectful attitudes and feelings
of awe toward the existing social order on the part of the
masses.

     These pressures produce a lower class that is ex-
tremely conservative, accepting the existence of strict hierarchy and a preordained low rung on the ladder for members
of that class.   These fundamental values instilled by religion
seem to change very little even when cholos or mestizos
adopt, in adult years, political ideologies opposed to the existing order.   The world-view of all classes (including the
middle and upper class, often called "mistis" by Peruvian
Indians) has much in common, perhaps explaining the powerful hold of beliefs instilled in early years.   Julian Steward
writes that natural phenomena are viewed as beyond human
control, being manifestations of divine will.   Man is regarded
as different from animals because he has a soul.   The
Church teaches that, even though sons of God, men were
created unequal, the lower classes being by nature inferior
and destined to serve the upper classes.   These differences
must be respected and efforts made by all to keep the existing hierarchy.   Life is sacred, but the life or death of a
person of the middle and upper class is more important than
that of someone in the lower ones.   All in all, it is a static
and conservative system of values.   As we shall see in the

following chapter, land and possession thereof plays a most significant role in determining where a person falls within the social order.

Peasant Invasions and Unrest

By reserving political activity solely to itself and through its control of the gains resulting from economic activity, the landed upper class (in which term is included the barely visible middle class) demands submission, respect and obedience from the lower orders. Manual work is held to be the obligation and destiny of the lower class. Due to its supposed social inferiority, the lower class is expected to render personal service to the upper. Commercial activity consists of everyone's trying to reap some advantages from the scant pastoral and agricultural production of the campesino.

It is not to be wondered at that, in relations between classes, there is ever-present elements of repressed aggression and potential conflict. Usually, conflict is deflected by use of humor or exaggerated forms of courtesy. Rebellions do occur, however, in the form of strikes and "invasions" of haciendas. The years 1961-63 were a period of unrest in rural zones, particularly in the south of Peru and in the Departments of Lambayeque and La Libertad in the north. The hunger of the peasant for land has been the common motive. Organizational effort by rural labor unions and peasant federations preceded the armed conflicts. Peaceful occupation of hacienda lands reserved to the hacendado was the weapon chosen by the peasant leaders. [9] With the passage of the Agrarian Reform Law in 1964, these landowner-peasant conflicts tended to subside.

The eruption of violence in Peru's rural zones represents an end-product of ideological currents launched by Manuel Gonzales Prada and Jose Carlos Mariátegui, among others, during the first decades of this century. Their teachings, made concrete in the Alianza Popular Revolucionaria Americana (APRA) founded in 1924 in Mexico by the Peruvian exile, Victor Raúl Haya de la Torre, led to an extended period of agitation, extending from 1931 to 1947. In recent years, Communism, in its orthodox form of the Communist Party in Peru and as Trotskyites and Fidelistas, has usurped the banner of APRA as the principal motor of rural violence. Communist Party's teachings have emphasized

prudence even while viewing the oppressed rural masses as
"the most efficient motive force of the revolutionary movement. "10   The Party argues that the working class and masses in the cities plays the decisive role, even though the
armed conflict of the revolution may begin in rural areas.

The Pervasive Poverty of Rural Zones

Conditions of the Peruvian rural mass led to an early
reform wave in the first decades of this century.   The effort produced little ameliorating legislation.   Regimes in
power since that time have refrained from announcing any
outright reactionary programs.   Often, the tactic has been
to argue that not only are reforms (such as those proposed
in the 1961 Alliance For Progress documents) desirable but
they have, in fact, already been accomplished in Peru.

The outstanding fact about this mountainous and desert
region is the prevailing poverty.   It has been said that "in
Peru, even the rich are poor!"   By this is meant that the
upper class, dwelling in the country and drawing its wealth
from haciendas or plantations, enjoys relatively modest in-
comes.   For most of them, their wealth supports a tolerable
living standard and perhaps permits education of their male
children abroad.   Nor is the Church itself noted for wealth.
Close students of Peru point to the meagerness of Church resources, despite the uninterrupted possession since Colonial
times by the Catholic Church of a substantial, but unknown,
portion of the country's land. [11]

Peru has all the characteristics of a culture of poverty.   Rather than thinking in terms of a wealthy, exploiting
class on top "milking the poor, " one is better advised to
look at a stratification system and set of values handed down,
almost unchanged, from the Colonial era, in seeking to explain the persistence of the landed elite.   A close look at the
economic system of rural areas shows that, for twenty years
or more, the traditional hacienda mode of production has
been deteriorating.   The political and social importance of
the hacienda system, on the other hand, and the strength of
its defenders in the National Congress and Central Government has not diminished.   Not wealth, but prestige and the
power that goes with it has been the main goal of Peruvians.
Buried deep in their pysche is what one observer called "the
fury of the Criollo against the white Spaniard. "   The Spanish
Laws of the Indies said that a man lost nobility if he prac-

tised manual occupations. Criollos (Spaniards born in the
New World) aped the Spanish upper class. They became
more rigid than the "peninsulares" (those born in Spain) in
maintaining elite values. Perhaps this was because of their
close tie and skin color affiliation with the non-noble mestizo
and Indian masses. Everyone avoided anything that implied
loss of noble status. The desire to identify with the elite
conditioned the whole educational system. Everyone sought
high status by entering only noble occupations--the army,
priesthood, higher administration and landed proprietorship.

Large Estate's Responsibility for Peru's Backwardness

        Our picture of the interior is not complete without a
summing up of the latifundio's regressive role. In Peru,
virtually all business, educational and formal governmental
activity is concentrated in the capital, Lima. With 1.5 million inhabitants (twelve percent of the country's population),
it far outranks the second-ranking city, Arequipa, which has
only one-tenth Lima's population. There is no real urban
life outside the capital. Isolation and backwardness, as we
have seen, characterize the entire expanse of the rest of the
country. Rural-dwelling Peruvians feel alienation towards
Lima. Those who can do so, e.g., officials "exiled" to an
interior town, long for the moment when they can return to
its languor and gossipy intrigue. Well-to-do landowners visit
their properties in the rural zone once a year, or less frequently, leaving them in the care of a mestizo administrator.
The Peruvian landed elite are characteristically absentee
landowners with all that this implies of neglect toward the
interior zone.

        Summing up what has been said above, it can be af-
firmed that Peru's archaic way of life and rural stagnation
is traceable directly to the latifundios. This is so notwithstanding the fact that the population is widely scattered in
small clusters and transportation is lacking. The institution
of the hacienda claims the best land and then wastes it. The
haciendas by their size greatly increase distances to be covered. The properties, thus, are responsible for the shortage
of roads and the scattering of rural dwellers. The estates
imprison their inhabitants in a rigid social structure. A hacienda fills all needs which remain at the primitive level of
a bygone era. One sees the master's large house at the
center, surrounded by draft and pack animals, a piece or
two of farm equipment, perhaps a truck (if a road exists,

since many hacendados prefer that no roads reach their property to lessen the likelihood of their subjects' fleeing to the
cities).   The workers live in miserable hovels at various
locales on the extensive property.   A few haciendas have
built schools, but learning to read and write has little practical value in this society and is soon forgotten.   Sometimes
a priest calls at the big house to offer blessings and "sanc-
tify" common law marriages.   Legal advice and protection
is provided by the administrator.   There is a storekeeper
occasionally as well as a small supply of medicines on the
estate.   Discharging its social function to rural masses who
demand nothing more, the latifundio fulfills so many needs
that villages and small towns have had little reason to develop in Peru.

        Isolating the peasants at a bare subsistence level,
failing at the same time to serve the educational and social
function of the small town, the latifundio perpetuates a form
of feudalism.   Peru's feudal structure is different from and
inferior to that of late medieval Europe.   It lacks the hierarchy of true feudal societies.   The big landowners are
lords, but there is no overlord like the medieval king.   The
national government in Peru, as elsewhere in Latin America,
has never succeeded in reuniting authority that became dispersed with independence.   Only substantial agrarian reform
(see Chapter VI) can restore the central authority now lacking in "our poor, disarticulated Peru, " as one member of
the seminars called it.

        Peruvians have long neglected the problem of agrarian
reform.   Most Peruvian planners have yet to be convinced
that survival of feudal social relationships hampers economic
development.   They dimly feel the need of integrating the
masses of Peruvians now outside the mainstream of the nation.   But they are happy to forget these peasant masses as
they are the backward, archaic, uncomfortable world of rural Peru.   What little money for development there is should,
they feel, be spent for better housing, education and health
services for the privileged urban minority.   Peruvians argue
that rural populations should not be overexposed to the amenities of urban life.   Rural isolation of the bulk of the country's population prevents wants from arising, in their view.
Latifundios with all their backwardness thus tend to minimize
pressure for immediate improvements in living conditions.

        In the discussions during the seminars of the landed
estate as an institution, the remnants of feudal forms of

property and landlord-tenant relations were roundly castigated. But few of the young elite representatives participating made any mention of abolishing or restricting the hacienda.   They put the problem of the latifundio easily out of their minds. Views were expressed that the backward people in rural zones are happy with their bare subsistence way of life under a paternalism that supposedly shelters them.   Recalling the squalor of rural migrants to the cities, they argued that the peasants are better off in their rural existence.

But, as will be discussed below, manorial society where all are under tight patriarchical authority is disintegrating.   To some, its "premature disintegration" is cause for concern.   One viewpoint is that the survival of the latifundios seems necessary to hold the Indian masses in check. Leaving the rural population locked in the relics of a bygone past appeared, in the view of some participants, as a way of eliminating them, of forgetting them, of abandoning them to fate.   The theme of what to do about the sixty percent of Peruvians who are Indians--leave them unnoticed within the grip of an archaic system or take conscious measures to incorporate them into a modern nation as Mexico has done-- has been the underlying theme of Peruvian politics for three quarters of a century.

<h2 style="text-align:center">Notes</h2>

1.   Harold D. Lasswell and A. Kaplan, Power and Society (New Haven: Yale University Press, 1950) use influence rather than power as the general term.   The operational definition here is taken from Karl W. Deutsch, "On the Concepts of Politics and Power, " Journal of International Affairs, Vol. XXI, No. 2 (1967), pp. 232-241.

2.   Frank Tannenbaum, "Toward an Appreciation of Latin America, " The United States and Latin America (Columbia University, New York: The American Assembly, 1956), p. 31.

3.   Jacques Lambert, Latin America, Social Structures and Political Institutions (Berkeley: University of California Press, 1967), p. 59.

4.   Daniel Cosío Villegas, American Extremes (Austin: University of Texas Press, 1964), p. 79.

5. Pan American Union, Estudio Económico y Social de
    América Latina (1963), p. 258. The annex to this vol-
    ume, entitled Sistemas Socioculturales presents a
    trenchant account of the hacienda system, explaining
    how it started, why it persists, tracing this to its util-
    ity in managing the large Indian populations of the
    Sierra. Other good sources on the hacienda systems
    include: International Labor Office, The Landless
    Farmer in Latin America (Geneva, 1957); José Matos
    Mar, "Consideraciones sobre la situación social del
    Perú, " América Latina, Rio de Janeiro, Ano 7, No. 1
    (January-March, 1964); Thomas R. Ford, Man and
    Land in Peru (Gainesville: University of Florida Press,
    1955); Francisco Ponce de Leon, "The Problem of
    Land Ownership in Peru, " Land Tenure, edited by
    Kenneth H. Parsons, Raymond J. Penn and Philip M.
    Raup (Madison: University of Wisconsin Press, 1963).

6. The important function of markets in permitting union
    organizers to reach the peasants is stressed in Richard
    P. Schaedel, "Etude Comparative des Societés Paysannes
    d'Amerique Latine, " América Latina (July-September,
    1966), pp. 38-39.

7. Alfred Metraux, "La estructura social y económica de
    las comunidades indias de la región andina, " Interna-
    tional Labor Office Review, Geneva, Vol. 59, No. 3
    (March, 1959), pp. 261-281.

8. Gabriel Escobar, "La Cultura: Sistema de Valores, "
    Lima, Plan Regional para el Dessarrollo del Sur del
    Perú, Vol. XXII, PS/F/50. Written by the coordi-
    nator of Andean Seminar No. 2 jointly with Richard
    P. Schaedel, this volume constitutes a thorough study
    of the values and attitudes of Peru's landed elite.

9. Hugo Neira, Cuzco: Tierra y Muerte (Lima: Popu-
    libros Peruanos, 1964), pp. 110-121. Neira was a
    leader of these rebellions and describes them in this
    book.

10. Partido Comunista, "Por la senda de Mariátegui, "
    Manifesto del IV Congreso del Partido Comunista
    (Lima, August, 1962).

11. J. Lloyd Mecham, Church and State in Latin America,
    A History of Politico-Ecclesiastical Relations (Chapel

Hill: University of North Carolina Press, 1966), pp. 215-216.

Chapter II

Rural Political Structure in Peru

In the Peruvian social structure, there are, for practical purposes, but two social classes, an upper and a lower.[1] The upper class is composed of hacienda owners plus persons who control the limited industry or commerce that exists. Members of the higher administrative hierarchies (prefects, banking officials, priests, military and police commanders) belong to this class. Normally, upper class Peruvians live in Lima or in one of the cities (Arequipa, Trujillo, Cuzco). The men occupy themselves in commercial life, management of properties or participation in politics. The women, aided by many servants, are concerned with domestic and family affairs, giving much time to religion. Careers in law and medicine are followed for the prestige and the influence they bring. Upper class individuals are generally conservative and tradition-minded. They are concerned mainly with the maintenance of their social status and the integrity of their families and properties. Gradually, a more dynamic sector of the upper class is making its appearance. One finds these individuals active in banking, commerce and industry.

An incipient middle class is making its appearance in the person of public functionaries, teachers, military officers, employees of banks and commercial firms and lower ranking members of the priesthood. In the middle class, too, are many members of the legal, medical and engineering professions. Often, they function as mayors, governors (a low ranking official in charge of a district), subprefects and justices of the peace. These people usually have strong regional or local identifications and make up a substantial part of the electorate.[2] Their highest ambition is to arrive at upper class status through acquisition of land or wealth in some other form. Women of this class occupy themselves in family matters, social work, nursing or teaching, and, not infrequently, medicine and dentistry. In the high value they place on status, in conserving what they have, in authoritarianism and dependence, in acceptance of Church con-

trol over family and educational matters, middle class representatives differ only slightly from the upper class.

Little has been written about the political customs and
habits that make up Peru's political culture. The best study
of local government in the country, written in 1964 by Allan
Austin, [3] omits any mention, for example, of haciendas, gamonales, jefes políticos, caciques, jefecillos, patrones.
These are who make up the actual government of the country
outside the capital. Instead, Austin writes strictly about the
formal structure, which has little to do with what actually
happens. The brief sketch of upper class values above suggests the rigid stratification system through which political
activity moves. The essential institutional factors are this
system, the political structure, the structure of families and
clans. Despite economic and demographic changes, these
institutions and the attitudes and values surrounding them remain unaltered from the Colonial era. It is the purpose of
this chapter to focus on the informal system of government
in rural Peru, in particular, the political role of the landowners. The patrón and gamonal constitute the particular
objects of inquiry.

Political Function of the Hacienda

It has been noted that rural areas in Peru bear re-
semblances to late medieval conditions in Europe. For
example, the process of enclosure (the passing of communal
lands into private hands), which produced so much strife in
16th century England, has remained a prime issue in the
Peruvian interior from the 19th century to the present. Politics increasingly turn on the struggle of the central government for control of the large landowners, the Army and the
Church. The problem of politics is seen by some as consisting of "revolutions that did not take place when they
should have." Government in Europe brought such independent power domains as the great landowners under control in
the revolutions of 1688, 1789 and 1917. This movement
from medieval to modern patterns has yet to occur in Peru. [4]

As in post-medieval Europe, the determining factor in
this archaic social structure is the "lord of the manor, "
i. e., the hacendado. He is the center of the system of
agrarian feudalism still prevailing in Peru. What is this
hacendado type like? What are the "system of rules" by
which he lives?

Tannenbaum, in his treatment of the latifundio, stresses the solidarity of the landowning class. The institution is
marked by a distinctive set of social relations and culture
forms. Chief among these is its control over sanctions and
force. 5 Its control over the principal sources of wealth in
the country make it a "power domain" of the first order.
The large property owner exercises power in his own right.
Usually the local political chief, the hacendado, exercises the
political functions for a given territory. A small group of
men, tied to him by family relationships and the patrón system, constitute the effective government. They use highly
personalistic and informal methods. These men create, in-
terpret and enforce rules that are binding on all members of
the collectivity. The system traces back to the Spanish tradition of authoritarian, centralized, bureaucratic rule. That
system left large territories as virtual fiefdoms of the fortu-
nate beneficiaries of the system of encomiendas. What is
seen today are the residues of that bygone era.

Historical Origins of Peru's Landed Elite

During nearly four centuries, Peru shared the common experience of a remote, undeveloped colony destined
solely to increase the wealth of the mother country. The
Indians constituted, wherever they existed, along with the
mestizos, "human machines to be exploited. " In the Spanish
domains, the pattern was set of a favored elite: education,
economic opportunity and political or ecclesiastical power
were the right only of the peninsulares. With independence,
the only change was that their place was taken by the creo-
les, the pure-blooded (or nearly so) Spaniards born in the
colonies. Like the colonial governors before them, the new
ruling class looked upon government as a source of booty and
personal gain. Government administration was largely pre-
occupied with money matters. Income came mainly from
customs duties, mine taxes, the sale of public posts and the
tribute (head tax) paid by the Indians. The Church received
the diezmo, or "tenth" paid also by the Indians. This fiscal
and administrative system of the Colonial and post-Independence epoch continues in Peru largely unchanged to the present day.

As we have seen, the large rural estate had its origin in the land grants and the reducciones or concentrations
of Indians similar to Indian reservations in the United States.
They were originally intended to civilize, indoctrinate and

organize the Indians, largely for revenue purposes.   The
reducciones in combination with the mita (forced Indian labor,
usually in the mines for one year every seven years) fostered the growth of the latifundio.   The Indian, usually in
debt after his year's mita service, returned to an abandoned
and uncultivated homestead.   Most sold their land for what
they could get from the Spaniards rather than continue their
unequal struggle.   Land titles were (and remain) unclear
throughout most of the highlands.   A periodic re-examination
of titles was a thinly disguised way of giving new title to
persons willing to pay.   The political world of the Indians
was that of the latifundio administrator, who in turn was and
is responsible to the gamonal.   This key personage is first
of all, according to Peruvian writers like Ciro Alegría and
José Maria Arguĕdas, a grabber of lands. 6   He is the owner
of vast lands.   He enjoys coercive power over hundreds and,
sometimes, thousands of unpaid serfs.   The world of the
latifundio took its present form in the 17th and 18th century.
A remarkable spurt of consolidation occurred in the 19th.
Despite its dead weight, inefficiency and inhumanity, noted
in a number of books by Peruvian writers, the system continues on in the present.   It is worth pausing to examine the
best known of these works to get at the mental world of the
large landholder as a social type.   To understand him one
must first understand the value system handed down from
Peru's past.

Persistence of Aristocratic Values

        Peruvians see themselves as a cultured people with a
rich heritage from Colonial and pre-Conquest times.   Spring-
ing from a profoundly conservative colonial world, Peru has
shown no originality in devising new social forms.   The ruling Criollo class broke reluctantly with Spain.   Perhaps because of this nostalgia, Peruvians have proved incapable of
creating a modern society.   Looking at the value context of
highland Peru, one finds four prime values all reflecting feudal relationships which suppose the underlying inequality of
men.   There is first the belief in hierarchy.   When Peruvians are involved in any social relation, their mutual hier-
archial situation is uppermost in their minds.   This is followed by paternalism, which implies the superiority of one
actor over the other.   Paternalistic and dependent attitudes
are common.   Being deeply ingrained, they color relations
within government and Church.   The hacienda owner expects
a personal loyalty from "his men. "   Although the landowners'

reciprocal responsibilities under the paternal system often go
unfilled, the peasants meet this with their tremendous re-
serves of fatalism (a favorite theme of theirs being a belief
that "God is punishing me").

Thirdly, one finds everywhere a strong authoritarianism.
Those who occupy the superior position develop a permanent
authoritarian behavior.   The elite member commands.   In the
face of authoritarian behavior, dissimulation on the part of
the peasant becomes a necessary skill.   One cannot disagree
overtly with the opinions of one's superior, yet one must get
on peaceably with him.   Fourthly, status is all-important,
for each relationship is a "status situation." Strictly contractual relations are not possible in Peru.   To enter into a
contract implies that the parties were previously independent
of one another and equal.   This condition is rarely realized,
particularly in the country's rural areas.

Value Attached to Land

In this near feudal, primarily agricultural society,
political power, prestige and wealth derive from the prime
instrument of production--land and the labor to work it.   In
a lengthy discussion of this topic, a leading Peruvian sociologist, Anibal Ismodes Cairo, declared the major preoccupation of Indians, mestizos, cholos and middle class alike was
to become owners of rural property.   Owning a piece of land
is more than a guarantee of livelihood in the event the political tables should turn.   It enables a man to exercise the
rights granted to the patrón or landlord, and denied the landless.   These rights include security, status in the community, freedom to act and speak freely, some degree of influence
in government and a share in its benefits.   Land assures access to education for one's children.   Only by becoming a
landowner can one benefit from government programs, such
as farm credit or irrigation improvements.   Ismodes stated
that, with a piece of land, the member of the lower class
can begin to plan his future.

Prestige and social security are directly related to
the property one owns.   Mario C. Vasquez, a leading Peruvian anthropologist, has written lucidly of the close connection between the haciendas and prevailing social values. [7]
The owner or lessee of a rural property is immediately i-
dentified as "rico," as a member of the local "society" or
aristocracy ("gente decente").   His peasants call him patrón,

and approach him only with hat removed and eyes cast down-
ward.   In parts of Peru, the "besa manos" is still common
as the proper form of salute, the peasant saluting the patrón
on his knees and kissing his hand.   To infringe these norms,
according to Vasquez, was until recently not permitted lest
it become habitual.

In political relations, the hacendado (even though his
property be a small one) is "known" and the friend of "everyone, " meaning the notables of the region.   In addition, he
has "connections" elsewhere, usually in the capital through
school chums and politicians from the area.   All these
friendly ties create for the landowner "la vara. "   This may
be defined as political, social, economic and religious influence.   In boundary disputes, which occur interminably and
with great frequency in Peru, the Indian communities and
small mestizo holders have learned that "la vara" can be a
potent factor on the side of the hacendado.   The local con-
stabulary and authorities side invariably with the one who
has most "vara. "   If a man is landless, or but a tenant or
squatter, his "vara" is nil.

"Gamonal" Benefits from Political Order

Peruvian tradition identifies the governing elite as being composed mainly of gamonales, so common is the latter
designation for one who is influential and rich.   In the two
best known "Indian romances" dealing with conditions in the
highlands, Alegría and Arguĕdas construct their novels a-
round several examples of this social type.   Both good and
bad hacendados exist in the pages.   The books are generally
tales of the progressive despoliation of the Indians.   The
landlord's or gamonal's land is pictured as being originally
acquired through some obscure process from a convent or
a monastery (indicative of the extent of Church holdings in
Peru).   A hard worker, cunning and without scruple, the
landowner shifts alternately from use of ruse and shrewdness
(offers of money) to resorting to violence.   He starts a
lengthy litigation over borders ("litigio por linderos"), producing an avalanche of stamped, official papers.   When matters are referred to Lima, no response is ever forthcoming.
In the books, the patrón always mobilizes the public authorities and local armed force at his pleasure.   Central government representatives such as Sub-Prefects, magistrates and
Army or police heads, feel the prudent course is not to get
in his way.   Meanwhile, respect for the patrón is taught by

the Church, whose local representatives are often dependent
upon the landowner for economic support. The peasants are
told to "maintain distance" from him. They are advised to
meet inevitable rebuffs at the gamonal's hand with patience
and submission. This is "God's will" in the order of the
universe fixed by him.

Alegría and Arguedas point out that much of this
"land grabbing" activity has been occurring since the turn of
the century. The result is that many of the larger haciendas
in Peru are of fairly recent creation. The process of latifundio creation described invariably culminates in the victory
of the patrón. He, as gamonal, is above the laws. They
cease to exist when they begin to embarrass him. The only
power that can arrest his movement is other gamonales.
Those who are stronger than he are able to risk long and
costly legal maneuverings. Sometimes, they mobilize more
powerful "vara." Eventually, in these novels, the gamonal's
career is climaxed when he becomes a Senator or a Deputy
with assured long tenure in the National Congress.

The essential feature of the gamonal's situation at its
climax is the grasping by one man (the "boss") and his group
of all favors to be derived from the political and administrative system. Good things flow to him from sources both
national and local. The gamonal names, revokes, displaces
functionaries within the administrative system at will. These
are usually found in the particular Ministry or offices subject to his direct control. It is in the gamonal's interest
and at his pleasure that roads, bridges, hospitals, schools
are laid out and built within his domain, which as we have
seen above exists as sort of an independent sovereignty. [8]

The picture is not all black, for both Alegría and
Arguedas point out that there exist good patrones, usually
called "mistis." These landowners protect the Indians and
mestizos dependent upon them, standing between them and
the representatives of the central government, e.g., in keeping them from military service. The good patrón provides
the Indians with work. A second type of patrón, the "vara-
yok" (a mixture of Spanish and Quechua meaning "man with
the baton"), usually is the chief of an Indian community.
Still a third type of patrón is the "tinterillo," usually a man
of mestizo origin, who with legal training, intercedes on be-
half of the peasants with the "mistis" or the civil authorities.
The Peruvian novelists make clear, however, that the gamonal, the representative type of the politico-socio-economic

system as a whole, enjoys all his advances at the expense
of the Indian.   The root characteristic of the socio-political
system I am examining is the spoliation and exploitation of
the large Indian masses existing in Peru.

Hacendado Aspirations

Seen through the eyes of the scions of the upper class
who attended the seminars described, the present socio-economic system has many admirable features.   The patrón assumes a paternalistic conduct toward his peasants.   He feels
he is keeping Christian principles to permit them to remain
on his property.   At the end of harvests, he sometimes
makes presents of chicha and aguardiente (two strong drinks)
to them.   The typical hacendado thinks of himself as a reasonable man.   He is content with the system which divides
whites, mestizos and Indians into separate and unequal
groups, each with its "place" in the scheme of things.   Owning land is not one of the rights of the lower classes, he
feels.   Occasionally, he believes it is unjust for the Indians
to be deprived of education and elementary sanitation, and
he sees no reason for preventing some amenity (a school,
for example) being established.   His sense of wrongness
"does not extend to a desire to alter the status quo."

The landowner's affection is lavished on his land, his
horses, his prize bulls and his several mistresses.   Once
acquired, a hacienda is almost never sold.   It is retained in
the family for generations.   "Recuerdo familiar" dictates that
the property symbolize family unity through the generations.
Vasquez writes that there is special fear that haciendas may
pass into the hands of campesinos.   Landowners in a given
region will join together to prevent this happening.   Many
haciendas are owned and operated by the Church, or let out
under lease by Church organizations.   Sometimes, to prevent a property falling into undesirable hands, it is deeded
to Church-affiliated institutions.

However hard a landowner may be with his peasants,
he is always generous with his friends, the Church, the
authorities and the politicians.   He sends acquaintances in
these groups gifts of his best quality products.   When they
visit the hacienda, they are given kingly treatment.   In this
way, many persons other than the hacendado-gamonal class
benefit from the institution of the hacienda.   To be proprietor of a hacienda, to handle one's peasants well and derive

maximum benefit from them while conceding them the least
possible in return is to be manly or "muy macho."

This life style of the hacendado class constitutes the
mode of life desired by most Peruvians, not simply aspiring
members of the landed elite.   Without exception, there is
no status higher than that associated with landed position.
The landed life is good because it distinguishes one from
the trader and the businessman.   It separates one farthest
from the common people who work with their hands, with
tools and in the process become dirty.   Love of the landed
life marks one as being of a superior breed.   Hence, as
Alegría and Arguédas have argued in their eloquent novels,
in a sentiment echoed by the members of the various Andean
seminars, owning land has both political significance and a
deep emotional importance.   It has produced a way of "playing the political game" on the part of the hacendado-gamonal
class that bears examining.

Peru's Informal Regional Structure of Government

The typical hacienda with the nearest town and the
Indian communities form a distinct sub-region.   Such regions
are created by the hacienda's relations with individuals,
groups and forces.   Although decisions affecting local events
are made outside, e.g., in Lima, it is through the local
landowner that they become effective, if at all.   Similarly,
the landowner's influence counts for a great deal in Lima.
Policies and actions from the outside have identifiable local
impacts through the manorial system.   Reciprocal currents
of influences flow between the manor house, the casa municipal, the departmental and national capitals.

It is these sub-regions, linked to particular haciendas,
which are the building blocks of Peru's informal structure of
government.   There are persons within each who participate
in varying ways in organizing and running things.   They
make the decisions regarding peace and order, collection of
taxes, public employment, distribution of "faena" tasks (compulsory road building), education and judicial concerns.   To
understand the politics of such an informal region, an outsider must seek to know who actually exercises influence and
makes the decisions.   To ascertain this, questions like these
were raised in the seminars: How do these hacendados or
their administrators exercise their political functions?   What
is their method and style of doing business?   Answers sup-

plied the evidence on which to base following tentative formulations of "rules of the game."

Rules of the Game

Rule No. 1--Strive to Secure the Dominant Position of the Landowning Aristocracy by Keeping the Great Mass of the Population isolated from All Decision Making Activity.

All thinking Peruvians have been struck by the numerical superiority of the Indians in their population. Mestizos
and cholos have been denied a share in the national patrimony, but the Indians have been kept in a state of utter subjection, economic and social. The stagnant economic situation
in the Sierra pictured in Chapter I keeps Indians and rural
mestizos on the margin of society. Moreover, it isolates
these groups one from the other. The end sought, consciously or unconsciously, is the neutralizing of the bulk of Peru's
population. This aim is facilitated by the geography, historical development and traditional pattern of life. Leaving
rural dwellers "out of account" eases greatly the landed e-
lite's task of monopolizing channels of political action and
control. Various mechanisms to accomplish this end results
in the insulating of rural Peru from the larger society.

Rule No. 2--Deprive the Whole Sector of the Rural Population from Access to the Land and the Resources Stemming from it.

Land in Peru without a permanent labor force to work
it is relatively valueless except for prestige and security
purposes, as Andrew Pearse and others have pointed out. [9]
Political power (through control of blocs of votes) and wealth
stem from having large numbers of peasants under one's
control. The value of the encomienda system lay in its giving rights to exact compulsory labor and tribute from Indian
populations. The unsatisfactory nature of a constantly changing labor force impelled the proprietor class to build up a
permanent class of laborers. The essential condition for
creating such a class was to deprive all but a tiny segment
of the rural population from access to land. In the present
as in the past, ability to get and hold labor matches the getting and holding of land as the twin pillars of Peruvian rural
social organization. The "unwritten rule" cited above shows
that practical purposes are served by upper class values and
attitudes.

Rule No. 3--Combine to Deny the Possibility of Social As-
            cension from the Lower Ranks.

As we have seen, the Peruvian scene is marked by
striking social, cultural and economic differences. Even at
the lowest level, these are discernable. At the bottom of
the heap are the wage laborers with no rights to use land.
Those with a permanent tie to a hacienda are considered as
slightly better off. Above these are those in a paternalistic
relationship with a patrón, expressed in the right granted by
a landowner for them to use a strip of land. Peasants holding land in their own right stand higher still. The emphasis
in the system is to "mantener en su sitio" ("hold one's
place") and to "guardar las distancias" ("keep one's distance"). Universally, the higher class looks with strong dis-
favor on upward mobility for the lower classes. Those who
attempt to break through the subtle barriers placed in their
way are accused of "exceso de ambición, " "deseo de figura-
ción" or "egolatría" (ego worship). As a result, able individuals without upper class advantages escape abroad or
lapse into resigned passivity.[10] In terms of politics, constant evidence of and reference to their inferiority tends to
prevent potential lower class leaders from arising. The
system has subtle but effective punishment for those talented
ones from below designated (and the Spanish language is
singularly rich in these epithets) as "refinado, " "recien ve-
nido, " "advenedizo" ("intruder"), "aspirante."[11] Where, as
happens, the rare lower class or lower middle class representative climbs to power or wealth (e. g., through military
or commercial channels), negative valuations are reversed
and he is rapidly absorbed into the traditional directing
class.

Rule No. 4--Endeavor to Monopolize all Interaction and Com-
              munication between the Rural Community and
              the Larger Society.

The typical large rural property is an autocratically
governed, quasi independent social entity. Isolation, lack of
communications with the capital, absence of roads serve the
purpose of centralizing all interaction in the hands of the
hacendado or his administrator.[12] Upper class domination
of the local population is enforced through their command of
communications, commerce and friends in the capital. The
peasants' only alternative is to accept the patrón's justice,
orders, trading arrangements and punishments. Where such
enforced isolation can be maintained, the hacendado-gamonal

class develops extra-legal forms of control, such as the un-
ionization of the patrones, blacklists (against "troublemakers"),
threats of dismissal, terror. As will be seen in the following chapter, at election time this monopoly of interaction and
communication enables the gamonal to deliver all the votes
of his peasants to a chosen candidate. One of the prices
paid for these votes is the guarantee that the gamonal will be
left alone by the government to administer his fiefdom as he
has in the past.[13]

Notes

1. Mario C. Vasquez, Hacienda, Peonaje y Servidumbre
   en los Andes, Monografías Andinas, No. 1, Lima; Vol.
   LVII, 1955, pp. 488-500; Richard N. Adams, "A
   Change from Caste to Class in a Peruvian Sierra
   Town, " Social Forces, Vol. XXXI, 1953, pp. 238-244.

2. Victor Andrés Belaunde, Meditaciones Peruanas (Lima:
   Talleres Gráficos Villanueva, 1963), pp. 88-90. A
   literacy requirement for voting, Belaunde points out,
   tends to be flexibly interpreted by the local authorities,
   permitting control of sizeable blocs of votes by the caciques. The subject is also dealt with in Jorge Basadre, La Multitud, la Ciudad y el Campo en la Historia del Perú (Lima, 1947).

3. Allan Austin, Estudio Sobre El Gobierno Municipal Del
   Perú (Lima: Institute of Public Administration, Oficina Nacional de Racionalización y Capacitación de la
   Administración Pública, November, 1964). The best
   study on formal government structures at Departmental
   and Provincial levels is Lizardo Alzamora Silva, De-
   recho constitucional general y del Perú (Lima, 1942)
   and Victor Graciano Maita, Gobierno Municipal (Lima,
   1946).

4. Richard Adams, The Second Sowing: Power and Secondary Development (San Francisco: Howard Chandler,
   1967).

5. Anibal Quijano Obregón (participant in Andean Seminar
   I), "El Movimiento Campesino del Perú y Sus Lideres, "
   América Latina, Ano 8, No. 4 (October-December,
   1965). Quijano describes the sanctions used against
   peasant leaders in the country.

6.   Ciro Alegría, El Mundo es ancho y ajeno (Minerva,
     Mexico, 1952); Jose Maria Arguĕdas, "Evolución de
     las Comunidades Indígenas," Revista del Museo Nacio-
     nal, Vol. 26 (Lima, 1957). Another useful study of
     society is William Stein, Hualcán: Life in the High-
     lands of Peru (Ithaca, N. Y.: Cornell University Press,
     1962).

7.   Mario Vasquez, op. cit., pp. 32-36. See also Henry
     F. Dobyns, The Social Matrix of Peruvian Indigenous
     Communities, Peru Project Monograph, Department of
     Anthropology (Cornell University, 1964), pp. 13-25.

8.   Oscar J. Alers, "Population and Development in a
     Peruvian Community," Journal of Inter-American Stud-
     ies (October, 1965), pp. 423-448. Dobyns, op. cit.,
     pp. 38-45 deals with these characteristics of the phe-
     nomenon of "gamonalismo."

9.   Andrew Pearse, "Agrarian Change Trends in Latin
     America," Latin American Research Review, Vol. 1,
     No. 3 (1966), pp. 49-50.

10. Prevailing middle and lower class attitudes are de-
     scribed in Eugene A. Hammel, Wealth, Authority and Pres-
     tige in the Ica Valley, Peru (Albuquerque: University
     of New Mexico Press, 1962). Peru is cited as rank-
     ing fourth in South America (after Argentina, Brazil
     and Colombia) in the number of engineers, doctors,
     social and natural scientists emigrating to the United
     States. (Committee on Government Operations, House
     of Representatives, 90th Congress, 1st Session, "The
     Brain Drain into the United States of Scientists, Engi-
     neers and Physicians" [Washington: U. S. Government
     Printing Office, July, 1967].), Table I, pp. 18-29.

11. Gabriel Escobar, "La Cultura: Sistema de Valores,"
     Lima, Plan Regional para el Desarrollo del Sur del
     Perú, Vol. XXII (1959).

12. For example, I learned during a visit to Ayacucho in
     1964 that the only communication between this major
     city and the capital of the country was a radio tele-
     phone for the exclusive use of the Prefect of the De-
     partment.

13. Sources consulted on the Peruvian landowners' relations

with the Central Government include: Richard Schaedel,
Gabriel Escobar, et. al., Funciones y Medios de Gobierno Local, Lima, Plan Regional para el Desarrollo
del Sur del Perú, Vol. XXIII PS/F/52; and La Organización Social en el Departamento de Puno, Vol. XXII,
PX/F/49. The effort in this endeavor to single out
and suggest landed elite "rules of the political game"
deliberately avoids many byways that have been pursued
by other scholars, e.g., the political behavior of the
military, the Church, labor union leaders and university students.   Regarding the Peruvian military's role,
much of importance could be said, as witness the fact
that some seventy-seven of the ninety-nine changes of
government since 1821 have been "unconstitutional,"
all but a few representing military intervention in politics.   A number of hypotheses have been gathered by
Robert D. Putnam in his "Toward Explaining Military
Intervention in Latin American Politics," World Politics (October, 1967).   Several apply to Peru.   Among
these are Finer's conclusion "where public attachment
to civilian institutions is weak or non-existent, military intervention in politics will have wide scope,"
(Samuel E. Finer, The Man on Horseback [New York,
1962], p. 21) and Finer's "military intervention de-
creases with the development within the military of a
norm of civilian supremacy" (Ibid., p. 32); Alexander's
findings that "the propensity for military intervention
increases with the habituation of the military to intervention" (Robert J. Alexander, "The Army in Politics,"
in H. E. Davis (ed.), Government and Politics in Latin America [New York, 1958], pp. 154-155; Huntington's implication that "social mobilization leads to military rule and that civilian rule depends on strong political institutions" by which he means effective political parties, political interest groups and civilian governmental institutions (Samuel P. Huntington, "Political Development and Political Decay," World Politics,
XVII [April, 1965], pp. 386-430); and Germani and
Silvert's articulation that "the likelihood of military
intervention is greater, the greater the cleavages and
the less the consensus in a society" (Gino Germani and
Kalman Silvert, "Politics, Social Structure and Military
Intervention in Latin America," Archives Europeennes
de Sociologie, II [Spring, 1961], pp. 62-81).   James L.
Payne's Labor and Politics in Peru: The System of
Political Bargaining (New Haven: Yale University
Press, 1965) links military intervention, civilian vio-

lence and employer-employee conflicts in an effort to
explore "rules of the game" as played by Peruvian
labor leaders.   Payne draws mainly on his finding that
"violence is the norm" in Latin American politics.
His main reliance is on interviews with Peruvian trade
unionists.   He treats at length the "rule" that organized labor threatens violence (i. e., strikes) at the same
time dickering with the military in order to force the
President of the country either to accede to its wishes
or face the possibility of removal by a military coup.
Payne's observations, although limited to but one aspect of the total political picture, are important in
that they suggest that all Peruvian political groups (including the landholding-commercial class which is my
concern here) periodically encourage interventions by
the military for their own short-sighted purposes.
None of these groups recognize that they are thereby
perpetuating a system that can best be described as
"praetorian" because of its similarity to the frequent
incursions of the garrisons into the seat of power during the Roman Empire.   Events since 1968 bear out the
vital importance of an inquiry such as this into the value
system and political role of the Peruvian military.

deterioration in the hacienda system's capacity to produce enough to sustain a rapidly rising population, both in the countryside and in the capital. The middle and lower classes, faced with these rigidities, seek to solve their problems through such means as migration, multiple jobs, religious faith and cooperation within the extended family. Only rarely do they think of political actions which will change their basic relationship to the governing elite.

Peruvians of all classes share a view of government that presents parallels to 18th century France or to England prior to the rise of industrialization. The chief legacy of the Colonial era in Peru is the tradition that the major proportion of the educated class depends for its livelihood on the public payroll. A copious administrative, religious and clerical bureaucracy existed throughout the Colonial epoch. From the 19th century on, a sizeable military bureaucracy was added to the others. Faced with restricted opportunities on the land or in commerce, Peruvians have traditionally sought government sinecures. Frequent turnovers in government have been welcomed in the expectation that they would lead to a place on the public rolls, followed by a modest pension. Changes in government had, and have today, an undoubted economic and social content, but the maximum expectations surrounding inauguration of a new government have been for "bureaucratic solutions, " i. e., increases all around in the number of offices and opportunities for employment. 4

Inapplicability of Usual Political Analysis to Peru

Basic to understanding the "game of politics" in Peru is recognition that the Central Government is still struggling for control of the large landholders, of the Army, of the Church. The movement from medieval to modern conditions, whereby these "power domains" (in Richard N. Adams' phrase) were brought under control of the secular state in Europe, has yet to occur in Peru and in much of Latin America. In England out of the confusion of the 16th and 17th centuries, local autonomies such as landed estates and private armies were merged into a system of control administered by a central government. Around and below this government there evolved a political system, i. e., "a persistent pattern of human relationships that involves power, legitimate rule and authority. " The developing English and American systems were regarded as democratic because the

opportunity to participate in decisions was widely shared, for
example, by economic organizations such as trade unions.
In Peru, as we have seen, participation was limited to a
few, a condition prevailing to the present day.

Legitimacy characterized the political system of England and North America because there was a general belief
that the persons holding power had good title to their position in the eyes of the people. [5] Legitimacy is based fundamentally on religious and philosophical beliefs. It establish-
es how people are recruited and trained for political roles;
how different groups are given a voice within the system;
how demands are combined and influence brought to bear;
how political information is communicated. In such a political system, one can analyze the "input, " i. e., the demands
placed on the political system to do certain things particular
sectors of the population want. The "output" consists of the
political decisions which are made, executed and interpreted
by different governmental organs. In a modern political system such as that of England or the United States, functions
are highly specialized. Different functions are carried out
by different structures and different men.

This model of a modern political culture finds no
counterpart in Peru. The revolution, as has been stated,
that should have brought it about "did not occur when it
should have, " that is, at the time of the breakaway from
Spain. Peruvian governments cannot be analyzed in terms
of the "demands upon them" on the one side or of "decisions
and non-decisions" on the other. They are not decision-
oriented. Decisional power often remains outside the central
government's sphere. This is seen, for example, in the
"veto" of the military over decisions of the civilian government. Nor is the state intended to serve public needs.
Historically, as shown above, the government bureaucracy
is conceived of as a means of providing livelihood for the
greatest number.

Some Guiding Concepts

There are, nevertheless, useful concepts to aid in
our effort to understand political processes in this culture.
The term apoliticals describes the mass of the population
which is for all practical purposes without a political role.
This apolitical stratum is extremely large due to mass illiteracy, isolation in the rural areas, lack of a minimum po-

litical sophistication, and fatalistic belief in one's inability
to influence decisions even through involvement. 6 This situation, it should be noted, is changing with increasing ur-
banization, popular restiveness and the organizational work
that is underway in the rural areas.

Besides the apolitical mass, there are the political
strata. These consist of middle and upper class people,
such as public employees, university teachers, lawyers,
engineers and the lower priesthood. They have some information about political events and participate in varying ways,
from voting to political action at election time on the assumption that their involvement has some relationship to decision. There are the power seekers who actively pursue
influence and power. Their motives may be personal self-
interest, or a complex of motives based on family tradition
or psychological deprivation. These individuals are landed
elite members for the most part. Then, there are the challengers to the power-wielders. This group, young intellectuals and a few disaffected members of the elite, will be
dealt with in a final portion of this study.

Finally, one may look at the powerful, the traditional
ruling element. Our chief concern, these are the persons
who, whether or not they actively seek power, have it.
Power in Peru, as this study endeavors to show, is most
often acquired by virtue of one's position as a large, hered-
itary landowner, or a higher ranking member of the administrative, banking, Church or military hierarchies. Land
appears to be the most basic resource on which their economic and political power is built.

The dilemma of government in Peru, facing all Peruvian Presidents, is how to effect one's will in the face of
traditional power holders who offer strong resistance to any
interferences in their long accustomed exercise of power.
As representative of the Peruvian upper class, he must act
within the rules laid down. Political life is considered the
exclusive preserve of the elite. Rule by a few families
could hardly be avoided in a country characterized by peasant masses living at a bare subsistence level. The governing elements cannot be effectively challenged by the small
middle class. Bourricaud points out that it is composed of
people strongly alien to one another without shared values
or a "middle class ideology. "7 It is the Peruvian President
who daily faces the challenge inherent in the existing system: How to be more than an "errand boy" for powerful,

behind-the-scenes rulers.   How has this dilemma been resolved?

Usefulness of the "Cacique" or Boss

In the scant available literature on Peruvian political
life, there are but few references to process, that is, what
goes on and how things happen.   José Carlos Mariátegui,
Manuel González Prada and Raul Haya de la Torre, all vehement critics of the existing socio-political system, are
generally silent on the process of politics as such.   They
are typical products of an educational system that emphasizes verbal skill and encyclopedic knowledge.   These writers define reality as pressing social problems on which
they propound solutions.   They do this offering a socialist
system of dogma opposed to the Church-directed, other
worldly dogma inherited from the past.   Victor Andres
Belaunde's interpretation of how the polity functions, mainly
through reliance by the traditional chief on top on "caciques, "
down below, is of particular interest.

Stressing the personalist nature of the system of
Presidential rule on Peru, Victor Andres declares that "the
personalist regime (el régimen personal) needs the support
of political forces whose collaboration is obtained by means
of concessions which constitute a limitation on its faculties. "
He goes on:

> The cacique . . . is a sui generis product of our po-
> litical sociology. In his Congressional form, the
> cacique is not a feudal lord and may not belong even
> to the agrarian oligarchy. . . . Generally silent, he
> lacks the faculties of a leader of the masses. . . .
> Starting as an electoral agent or a modest lawyer,
> filling vacancies in the delegation, he emerges as a
> property owner due to the favors received from the
> government. He consolidates himself and becomes
> a political force, giving the government his vote and
> receiving from the government all kinds of protection
> and influence in his electoral district.
>
> The government . . . gives him support, believing
> it is winning an effective influence in the province.
> . . . The cacique is agent of the central power in
> his province, a collaborator of the personalist re-
> gime. Eventually, the cacique consolidates his po-

sition, usually taking a high place as a Congress-
man.   Solidary in defense of joint interests with
the government in power, he becomes a political
factor to be reckoned with. [8]

In Victor Andres' terminology, the cacique is different from the gamonal, although in practise the two may
overlap.   He becomes a political force (as do similar political bosses in American society) by giving the central government a bloc of votes in return for all kinds of protection
and influence within his own district.   A sharp, close student of Peruvian politics, Francois Bourricaud traces the
development of caciquismo (as the whole complex of relations
centering around this individual is called) to the fact that political organizations are simply the personal following of one
powerful person, usually a presidential candidate.   If the
candidate is reform-minded, he will be faced by demands
for remaking the entire system of government in taxation,
administrative practices and the like.   The Peruvian idea of
reform (e. g., of Haya de la Torre) is to set things right
once and for all, often by embarking on some grandiose
scheme.   (Former President Belaunde's plan to open Latin
America's heartland by building the highway known as the
Carretera Marginal de la Selva comes in this category.)
However, habits deeply ingrained in the Peruvian psyche
work against such simplistic solutions.   Prevalent bad humor, pessimism, cavilling, mutual distrust combine with behind-the-scenes opposition to prevent a joining of forces.

In such circumstances, a political ally in Congress or
in the provinces can be most useful.   The newly elected
President may be able to trade off one part of his program
for support for other parts.   He may postpone some actions
to be able to move ahead on others.   He may present the
opposition with an issue that he thinks will divide it.   He
may try throwing successive sops to leaders from different
regions of the country.   Placating a series of factions or
groups one by one is a frequently resorted to tactic.   But
through it all, the cacique constitutes a principal means for
working the President's will.

Sources of the "Cacique's" Power

The gamonal derives his power from control of land
and the ability to wreak deprivations on those who oppose
him.   The cacique, on the other hand, gets his strength from

control of government favors, most often jobs.   Each can
claim the allegiance of greater or lesser numbers of other
men, delivering blocs of votes at election time.   The relationship with these followers is extremely personal.   Mixed
with sentiments of loyalty and the expectation of favors on
the part of the followers is the demand for unquestioning
obedience to the boss, especially at election time.   Of all
advantages thus acquired, government jobs are the most
prized.   The most firmly entrenched caciques gain a patron-
age control over entire ministries as well as the available
jobs in their district. [9]   No sharp distinction is made between the official and private sphere, the public and private
patrimony of the cacique being one and the same.   The government functionary owes his primary loyalty to the powerful individual who placed him there.   In return, the functionary holds his government job to be a personal right, independent of any concept of public interest, bestowed on him by
the cacique.   Elections become, in Peru as elsewhere where
these attitudes prevail, mainly a scramble for public posts,
with the newcomers turning out the old crowd, at districtal,
provincial and national levels.

Placed strategically in the political process, the
cacique (sometimes simply called patrón in Peru) is the reg-
ulator of public favors.   He courts the various ministries
and obtains all sorts of "manna" for his particular department.   As was noted in the preceding chapter, control of
communications is an important source of his power.   It is
through this powerful personage that the leading political figures of Lima communicate with the province.   The cacique
tries to be a "friend" of the President.   He tries to render
himself indispensable both to the President and to the people
of "his" province. [10]

His durability, contrasted with the ephemeral character of Presidents and ministers, is a noteworthy characteristic.   The cacique accommodates to all regimes and each
succeeding regime accommodates to him.   Politicians, of the
type who assume presidential or ministerial posts, have traditionally enjoyed little stability in their political careers.
Peru is a difficult country to govern, as is shown above by
the fact that from 1821 to the present-day, there have been
ninety-nine governments of which only twenty-two entered
office constitutionally and only twelve were able to carry
through to the end of their appointed term.   (Until 1872, all
Peruvian Presidents were military men, and the tradition of
caudillo rule continues strong to the present time.)   Politic-

ally active individuals (los políticos) form something of a
class apart, even though their ties to the landed elite (which
Peruvians identify as la oligarchía) are quite intimate. [11]
The typical leader's political fortunes go up and down.   By
contrast, the system favors the entrenched cacique, the defender of local interests.   The more specific and narrow the
departmental or provincial interest that he is protecting, the
greater his staying power on the national scene.   He is either
a "local notable" of the type analyzed in Chapter II above, or
he is the protegé of a leading member of the upper class.
A study of Congressional representation during the two administrations of President Prado (1939-1945 and 1956-1962)
shows several instances of entrenched Senators whose parliamentary mandates correspond with the Presidential terms. [12]
Most often, the cacique caps his career in the Senate.   The
Chamber of Deputies, by contrast, shows marked changes in
composition, it being estimated that eighty to ninety percent
of the Deputies change from one Congress to the next, compared to some sixty percent of the Senators. [13]

Effect on Central Government

        During discussions in Lima preceding Andean Seminar
II of the important municipal elections of 1963 (the first in
almost forty years), Bourricaud said, on the basis of his
studies of the region, that political life in the country re-
duces to a series of transactions over time.   These are between a presidential candidate (or later Chief Executive) and
his agents and the numerous "bosses" with whom he must
deal.   These caciques place at the disposal of the candidate
who bids highest for them the votes of their friends, followers, relatives, compadres and campesinos.   (Under Article
86 of the Constitution, the right to vote is reserved to those
who can read and write, a consideration subject to liberal
interpretation by local notables who control the registers.)
This means that these leaders must exercise a rigid control
over their followers.   The game will not interest the politicians if they must negotiate revocable contracts with a number of little chiefs (called jefecillos), who are unable to deliver the votes.   The political class (i. e., those aspiring to
or promoting a candidate for high office) finds itself largely
at the mercy of the caciques, for the latter do not join in or
support political parties.   Caciques often prefer that the politicians dispute for the votes they control before very delicate alternatives.

An explanation for the weakness of political parties
in Peru (as in most of Latin America) can be found in this.
Their failure to develop lies not alone in personalismo, but
in the prevailing system of caciquismo. The politicians
generally find themselves at the mercy of a prevailing indifference and apathy within the narrow electorate. Group solidarity lies behind the patrón, not with a party. Even in
power, political parties such as President Belaunde's Acción
Popular are unable to satisfy the needs of their "clientele"
because the distribution of favors, as was noted above, so
often rests with the caciques. A related consideration is
that the new President and his followers are unable to win
lasting loyalty on the part of the masses because it is the
cacique rather than the President (with rare exceptions) who
staffs the middle and lower echelons of the bureaucracy. It
is these bureaucrats who must carry out the new President's
will or who can, just as easily, sabotage or ignore it. In
consequence, little that is of benefit trickles down to the
masses, despite the supposed power of the President to carry out new measures and effect reforms. I shall examine
this aspect in more detail in Chapter VI, illustrating the
working of certain "rules of the game" of Peruvian politics
as shown by the movement toward agrarian reform.[14]

The system described of electing Presidents as well
as effecting their will over the vast expanse of Peruvian territory through a multitude of "bosses" has far-reaching consequences. Like the control of wealth through hacendado-
gamonales, the conduct of the bulk of political activity through
caciques greatly weakens the power and accountability of the
central administration, i.e., the Government. Lending itself
to behind-the-scenes alliances, deals and manipulations, the
system of caciquismo perpetuates the power of the landed
elite. If the experience of Mexico is a guide, the power of
provincial bosses can be broken and the authority of a central government strengthened only by the creation of a mass-
based political party. Thus far, the practitioners of politics
in Peru are ideologically indifferent, content to play the game
of giving votes to him who offers the most concrete advantages. New forces are appearing on the scene, however,
bent on radicalizing politics in a revolutionary sense. The
outcome of this radicalizing tendency will determine the evolution of Peruvian politics in decades to come. More will
be said about this development in the last chapter.

The "Rules" as Seen by Central Government

Over the years, there has developed a tacit set of rules centering on the President's place and function in the Peruvian political process. The subject is one of considerable fascination and importance. However, our attention is focussed on the landed elite. In consequence, only a few of the more significant "rules of the game" viewed from the perspective of the central government will be offered here.

Rule No. 5--Develop a Solidarity between the Regionalism of the Caciques and Gamonales and the Centralism of the Government.

Federalism has rarely been espoused as a doctrine in Peru. Mariátegui points out that those favoring federalism have been the ones momentarily in disgrace with the central power. Decentralizing has always meant augmenting the power of the gamonales, whose principal preoccupation has been to strengthen their feudal positions. Following the many decades of military caudillo rule in the 19th century, there appears to have developed a tacit understanding between holders of the executive power and the "bosses." Centralizing tendencies (best evidenced in the concentration of virtually all the country's public expenditures on Lima) on the part of the government are not opposed provided the caciques and gamonales remain the principal instruments of the government. The caciques are converted into the instrument of the central regime, at the same time being confirmed in their power in the provinces. They renounce any grievances against their "allies" in the capital city. Thus, the system comes to serve the aims of both parties, to the detriment of any real popular participation in affairs of state or any effective distribution of government largesse to the outlying regions. Graphic illustrations of how this arrangement, which has characterized Peruvian politics for more than a century, fosters the stagnation of the countryside were offered during discussions of the municipio in the seminars from which data for this research has been drawn.

Rule No. 6--Strive to Maintain the Upper Hand by Means of the Competition for Government Favors.

Political fights and hatreds in Peru have been due basically to struggles for "booty" in the form of grants, jobs, rewards, credit, honors and other largesse from the central

government.   Rulers who have survived the longest time
(e. g., President Leguîa who governed from 1919 to 1930)
have been the most skillful in manipulating distribution of
these favors.   Some families are surfeited while the members of others who oppose the leader are exiled.   As we
have seen above, needed support from various quarters follows upon the granting of concessions or favors to them.
This "art of politics" does not differ from that practised by
skilled politicians everywhere.   However, this aspect of the
game tends to pre-empt and overshadow all others, wherever the tradition holds that the state exists solely for booty.
In the following chapter, I shall attempt to show how the
hand of the President is strengthened by the fact that the upper class is divided among competing economic groups, enabling him frequently to play off one against another.   Favors follow proof of one's loyalty to the chief.

Rule No. 7--Take Care to Publicize One's Reforming Inten-
            tions upon Assuming Power.

        Players of the game of conservative, elite politics in
Peru have done so with such success during the past half
century that they are convinced that, as Bourricaud states,
"with a little luck and much skill" they can save the essentials of their position.   The three pillars of the ruling class
--the Church, the military and the landowning, commercial
families--are united in this belief.   Leading spokesmen of
the political elite pay lip service to reform.   Legislation is
passed. [15]   Patrones, Church and government functionaries,
however, join in preventing its implementation.   Voluntary
associations, political parties, labor unions which might succeed in making a reality of a reform proposal enjoy, at
best, an unstable, precarious existence.   This is so because
there is fear that they might tend to take on an independent
existence and work a real change in the social order. [16]   By
co-opting their leaders into the upper class, their effectiveness is diminished.   All this takes place, however, behind
the facade of an apparent reforming zeal on the part of new
leaders, military or civilian, upon assuming office.

Rule No. 8--Diminish the Power of Congress

        The prevailing weakness of parliaments in Latin A-
merica is an outstanding characteristic of politics in the
area.   The Peruvian Congress, through the electoral system
as well as social order generally, has always been weighted
in favor of the gamonales, the caciques and other elements

most dedicated to local interests. 17   Where a President cannot exclude oppositionists by exile or other means, the tactic has been to pack Congress with his own followers.   This is accomplished through deals with the "bosses" described above whereby candidates are named who will do the bidding of both the hacendado-gamonal and the President.   The result of these tactics plus the provincial orientation of most members of Congress is to create a legislative arm subservient to the executive.   No tradition exists that Congress should represent a constructive opposition to the executive. Thus, the constant effort is to remove oppositionists from Congress rather than create a healthy, informed opposition capable of offering constructive criticisms and alternatives. The overall result of this constant weakening of the legislative branch is to reinforce the powers of the political elite or the "oligarchy" against forces of change that are at work in the society.

Notes

1. R. Coulbourn (ed.), Feudalism in History (Princeton: Princeton University Press, 1956), p. 4.

2. President Manuel Prado, at the end of his first administration in 1945, received a 50, 000 hectare grant of land at Huallaga in the eastern Andes from the government, as cited in Wolfram U. Drewes, "The Economic Development of the Western Montana of Central Peru as Related to Transportation, " Peruvian Times (Lima, 1958).

3. Gabriel N. Escobar, Organización Social y Cultural Del Sur Del Perú (Mexico D. F. , 1967), pp. 154-156.

4. Emilio Romero, Economic History of Peru (Buenos Aires, Editorial Sudamericana, 1949), p. 446.

5. Martin Needler, "Putting Latin American Politics in Perspective, " in Inter-American Economic Affairs (Autumn, 1962).   "Government" herein is not synonymous with "political system. " For governments, "to remain in power becomes the all important objective, " as Needler says.

6. David Barber, Yale University.   (Talk given to members of Andean Seminar IV, 1966).

68   Wealth and Power in Peru

7. Francois Bourricaud, "La Oligarchía Peruana, " ECO-
    Revista de la Cultura de Occidente, Bogotá, Colombia,
    No. 68 (December, 1965), pp. 198-200. For a con-
    trary view of the Peruvian middle class, see Frederick
    B. Pike, The Modern History of Peru (New York:
    Frederick A. Praeger, 1967), pp. 320-331. Pike sees
    many revolutionary groups trying since the 1890's to
    introduce sweeping reforms into Peruvian institutions.
    It is the moderate faction of former oligarchies, he
    holds, that has exerted lasting influence on Peru's de-
    velopment in recent decades. Pike's position is that
    real political power had fallen by the mid-1960's into
    what is actually a middle class led by President Fer-
    nando Belaunde Terry.

8. Victor Andres Belaunde, Meditaciones Peruanas (Lima:
    Printed by Talleres Gráficos Villanueva, 1963), pp.
    244-249.

9. Mario Alzamora Valdez, "La Renovación de las Muni-
    cipalidades, " Monografías del Seminario Andino, Mon-
    ograph No. 10 (1964).

10. Francisco Fernandez Vidal (Mayor of the town of
    Ayacucho) "Autonomía municipal y desarrollo regional, "
    Monografías del Seminario Andino, Monograph No. 12
    (1964).

11. Commentary by members of Andean Seminars I and II,
    January and September, 1964. Chapter VI examines
    selection of Cabinet members during the decade 1956-
    65 to ascertain whether politically active individuals
    (thus defined) are drawn disproportionately from the
    class of large landholders.

12. Arnold Payne, The Peruvian Coup d'Etat of 1962; The
    Overthrow of Manuel Prado, Political Studies Series:
    No. 5, Washington, Institute for the Comparative Study
    of Political Systems, 1968, pp. 19-31.

13. Vice President Edgardo Seoane, personal conversation
    in Lima in 1964.

14. A number of individual papers submitted in Andean
    Seminars I, II and III dealt with agrarian conditions
    and throw light on the tactics used in rural zones by
    elite representatives.

15. Examples of reforming legislation are cited by Victor Andres Belaunde and Frederick B. Pike, most being changes in electoral laws. A polemical account of the attempts at change and the "oligarchy's" opposition thereto appears in Cesar Augusto Reinaga, La Fisonomía Económica del Perú (Cuzco, 1957).

16. For a description of these organizations see Richard Patch, "The Peruvian Elections of 1962"; "The Peruvian Elections of 1963 and Their Aftermath," New York, American Universities Field Staff Reports.

17. Sandro Mariátegui (son of José Carlos), conversation in 1964 in Lima in connection with planning of Andean Seminar II.

Chapter IV

Persistence of Value Patterns

A vital consideration in assessing Peru's landowning class, particularly political socialization practices, is the religious and educational ideals of the landed elite. Always a vital force in Peru, the Catholic Church has maintained its closeness to both the government and the conservative upper class. Over the past fifty years, its hold over the educational system has been only slightly relaxed. In this chapter, I shall examine the role of the Catholic hierarchy in perpetuating the dominance of the ruling elite. The subject warrants examination for, since J. Lloyd Mecham's classic study on the relations of Church and State in Latin America, little has been published on this vital aspect of Peruvian life.[1]

To the mass of the population in rural and urban zones, the Church offers its frequent processions, its intercessions with the Divinity and the baroque grandeur of its many cathedrals. The middle class comes in contact with it through the Church's schools and colleges and regular attendance of its women at mass. Its real influence seems to be reserved for the upper classes, however.[2] A strongly conservative force, the Church exercises a strong and direct influence on politics. The minds of the elite are carefully molded toward attitudes favorable to the Church world-view and power position, during the long years of adolescent education.

The intimacy between the Church and the Peruvian upper class has been an unvarying characteristic of Colonial, post-Independence and modern eras in Peru. Constitutionally, the Church forms part of the national government. Construction of churches and part of the salary of priests are paid from tax funds. The best high schools have been religious. There are chaplains for every national secondary school. The Church's great influence stems from its being the official religion.[3] The constitution does not permit priests to vote but it does not exclude priests from political office.

Owing to its traditional position close to the center of political power, the political role played by the Church is all pervasive, enabling it to exercise powerful controls over what, in other countries, are held to be non-religious subject matters. To gain proper perspective on the changing but still dominant place of the Church in molding elite values, let us look at the place of religion, not simply the Catholic Church, in Peruvian culture as a whole.

Religion plays a vital part in the lives of Peruvians, high and low. To Peruvians, religion has a two-fold aspect: one is the visible part of going to church, saying confession, taking part in religious ceremonies; the other consists of the hidden experience of one's psychic life, the deep well-springs of a person's character. Some of the externals of religion are described below, but my objective lies mainly in describing a representative "ideal type" of the younger elite. This figure is the "Church-politician" who guides the Church's intervention in politics. Mecham says:

> There is a strong tradition of clerical interference in political matters. . . . The counseling of parishioners as to how they should vote, and the influencing of legislation and governmental offices, are recognized as legitimate and necessary activities on the part of the clergy. The Church . . . is still accustomed to make use of its organization and discipline to apply pressure when and where it chooses and it usually works through individuals. [4]

Historical Development of Church Role

With such a tradition of intervention in politics, the Church has played a preponderant role throughout Peru's history. The country inherited from Spain a central political organization. Initiative and the ultima ratio resided in the state. But the state, in turn, was largely dominated by the higher clergy. It is not too much to say that the pattern, which fitted pre-Conquest Peru, prevails in this country to the present day. In the Inca empire, there was an absolute ruler, frozen and caste-like social classes, a priestly caste and a conscript army. Julian Steward points out that a national religion and a priestly class developed because of increasing populations, larger irrigation works and greater need for social coordination. Religion supplied the integrating factor. [5]

With the Conquest, Spaniards took over the key positions in the political and religious hierarchy. Spanish law was imposed to the extent necessary to maintain the Spanish institutions. The Catholic Church completely replaced the Inca sun cult, for Catholicism could not, and does not today, tolerate a rival national religion. All inhabitants became nominal Catholics, accepting the Christian God and saints and contributing to Church support. The natives of Peru did not abandon local shrines, ancestor worship, household gods and other forms of religion. The Catholic fathers were content to regard these practices as mere "paganism. "

A brief historical resumé shows the intimate tie of organized religion at various epochs to the upper class and to the government of Peru. Under the Viceroyalty, numerous convents, seminaries, churches and "public benefit societies" were established which permitted a sizeable portion of the arable land to pass gradually into the hands of the Catholic Church. The 18th century travelers, Juan and Ulloa, in their famous Noticias Secretas, remarked on the wealth of the clergy in Peru, noting "there are but few who do not pay rent to the Church, either for their houses or for their farms. "6 The clergy, during the War of Independence, was pro-Spanish throughout, fearing loss of their land and privileges. After independence, the Church shared power with a succession of military rulers and later civilian leaders, taking an active role in politics. Some reforms were introduced, most notably the abolition of the diezmo, or feudal tithe. In 1859, it was provided that the archbishop, bishops, dignitaries and canons in cathedrals should be paid from the national treasury. In contrast to Mexico where the situation until the middle of the 19th century was, in many respects, identical to Peru's, no voices were raised in opposition to the accumulation of wealth and large propertied interests by the Church. 7 A review of late 19th century writings by Mecham showed no one voicing the conviction that the dominant economic position of the Church organization curbed individual opportunity. Mecham remarked on the striking absence of liberal opinion and of leaders capable of raising the Church-State issue in Peru. Only later, at the turn of the century, did Manuel González Prada, the strongest anti-Church voice, publish his diatribes against the Church. He rested his case less on the Church's wealth and landholdings than on the fact that it jeopardized political freedom. 8

If the experience of Mexico is a guide, as much as one-half of the arable land of Peru may lie under "mortmain"

and be for all practical purposes removed from production.
To the Church hierarchy in Peru, the political aspects of
nationalization of land are viewed as extremely important.
Disamortization of Church properties would destroy the political influence of the Church.   It would reduce the sources
of income that enable them to take over responsibility for
elementary, secondary and much college education.   Thus,
any talk of a disamortization law has invariably stirred up a
veritable hornet's nest of clerical and conservative opposition in Peru.   The attack on its property is regarded as a
"sword's thrust at the very heart of the Church."

    The Church views control of its lands as a most vital
consideration.   A modus vivendi established by a Papal Bull
in 1874 vested title to the vast ecclesiastical holdings in the
Church without any restrictions whatever.   It is recognized
as independent possessor and administrator of its revenue-
producing properties as well as its churches, monasteries
and convents, scores of primary and secondary schools, seminaries, many hospitals and the Catholic University of Lima.

    Since the passage of the Law of Free Disposition of
1901, the Church may again freely acquire property.   There
is a provision in the civil code permitting the inheriting of
real estate by the Church.   The Church has been able to
build up large and valuable holdings of urban property in addition to its country realty. [9]   With an increased income, it
has been able to embark on energetic programs of support
at election time of its political allies.   Mecham concludes:
"It is remarkable that, notwithstanding the vast ecclesiastical
holdings of urban and rural estate, this condition has not
been a matter of popular concern."   Since public opinion is
formed by the elite, it is worth examining more closely the
impact of Catholic education and teachings on the minds of
elite members.

World-View Instilled in Elite Youth

    By "world-view," is meant an individual's concepts of
what is good and bad, proper and improper in life.   The
term includes his conception of the nature of the world.   Is
it threatening or non-threatening, orderly and manageable by
him or not?   Elite members, no less than the lower classes,
have been furnished with a set of beliefs, practices and in-
stitutions--in a word, a religion--which is their shield a-
gainst what is not understandable nor controllable in their

lives. To find the ultimate political values of the Peruvian
landed elite, a study of their religion can be most productive. The overall impression is one of their being molded
into a single type of intellectual habits and orientations,
which can be called "Catholic mentality." Much of the persistence of the upper class system of values can be traced
to the imparting of this mentality in the process of a Catholic upbringing. Several components of this world-view have
been identified:

A. Belief in Rightness of Existing Social Order--The
ethos of the present-day Peruvian upper class member reflects a long process of socialization into a well-defined system of mores and beliefs instilled in him since the age of
four or thereabouts. It mirrors the stream of spirituality
of Spanish Catholicism. In that system, existing social and
economic structures are products of the will of God. The
necessary imperfection of social organisms is a consequence
of original sin. Innovations or radical change are, therefore, to be condemned. As long as the masses of the poor
accept the system as right and just, there is no problem.
The poor should take comfort in the thought that death is the
great equalizer and that, in fact, they might be better off
than their patrones after death. The result is a kind of fatalism that is characteristic of rich and poor alike: The
system is foreordained; it is all God's doing; one simply accepts the system and puts all his faith in God's mercy. The
important thing is one's "goodness of intention," owing to
man's inability to control or transform his environment. Instead, leave everything "in God's hands."[10]

B. Respect for the Priest and his Authority--Young
Peruvians recalling their elementary schooling report almost
a monastic discipline. A simple enforced conformity, it is
presented as "virtue" and "self discipline." Learning the
Catholic cosmogony, they are taught in memoristic fashion.
The system of teaching is a method of disputation rather
than observation, communicating to the young person in au-
thoritative and orderly fashion all the doctrines and opinions
established by Church fathers. The important thing is to
adapt things to an accepted norm. That norm is "revealed
knowledge" which is superior to all experimental analysis,
for revelation traces to God and God is the primary source
of all things. The teacher explains the proposition to be
established. Opposing opinions are then refuted. Finally,
one reaffirms the thesis desired to prevail.[11] Where the
adequacy of an argument or course of action cannot be dem-

onstrated rationally, assent is secured by referring to values
or truths that transcend the judgments of the persons involved.
The priest's or nun's function is that of both a spiritual and
temporal authority to the young scion of the elite (and to others attending the school).   Conflicts within one's mind are
obviated by submission to authority.

     C.   Disdain for Fact-Finding--The educational system
does not teach the experimental approach to truth.   (The word
empírico--empirical--to this day, tracing to the meaning
given it in 18th century Spain, conveys to most Latin Americans the idea of "charlatanry," "deception.")   The idea of
acceptance or rejection through the application of one's own
human reason makes little headway.   The experimental method runs counter to the notion that anything implying work
with one's hands is to be avoided.   The child is taught that
"he is a well-fed, God-fearing, elevated person who is not
only equal to but also rather superior to all other people."
He is taught that work is to be avoided, but that "employment" (empleo) is to be sought, as a sinecure well deserved
by someone of his rank in society.   Occupations that imply
manual labor, such as civil engineering or field research,
receive few adherents.   One admires instead skill in verbal
expression, encyclopedic knowledge, a passion for ideas.
"Reality" is, according to one seminar member, "the explanation of the social problems of the country by some intellectual of note who has used some system of dogma to arrive
at his conclusions."   A prevailing ideology replaces for some
the authority and dogma of the Church.   But the mode of
thinking remains unchanged.

     D.   Acceptance of Church's Worldly Role--Along with
the nearby haciendas, the center of influence in Peru's interior towns is likely to be the local church, always the biggest and most imposing structure in town.   It is at one and
the same time the religious, social, cultural and artistic
center.   Rarely is it an active center because the Peruvian
Church suffers from a grave lack of priests, despite the
numbers of Spanish and North American priests working in
the country.   This has reduced the educational, cultural and
political functions of the Church somewhat.   The underlying
belief system that is taught the landed elite regarding the
Church as the arbiter and judge of all acts has not changed,
however.   Cultural, spiritual and Christian humanistic values
are emphasized, but the medieval concepts of the Church's
responsibilities remain strong.   As in medieval times, the
Church "gathers to itself, as the sole respectable and ultimate

end, all human actions and occupations. " It teaches disin-
terest in material goods, an indifference to present life, res-
ignation in the face of one's own or other people's misery or
want. [12]

Traditionally, as we have seen, the Church has denied
an independent existence to the Peruvian state, arguing that
political leaders are subject to its conceptions of morality.
This pretension on the part of the Church, in the realm of
politics, has been at the root of the still unresolved Church-
State conflict which reached prominence in Peru in the early
1900's and has since subsided.   Generations of the Peruvian
elite have been educated to accept the Church's definition of
its heavy responsibilities in secular matters.   In terms of
relative importance of acts of merit, to cite an example of
this process, children are taught to view the protection,
care and feeding of the local priest as of primary importance,
followed by repairing or beautifying of the Church and participation in the various religious festivals.

E.   Impact on Government of the Ideal of the Catholic
Family--Despite gaps between practice and theory, many
items of behavior derive from the Catholic family ideal
taught the elite and the masses.   The ideal embraces the
sanctity of the family unit, abhorrence of divorce, the father
as the final arbiter of conduct, the inferior status of women.
It is strengthened by the fact that the practice of religion is
largely left to women.   Religious belief in the upper class
male appears to be limited to outward observance of the
forms of Catholicism.   In the doctrines of the Church on the
family, questions of courtship, marriage, divorce, religious
observance, marital relations, education of the young and
death are held to be the exclusive concern of the Church.
Increasingly, the Peruvian state has asserted itself in most
of these areas.   Still, the ideal is that of the "Catholic family. "   Because it motivates much of the behavior of the upper classes and of those farther down who aspire to a more
exalted position in society, the ideal is of political importance.   The ideal acts as a social cement.   It is a set of
reciprocal obligations that begin at the cradle and end at the
grave.

Peruvian politicians feel constantly the strong bond of
family unity.   Ties of blood are of first importance in all
matters, public and private.   The upper class relies heavily
upon the family group to dispense economic and social position, including access to government posts.   There are for-

malized rules that determine deference among kin, ceremonial practices, intermarriage and preferential mating, economic responsibilities and, to a limited extent, one's stance
in politics. A second characteristic affecting political life
is <u>male subordination to the family.</u> A young man obeys and
protects the family. Once married, unless he is the eldest
son, he is drawn into the orbit of his wife's family. He is
free to show what he can make of himself, but his primary
obligations are to one's family, his own and his wife's. In
dispensing jobs, "charity begins at home" and one favors
certain people because of one's personal links to them. Within the framework of the extended family, a man is free to
be himself, to assay business, political or amorous adven-
tures. Should they fail, they will not disqualify him from
receiving the help and admiration of his family. Above all,
if he occupies an important government post, all members of
his family, however remote, expect to benefit.

F. <u>Continuance of the Family Through Generations</u>--
As with landed elites everywhere, residence and family affiliation tend to follow lines of property. The upper class
marital union is often determined by economic and social
considerations, usually revolving around landed property, the
hacienda. The continuance of the family name, symbolized
often by a particular rural property, through the indefinite
future is regarded as a matter of first importance.

G. <u>Interlocking Ties of Elite Families</u>--This is an
especially significant characteristic. Among well-to-do Peruvians, personal ties extend, besides vertically back to preceding generations, horizontally in four ways: blood, marriage, ceremonial (the godparents or <u>compadrazgo</u> system)
and friendship. To be outside these relationships is to be
outside the society. A member of Andean Seminar III
phrased it thus: "I was raised with the distinct impression
that if a man didn't fit one of these four categories of relationship, he simply didn't exist. "

Church-Politician "Rules of the Game"

The preceding paragraphs set forth impacts on elite
values of a socialization process dominated by the Catholic
Church on the one hand and the family institution on the other. Summing up, the Churchmen of Peru see dogma and a
politically active Church as a prime way to exclude disintegrative forces. They see it as a means to preserve tradi-

tion and maintain some sort of social unity. From Simón
Bolivar onwards, this service of the Church has received
recognition from Latin American statesmen who, fearing social chaos, have welcomed active Church interventions in the
secular sphere. [13] For its part, the Church through its control of the educational system has spread a world-view to upper and lower class alike that includes a perception of un-
controllable forces around them restricting and dominating
their lives and requiring active Church intervention. The
members of the elite find protection from these forces in reliance on the Church and in their economic power.

The conservative Church-politician sees an ideal society resting on the twin pillars of the Church and the Army,
with the constitutional regime ultimately dependent for its
continuance on the support of these two power domains. In
this conception of society, special privileges, absence of liberty of conscience and domination by an upper class constitute the rocks on which the social order is built. No examination of the assumptions on which the structure of society
is based is to be permitted. The dominant conservative elements in the Church, in the Army and among the landholding elite rarely give public utterance to convictions such as
these. Yet, such a world-view as this, according to informed
members of the younger generation of Peruvians, underlies
much of the present-day social and political reality in their
country.

Study and discussion of how the Catholic Church has
"played the game of politics" in Peru offer some valuable insights into political practices in the country. An attempt has
been made to place these unspoken rules into words in the following formulations:

Rule No. 9--Do Not Encourage Competitive Politics

A profoundly conservative institution, the Catholic
Church's conception of its political role is one of energetic
protection of its own interests and support of its political allies. As one of its primary beneficiaries, the Church sus-
tains the feudal land system. At the turn of the century, an
attempt was made by the early 20th century reformers (Manuel Gonzalez Prada, Manuel Vicente Villarán and Mariano
Cornejo) to introduce a competing view of politics. [14] To
them, politics meant a struggle for freedom of thought and
speech, the extinction of clerical participation in affairs of
state, the nationalization of great areas of land held by the

Church. They sought the normal participation of laymen in
government, largely through a revitalized Congress. Implicit in this view of politics was the equality of all Peruvians,
high and low, before the law, a reform of higher education
to permit intellectual progress and training in the industrial
arts. Their efforts, had they been successful, would have
set Peru on the path to modernity. Gonzalez Prada, in particular, believed that there was no solution to Peru's political problems without destroying beforehand not only the political but also the social and psychological influence of the
Church. [15] A modern history of Peru would have to probe
deeply into Church influence during the past sixty years to
ascertain how and why the efforts of these reformers produced so little change in the basic structure of the country.

     To the Church-politician, efforts to establish a ration-
al, laicized society resting on a conception of the dignity of
the individual is competitive politics, a divisive and potentially disintegrative threat to be warded off at all costs.   Interest groups, e. g. , peasants' unions, and political movements aimed at organizing or mobilizing the mass represent
dangerous competition.   The influential Church-politician, as
cited above, relies on personal intervention at all levels of
the government administration, including the Presidency itself, as the principle vehicle of action.   Thus, he does not
understand nor welcome political techniques that involve mass
organization.   These are alien to his style of rule, a point
amply demonstrated by members of the Andean Seminars who
had had direct contact with the thinking of conservative
Church-politicians. [16] The latter distrust mass movements
and mass agitation as potentially subversive and difficult to
control.

Rule No. 10--Discourage the Study of National Problems by Elite Members

     The end product of the educational system are individ-
uals "whose value systems have not kept pace" (with the demands of modern life). [17] The typical scion of the elite is
"incurious, unconcerned, content to avoid taxes and social
responsibility, to hold land idle, to reject labor organization. "[18] Holding that the principles that rule society are
immutable and untouchable, the Churchman-turned-legislator-
and-educator rejects as "fables" (novelerías) the effort to apply free inquiry to natural and social problems.   As pointed
out above, the mentality inculcated turns away from objective,
painstaking inquiry toward becoming a skillful expounder of

or a propagandist of a philosophical system. Thus, no tradition of study of national or public questions develops, nor
does there emerge a segment of the elite interested in fos-
tering democratic, non-authoritarian values. The effects of
this absence within the upper class of the kind of informed
criticism that opened the door to modernity in other societies
are incalculable. The subject is worthy of a special study.
Suffice it to say that, lacking such leaders, the Peruvian middle class has failed to develop a system of original values,
distinct from and in opposition to those of the traditional,
conservative elite. This has meant the effective "neutralization" as a political force of the middle class.[19]

Rule No. 11--Retain the Essential Functions of Society in the Hands of the Church

Education of the young, control over land as the chief
source of wealth, performance of the crucial rites in the
lives of individuals (at birth, marriage, death), passing on
candidates for high office may be viewed as the "essential
functions" of organized society. A basic "rule of the game"
seems to be to keep these powers firmly in the hands of the
Church. Drawing on Inca and Hispanic practices, the Church
hierarchy has always disposed of sufficient power to keep the
formal government administration at arms length in most
such matters as these. A decline in Church influence has
taken place in Peru as elsewhere. Nevertheless, the Church
through skilled political maneuvering has been able to insure
that governmental authority is used in such a way as not to
breach the status or privileges of the Church. Illustrations
of this are abundant in recent Peruvian history, an example
being the agrarian reform legislation which will be examined
in detail below. Not by governing itself but through those
who are its fervent supporters (e. g., President Leguía in
1919-30) does the Church prevent decisions being taken that
are contrary to its interests. Given the socio-political and
economic importance of the family, the Church's function as
arbiter of all matters affecting this institution also gives it
power not to be overlooked.[20]

Notes

1. J. Lloyd Mecham, Church and State in Latin America,
    A History of Politico-Ecclesiastical Relations (Chapel
    Hill: University of North Carolina Press, 1966 edi-
    tion), pp. 210-224.

2. Father Rafael Baquedano, a participant in Andean Sem-
    inar IV, cites studies made in Venezuela to show that
    the bulk of the priests in Latin America minister to the
    well-to-do, leaving little time for the poor. Roberto
    MacLean y Estenos, Sociología del Peru (Mexico, 1959)
    provides valuable perspectives on the Church's broad-
    ranging impact on Peruvian life and thought.

3. Article 232 of the Constitution of 1933 permits freedom
    of worship but explicitly protects the Roman Catholic
    faith. In practice, Protestant orders have been success-
    fully opposed in their efforts to establish schools or
    missions in Peru. In this connection, see James G.
    Maddox, Technical Assistance by Religious Agencies in
    Latin America (Chicago: University of Chicago Press,
    1956).

4. J. Lloyd Mecham, op. cit., p. 215. The capacity of
    the Church for exercising influence and/or political
    power is examined by David Apter, "Political Religion
    in the New Nations," Old Societies and New States, ed-
    ited by Clifford Geertz (New York: The Free Press
    of Glencoe, 1963), pp. 57-104.

5. Julian H. Steward (ed.), The Handbook of South Amer-
    ican Indians (Washington, D.C.: Smithsonian Institu-
    tion, 6 vols, 1946-1950). "The Contemporary Quechua,"
    Vol. II, pp. 441-470, by Bernard Mishkin, provides
    information on religious practices in rural zones.

6. Jorge Juan and Antonio de Ulloa, Voyage to South Amer-
    ica (New York, 1964). The work was first published
    in 1735.

7. The author personally observed the sizeable wealth ac-
    cumulated by the Church during the colonial era, most
    of which still remains inert in the recesses of cathe-
    drals and convents. While in Cuzco in 1967, he vis-
    ited the interior vault (opened once daily to tourists)
    of a 17th century convent and there saw a five foot
    high statue in gold encrusted with hundreds of diamonds,
    rubies, pearls and other precious stones. It had been
    constructed, he was told, between 1709 and 1750 "as
    an adoration of God," the churchmen converting rents
    and tithes into precious stones. Its value was placed
    at well over a million dollars according to a leading
    Cuzqueño businessman. I was told that most larger

churches in Peru have similar, extraordinarily valuable
objects of adoration under lock and key deep within
their recesses.

8. Manuel González Prada, Horas de Lucha, 2d ed.
    (Callao, 1924); see also his Figuras y Figurones (Paris,
    Bellenaud, 1937).

9. F. M. Stanger, Church and State in Peru, HAHR, vii.
    (Hispanic American Historical Review, 1927), pp. 410-
    437. Dr. Anibal Ismodes Cairo pointed out to the au-
    thor examples of large urban tracts and apartment
    houses in Lima owned by the Catholic Church.

10. Father José Gomez Izquierdo, participant in Andean
    Seminar I, cited these aspects of the Church during
    extended talks with the author.

11. Mariano Picón-Salas, A Cultural History of Spanish
    America (Berkeley: University of California Press,
    1965), pp. 107-108.

12. Gino Germani, Política y Sociedad en una Época de
    Transición (Buenos Aires, Edit. Paidos, 1962), pp. 69-
    127. Germani emphasizes the difficulties of science
    or scientific personalities developing in Latin America
    because of the prevailing sacral culture.

13. Daniel A. del Rio, Simón Bolivar (Clinton, Mass.: Co-
    lonial Press, 1965), pp. 128-136.

14. Leopoldo Zea, The Latin American Mind, trans. by
    James H. Abbott and Lowell Dunham (Norman: Univer-
    sity of Oklahoma Press, 1963), pp. 188-196.

15. Manuel Gonzalez Prada, Nuevas Páginas Libres, chap-
    ter on "Catolocismo y Ciencia" (Santiago, Ercilla,
    1937). His Instrucción Laica, 1892, shows his effort
    to offer an alternative to Church instruction of the
    young.

16. Camilo Torres Restrepo, Camilo Torres, por el padre
    Camilo Torres Restrepo (1956-1966), Sondeos No. 5
    (Cuernavaca, Centro Inter-cultural de Documentación,
    1966). Camilo Torres was interviewed and accepted
    for Andean Seminar I in September, 1963, but the par-
    ticipation of this highly intelligent Colombian priest was

cancelled at the last minute, the stated reason being
the pressure of his other duties in Bogota. His radicalization and sudden death occurred about two years
later. Torres' criticism of the Church may be said
to apply to Peru.

17. Kalmen Silvert, La Sociedad Problema: Reacción y Re-
     volución en América Latina (Buenos Aires, Editorial
     Paidos, 1963).

18. Simon G. Hanson, quoted in William V. Antonio and
     Frederick B. Pike, Religion, Revolution and Reform,
     op. cit., p. 187.

19. Francois Bourricaud, "Structure and Function of the
     Peruvian Oligarchy," Studies in Comparative Interna-
     tional Development, II, No. 2 (1966), pp. 27-29.

20. Implicit in this treatment of the Church's socializing
     influences on youthful elite members is the assumption
     of a close identity of interest between the Church and
     the landholding elite. Many Churchmen, especially up-
     per clergy, are sons of the landowning elite. How-
     ever, the matter is, in a sense, irrelevant in a society
     where, as Ivan Vallier says, the whole traditional Cath-
     olic system is "sponsored, protected, supported and
     cradled by the total society, especially its political ma-
     chinery" . . . where "all the neighbors were baptized
     Catholics, so were the people of the next village, so,
     too, were the patrones and slaves, peasants and mili-
     tary officers." See Ivan Vallier, "Religious Elites:
     Differentiations and Developments in Roman Catholi-
     cism," in Lipset and Solari, Elites in Latin America,
     op. cit., p. 196. Vallier adds: "The reference group
     of the traditional elite within the Church is the upper
     class, from which many of them come." (p. 203) In
     Latin America's religiously-based social order, the
     dominant Catholic ethos will, according to Vallier and
     others, continue for a long time to come to be the
     core of the culture. Information on the socio-economic
     origins of Peru's clergy is exceedingly scarce. No
     mention of clerical education or social origins appears
     in the most detailed study to date of the Peruvian
     Church: Isidoro Alonso, Gines Garrido, Mons. Dammert
     Bellido and Julio Tumiri, La Iglesia en Perú y Bolivia
     (Bogota and Friburg: Oficina Internacional de Investi-
     gaciones Sociales de FERES, 1961), pp. 11-151.

Chapter V

Political Socialization Within
the Peruvian Elite

Because young people are singularly impressionable,
the habits and attitudes instilled by the Church-directed educational system in the earliest years last many Peruvians
for a lifetime. Other influences are at work, however, and
these will be dealt with in this chapter. The word "socialization" describes the process by which a cultural tradition
or social system is passed on from one generation to the
next.[1] "Political socialization," the object of inquiry here,
relates to the political attitudes and habits (sometimes called
the "political culture") that are passed on from parent to
child. Besides our parents, brothers and sisters, family
elders, childhood friends, neighborhood cronies, schools and
churches exert influences that mold our attitudes and values
in formative years. They discipline us, make us want to
live up to the expectations of others. The appraisals of others are organized into a pattern which we call our "conscience." What can be said of the Peruvian elite's distinc-
tively Peruvian approach to politics? Is there a distinct
"elite politician personality" (similar to the gamonal, cacique
and Church-politician) noticeable among the country's politically active upper class members? What memories does he
carry into adulthood from early childhood? How is the child
taught to view the world by his parents?

Speaking in terms of politics, what is "socialized" is
first of all a social system, a structure of symbols. Later,
a set of power relations and attitudes and, finally, a collection of "rules of the game" of politics are communicated to
the young. These patterns persist through the decades and
centuries, as shown by Tocqueville's masterly description of
American democracy. Learning to adjust to the group, the
individual acquires social behavior of which the group approves. The particular sub-culture of the society into which
the child is born is "internalized" within him. Socialization
occurs as an arbitrary process in infancy. As a person
grows up, he learns more consciously to accept or reject

values and preferences.   What he accepts or rejects becomes
his political culture.

Values Found in Peruvian Society

It is worth recalling that at no time in the history of
Peru has there been a peasant revolt (with the possible exception of the Tupac Amaru uprising in the 18th century) that
had violent overthrow of the existing system as its goal.
The lower class has accepted the existing order.   This includes the upper class that bulks large in the peasants'
world.   The prevailing relation of the campesinos and the
elite has not been one of oppressor and oppressed, despite
what has been said above about the nature of their relationships.   Resentment or hatred of the rich does occur.   However, this seems to result, in the view of knowledgeable
Peruvians, most often from failure of an upper class individual to preserve the traditional patterns of conduct ap-
proved for both peasantry and elite.   The socialization of upper class youth towards accepting a superior position in all
matters does not happen against the backdrop of a sullen,
resentful lower class ready to revolt.   Instead, it occurs as
the right, the natural, the accepted way.   The rich should
be generous.   The patrón, or his son, should not abuse his
power.   This is the background, reminiscent of noblesse
oblige, against which the socialization process takes place.

What, in general, are the values and attitudes instilled
in elite youth, above those cited in earlier chapters?   Male
exemption from work has been stressed.   Work is something to be avoided, while leisure is valued, to be interrupted
only occasionally by work.   Not producing anything, but rather congenial human relationships is what is assiduously pursued, at one's club, among one's cronies at a cafe, within
the extended family, in one's government bureau where one
spends two or three hours a day.   Leaving work-a-day responsibilities to the womenfolk, upper class Peruvians (and,
emulating them, middle and lower class men) devote much
of their time to congenial social pastimes.   Only the Indian
and the mestizo-Indian mixed blood or cholo are expected to
work.   Life for the upper and upper middle class develops
a sociable, friendly, lively charm.

The pursuit of manliness, as shown in the discussion
of the hacendado, ranks high in terms of what the young
member of the elite is taught is good, desirable and ideal.

This is the value called <u>machismo</u> or <u>hombría</u>. It involves
approval of male sexual <u>conquests</u> and <u>the ability</u> to maintain
a succession of mistresses. Also related to the quality of
masculinity is a touchy pride, a command of eloquent language and a readiness to redress personal wrong. To be
successful in politics, an elite member must be considered
<u>muy macho</u>.

Different from the ideal of masculinity is the <u>desire</u>
<u>for dominance</u>. Despite all the advantages granted <u>them, life</u>
for most Peruvians of white or mixed blood is hard and more
so the further one goes down the social scale. The forbidding natural environment (virtually all of Peru is desert,
high mountains or impenetrable jungles) intermingles with the
exploitative social order to produce people with many frus-
trations and latent aggressions. There is a high capacity for
struggle in Peruvian society. But this is not directed against
the natural environment (nothing akin to the "frontier spirit"
can be found in Peruvian history). A shrewd, pseudonymous
"N. VonFutte," long resident in Peru, has characterized the
outstanding characteristics of Peruvians, high and low, as
"an unused, dormant reserve of combativeness, a deep sedi-
ment of unemployed aggressiveness that, since it cannot be
exercised against nature, simply and fully takes itself out on
people and things as an escape valve. Instead of doing something in favor of something, one acts against something. Everyone recognizes that this combativeness may display itself
at any moment and in any way. This display is regarded as
perfectly natural." The desire to dominate is never openly
expressed. Nevertheless, it motivates much individual behavior. Perhaps the trait explains some of the behavior of
<u>gamonales</u> and <u>caciques</u> dwelt upon in preceding chapters.

In contrast to the foregoing is the <u>cosmopolitan</u> out-
<u>look</u> coupled with a tradition of liveliness, <u>vigor, sprightli-</u>
<u>ness</u> and wit (expressed in the phrase <u>viveza criolla</u>) that is
acquired and demonstrated by many members of the elite as
a result of their upbringing and, frequently, foreign education. The "<u>vivo</u>" type of person is felt to be more modern
and intelligent. He merits and receives respect and honor
from his compatriots. Such a person is often found among
politically active sectors of the upper class. The intelligent,
well-traveled <u>Limeño</u> is a charming, attractive personality.
One notes the surface combativeness, but beneath this is a
democratic humanity and cordial equality. This type of person will be discussed in more detail in the chapter dealing
with the Peruvian "counter-elite."

Before passing on to more generalized aspects of the
political culture, mention should be made of the distrust of
learning inculcated in the young elite member. As was
pointed out in the preceding chapter, under the prevailing
power and value structure, the intellectual life is not encouraged. The questioning, inquiring, critical mind faces much
overt hostility in a society that places high value on dogma
and orthodoxy. Few Peruvians have learned to "live dangerously" in an intellectual sense, seeking to arrive at their
own individual perceptions of truth. The pressures to conform to existing norms are great, not least of which is the
"anti-intellectual" climate remarked upon by more than one
participant in the seminar gatherings. Ortega y Gasset defined politics as "the process of arriving at and the knowledge of what, within a society, the State should do." Victor
Andres Belaunde points out that very rarely has the so-called
directing class actually directed the progress of the State in
the sense of knowing what should be done. He traces this to
their ignorance, dilletantism and closed minds.[2] New ideas
are greeted by a conspiracy of silence, if not ridicule, he
says.

Instead of bringing the young into closer touch with
the national reality, education pursues a "decorative intel-
lectualism," the cult of the "bachiller" and the "doctor."
There is a universal desire for the symbols of learning, but
not the substance. A visitor to Peru sees the high status of
titles such as Doctor, Licenciado, Ingeniero, Arquitecto in
the excessive use of the symbols. Letters and nameplates
display the information. Men are careful to address each
other in the ceremonial fashion. University positions are
valued for their great social prestige. Knowledge, however,
is reduced to a set of ready questions and answers, beyond
which there is little to be added or learned. The spirit of
inquiry is absent from the educational system.[3]

Aspects of the Political System

The kind of politics into which upper class Peruvians
are socialized has been characterized as "elite politics" because the political system appears to be controlled by a
landed elite. Another way of stating this is to say that politics are the preserve of a small aristocracy, acting through
associations of landowners and commercial interests, the
Church hierarchy and the armed forces. Power still rests
with these groups, although increasingly middle and lower

class voices are being heard. The stage of "mass politics,"
i.e., a system of politics based on extensive popular participation, has not yet arrived. It may be argued that the advent of shaker Haya de la Torre's A.P.R.A. on the scene in
the 1930's represented the advent of democratic, participa-
tory politics. A close look at A.P.R.A.'s leadership, including Haya de la Torre, shows that this is not the case.
These individuals are almost without exception members, al-
beit dissident members, of the upper class.[4] Political systems are democratic, in part, because the opportunity to
participate in decisions is widely shared. The politician ar-
ranges and holds together compromises among competing
groups. In order to get action for his policies, the democratic politician finds it often necessary to mobilize mass
support. He must dramatize the need for, or alternatively
the dangers of, change. He is an expert in political bargaining. This kind of behavior does not occur in Peru. In an
era of "mass politics," as George Bernard Shaw put it, "the
politician who once had to learn how to flatter kings has now
to learn how to fascinate, amuse, coax, humbug, frighten or
otherwise strike the fancy of the electorate." If the fancy
of the electorate can be struck, if it has confidence in a
leader, then the mass rallies to his support. The mass
type of politics, characteristic of political life in advanced,
industrialized, democratic countries, is not the one that the
young members of the Peruvian elite become accustomed to.
What, then, are the prime features of the political system he
does get used to?

        A first difference lies in the approach to problems.
In the United States, for example, our approach to change is
pragmatic and experimental, moving from one major issue
to the next, trying out a solution to see how it works in
practice. The pace of political change tends to be slow and
steady. Sometimes, the pace is agonizingly slow; but rarely
does it move forward at a dangerously rapid rate. Within
Peruvian culture, political happenings are posed in different
terms. At election times, there is usually the "legal candidate," supported by the Church, the Army, the bankers,
landowners and industrialists. His platform is the continuance of what is. His opposition is a candidate backed by
other segments of the elite, with greater or lesser middle
and lower class support. The candidate of reform builds
his campaign issues on short-run emergencies or, alternatively, the idea of setting things right once and for all, by
reforming in a revolutionary way (e.g., A.P.R.A.'s solutions). However, the deeply ingrained habits of the popula-

tion, coupled with a subtle but powerful defense of the status quo, work against the oppositionist and his simplistic solutions. The result is no progress, either on a large or small scale. One Peruvian called this frequent result "a latent pact with God," tracing the immobility in the political system to "a failure to adopt conclusive attitudes," to "a certain abandonment of things, a discontinuity of processes."

Personal Influence Networks

A second aspect of the country's political life with which the young person becomes familiar is that politics is a matter of personal favors, either asked for or received. Things happen only in response to interventions. Administrative activity consists of short-term, unsystematic measures, responding to pressures from this or that source. As was seen in Chapter III, the power of initiative often rests, as in the United States of a century or less ago, with the local caciques in each province and municipality (or in the barrios of a city like Lima). When a neighborhood is subjected to a natural disaster, when something is desired from the government, or when it is simply a matter of jobs for one's adherents, the caciques (bosses) or patrones provide both the channel and the influence required. In the Peruvian political environment, a forceful personality and a network of personal ties, based on services done for those above and below one, is the essential ingredient for successful action.

Resistance to Leaders Weak

Leadership styles differ. Leaders in aristocratic political structures like Peru enjoy much independence. They are accorded wide authority to do as they think best by followers who place their fates in his hands. Power, once acquired in this country, seems to carry all before it, to be greater than anyone had expected. An example of this is the "mandate" given a new President, like Belaunde in 1963, to undertake sweeping measures, although his election was by only a plurality of the vote. This power, on closer inspection, turns out to be the lack of external resistance to the leader. The reaction of the political environment, i. e., in congressional and press criticism, is mild, if not favorable to the newly elected leader. The absence of effective law and regulations and of an organized opposition are important elements in the apparent excessive power accorded

the individual. Related to this is the Peruvian penchant for
trying to smooth over the danger inherent in the individual
leader's exercise of power by seeking friendly contact with
those close to him. Why, then, do not great things happen,
in the face of the apparent power enjoyed by a new President,
for example? The answer seems to be that the appearance
of power is greater than the reality of Presidential power in
Peru.

Features of Existing Parties

In Peru political organizations spring to life, exert
immense short-run energies and then fade away. The election of 1956 was an example of this. With the exception of
A. P. R. A., Peruvian political parties are little more than
labels for individual candidates. The local affiliates, when
they exist, are mere bands of "hopefuls" hanging on the
coattails of a national politician. They have only tenuous
connections with the nationwide party based in the capital, in
part due to the extremely poor communications system in
Peru. Party loyalties are unstable. A man or a group can
be identified with the "legal candidate" one election and with
the "opposition" the next. This situation reflects the "behind-the-scenes deals" that were treated in some detail above.
Candidates themselves experience little difficulty in switching
from one label to another. The idea of a political party as
a team of candidates, sharing certain purposes (victory at
the next election) is notably absent. Parties in Peru have
traditionally represented only the personal following of one
powerful individual. The situation reflects an underlying psychological reality: dependence at all levels on one strong
individual for all decisions. He may be the patrón, the
cacique, the ministro, the padre, the jefecillo, the presidente.
All things wait for the sign from him.

Impact of Women and the Family on Politics

The extent to which political ideals and values are
instilled by the Church and the educational system was
touched upon in the previous chapter. No understanding of
political socialization is possible without recognition of the
importance of the Peruvian woman (the Catholic wife-mother)
and of the extended family structure in this process. A
player of the game of elite politics must ask himself: What
groups ought I to give the same consideration as I give to

myself? What lesser degree of attention is to be given to
groups farther away? The family, an institution of great
importance in Peru as elsewhere in Latin America, tells
him to whom he is united by moral, economic and religious
bonds. It defines his social rights and obligations. The
family group is his principal unit of cohesion within the upper class. In the entire hierarchy of Peruvian social values,
to be "respected" ranks near the top. Respect flows from
one's family name. If it is among the forty or so most il-
lustrious upper class families, he is immediately accorded
precedence in all things. Thus, the family nourishes one's
sense of self, of being someone. The upper class Peruvian
may be many things in his lifetime--writer, banker, con-
gressman, diplomat, high official. But he feels first, last
and always that he is of a certain family. This fact defines
him as a person. He achieves early in life a sense of identity, of belonging. To the upper class Peruvians, the family is the basis of their society. [5] It prescribes his manners
and his daily round of activity. Without exaggeration, the
family is the first fact of his existence. More important,
much of the content of collective activities such as politics,
religion or banking and commerce interweaves around family
ties, obligations and rewards.

In all this, the upper class in Peru enjoys an inesti-
mable advantage over the middle class and, above all, the
lower and lowest classes. The upper middle class family
may approach that of the elite in its cohesion. But the word
"family" conjures up different images to those lower on the
social scale. For many Peruvians the concept of family is
the nuclear family. The father (absent to a very high degree
in the lower classes) the mother and the children constitute
a group which functions independently. It takes care of its
own needs, without seeming to take much interest outside the
immediate family circle. As a result, relations with other
relatives are weak. New families are formed with each
generation. This sharply contrasts with the families of the
upper class which continue through many generations. The
kinship felt by the hacendado with the alcalde of the neighboring town, even if he does not know him personally but only
that he is a member of gente decente, provides a strong
bond of cement in the upper class world. It generates an
in-group feeling which is quite strong, giving solidarity to
the elite elements as a class. The situation is different
even at the relatively affluent middle class level. Ties exist
and may be based on compadrazco, friendship, neighborli-
ness, economic advantage, or, in fact, on family or kinship.

But middle class in-group feeling is weak or non-existent.

With upper class or cacique control of government
jobs, the middle class has few economic "plums" to distrib-
ute among its members.   The break between generations is
a noteworthy feature at the middle and lower rungs of the
ladder.   Different generations have little in common in part
because there is nothing--neither goods, nor land, nor sta-
tus--to inherit.   Essentially, each generation must supply
its own needs.   It is awareness of the lifetime advantages
that upper class members enjoy automatically, so it seems,
that makes the middle class cling to the "life ideals" and
values of that class rather than striking forth to develop new
aspirations and patterns of its own. [6]

Indirect Influence of Women

Even in male-dominated Hispanic culture, political institutions and behavior mirror the kind of woman who is
predominant in such societies.   Peruvian women were late
in receiving the vote, being accorded it only in the 1960's.
Only an estimated five percent of Peruvian functionaries
were women as recently as 1967. [7]   R. J. Owens states that
Peruvian women have not felt it necessary to participate in
government directly, through the vote and job-holding. [8] This
may be because their indirect influence on political and educational matters through intimate alliance with the Catholic
Church has sufficed from their point of view.   In setting the
tone of Peruvian society, the ideal of the "Catholic wife-
mother" appears to have wielded great influence.   Thus, one
often finds at the top of the upper class extended family
structure a woman, a matriarch (usually a grandmother),
sharing if not superceding the power of the patriarch or
patrón.   It is worth treating the significant phenomenon in
some detail, for the light it throws on the inner workings of
Peruvian society.

A Catholic marriage is the goal of all young upper
class women.   The highest status she can aspire to is that
of married woman, respected and obeyed as reina y senora.
The mother or grandmother is a symbol of family solidarity,
around whom everyone rallies on feast days, saints' days
and at time of births, marriages or deaths.   Competition for
husbands in the upper class leads to early marriages.   A
woman of twenty is often considered a quedada (spinster) if
still unmarried.   A prime function of the wife-mother is re-

ligious observance, which explains her closeness to the
priests.   The Church insists on the strict Catholic upbringing of the children, and looks to the wife-mother to enforce
this stricture.   The pressures from the Church plus youthful marriage lead to numerous children at this upper level
of society.   Childbirth is considered a divine benediction and
an assurance of future security and respect for the parents.
To restrict birth, the Church teaches, is immoral.   Moreover, it menaces the economic progress of the family.   In
consequence of the resulting large families, there is always
an ample supply of young members of the elite to occupy any
job openings that may result from turns of political fortune
or the establishment of new public organizations.   For those
women of the upper class (or the middle class) who fail to
arrive safely in marriage or who break the rules of the
strict Catholic family, there are few places of refuge.   A
convent is one and, increasingly, the possibility of self-sup-
port through public or private employment.   The mother of
an illegitimate child, for example, finds herself outside the
culture.   Social pressures restrict her generally to maintaining a permanent liaison with a man as a secondary wife, becoming a nun or an inhabitant of a barrio de tolerancia
(which districts exist even in the smaller towns).

        The foregoing is not to be taken to imply that the up-
per class women take the place of the dominant and respected
male family heads.   Women do lead a circumscribed adoles-
cence.   There are no women politicians of note.   In marriage and, in general, in society, their place is still one of
subjection.   The necessity to marry is so great that women
accept the male proclivity to a succession of mistresses and
secondary wives.   Few achieve a spirit of camaraderie in
their relations with spouses.   Education has traditionally been
denied to Peruvian women of the landed elite.   It is still the
common belief that women belong in the home and need only
certain domestic skills and a minimal education.   Peruvian
women are usually pious and sometimes fanatical, and readily
accept the guidance in political matters offered by the Church.

Molding the Values of Peruvian Men

        Woman's place in the political and socio-economic
picture which I have painted is something more subtle, and
more lasting.   Peruvian scions of the upper class early
come under the influence of the clergy through religious instruction which is compulsory in the schools in this over-

whelmingly Roman Catholic country. They are doted upon
from earliest years by adoring mothers, sisters and aunts.
Their characters are largely formed by these two influences:
the clergy and the womenfolk of Peru. It is in fulfilling this
task of socializing the young that the wife-mother bulks large
in our analysis of political socialization. She teaches him
that the family group forms a world of its own which is regarded as opposed to the world beyond. One's loyalty is con-
fined to the members of his family, and to a lesser extent
to his class. Everyone outside it is a stranger. The wife-
mother and the family, as a result, are interwoven with the
country's cultural and political characteristics.

Extended Family's Impact on "Rules"

What are some of the "rules of the game" that the
Peruvian landed elite members learn, what "answers" are
communicated to the political aspirant, through constant ex-
posure to the extended family? As has been shown, the dominant patriarchical or matriarchical Catholic family explains
much about the politics and the still essentially feudal social
structure of Peru. What does the institution tell a person
about "how to live"?

Rule No. 12--That Class Solidarity Comes First is Taught at an Early Age

The young male or female member of the landed elite
learns early that he or she is of a special breed. A variety
of prejudices are instilled against the mestizo, cholo or Indian segments of society, much as the southern white in the
U.S. South has traditionally acquired feelings of superiority
toward the Negroes. The elite individual learns that Indians
are subject to the caprices of landowners. These attitudes,
in time, develop into a strong in-group feeling of class solidarity. As pointed out already, the fact that over sixty
percent of the country's population is Indian, and perhaps
twenty-five percent mestizo, puts the elite in a defensive position numerically. The writings of José Carlos Mariátegui
made clear that the conflict at base is between the mentalities
and ideology of the landowning class, i.e., the elite, and
those who favor the Indian and can mobilize mass support.
That writer and thinker argued vehemently that the liquidation
of the colonial, feudal order symbolized by this elite is the
first elemental condition of progress in Peru. As a result
of its deep-rooted sense of insecurity, the upper class has

developed a number of defensive tactics (in effect, the "rules of the game" that are being examined here). In acquiring a sense of belonging to the ruling class, Peruvians learn that the Indians must be kept down, that they have no rights, that to exploit and exploit them is normal and just. When protective laws are passed, the Peruvian establishment combines and connives to break them. They argue to themselves that the solidarity of the upper class requires this. One notes also the absence of concern for the peasants' social and economic interests at all levels of government--municipal, departmental and national. When Indians or cholos (or sometimes middle class individuals) finally gain a hearing with some official, often after trudging for many miles and waiting many days, the most common result is for the official to end the matter by shouting down the peasants or saying "come back tomorrow!" To other members of the elite, such practices are viewed as essential to maintain the dominance of the upper class. But to those outside that class, things seem as if there existed an accord among all the great families, including the military chiefs and the upper echelons of the Church, to the end of keeping the mass of the population down. This feeling is given voice in the declarations of the Peruvian Community Party. The one issued after its 1962 Congress began by stating that the Peruvian oligarchy is "a closed group, a foreign body, a cancer which can be carved out by a surgical operation. "

Rule No. 13--Treat the State and the Public Treasury as the Elite's Own Property

I have noted above that Peru's politics are "elite politics. " In essence, this means that young Peruvian elite members learn that all political action is reserved to their class by right. Historically, the feeling seems traceable to the fact that wealth and economic power derive from favors conferred by the state, not from one's own efforts. From the beginning, land and labor to work it depended on one's standing first with the king and later with the republican government in Lima. Sharing political control meant splitting the benefits that flowed from the state among ever greater numbers of claimants. This point is stressed by Victor Andrés Belaunde in his caustic commentaries on the Peruvian political system. The ruling class has thus been divided into competing clans or economic groups. It has, however, joined forces when new elements demanded a portion of the rewards, e. g. , the part of the populace that rallied to A. P. R. A. 's banner. Mention has been made that when government jobs are to be handed out, the upper class looks out for its own, gaining the lion's share. One shows one's solidarity by assigning posts in government and in public and private enterprises not to the most competent people but to those among one's relatives (or the relatives of one's friends) who need them the most or who will be most thankful for them. Important openings for profit are kept to the top man, his administrative staff or an inner group of cronies.

Rule No. 14--Keep a Foot in Both the Antique and Modern Worlds

La tradición carries great weight in Peru. Memories of the great Inca Empire coupled with the evidences of Colonial times that abound in Lima give Peruvians a nostalgia for the past. With rare exceptions, upper class Peruvians live happily in both worlds: the Colonial, feudal order of the past and the cosmopolitan, bustling order of the present. The landowner typically straddles both existences. If encountered in the city, or in New York or Paris, he is worldly, witty, up-to-date in manner, dress and speech. Yet, if met at his hacienda in the Peruvian Sierra or in one of the barren valleys along the coast, he is wholly traditionalist in manner and outlook. He takes pleasure in his Indians bringing him small gifts or performing gratis some menial service. Careful to comply with his contractual obligations in the world of commerce, trade or banking, in his dealing with his peasants he is often capricious, harsh and without scruple, preferring verbal agreements with them that he can break at will or when interest suits. As a feudal lord, he idealizes the past. The fact that his hacienda is 300 or 400 years old, that some of the furnishings were brought from Spain in the 1700's is a source of great pride to him. [9] The characteristic landed elite member is "a man split between two worlds." Much of the political stress evident in Peru today, and in neighboring republics, stems from the conflicting attitudes within an upper class drawn simultaneously toward the ways of an unfamiliar, modern, democratic, industrial order and toward the warm, humanistic, stratified, traditional system in which they have been nurtured.

Notes

1. Herbert Hyman, Political Socialization (Glencoe: The Free Press, 1959), pp. 9-14. Examining the alternative psychological perspectives of politics, Hyman calls

for studies of the socialization of elite, mass, deviant groups and social movements. He focuses on <u>partici-pation</u> or involvement in politics, and on <u>goals</u> of action, viz., toward radical, conservative, democratic or ameliorative forms. His stress is on case studies of political behavior and on processes underlying particular socialization patterns. Other works on political socialization include: H. Eulau, S. J. Edersveld and M. Janowitz, <u>Political Behavior: A Reader in Theory and Research</u> (Glencoe: The Free Press, 1956) which contains illustrations of the application of psychology by political scientists; Sidney Verba and Lucien Pye (eds.), <u>Comparative Political Culture</u> (Princeton: Princeton University Press, 1966). A useful work showing how normative values are internalized within the individual is Robert F. Lane, <u>Political Ideology</u> (New York: The Free Press, 1962). A perceptive article dealing with political socialization is Kenneth Walker's "La Socialización Política en las Universidades Latinoamericanas," <u>Revista Latinoamericanas, de Sociología,</u> 2 (1965), pp. 200-219.

2. Victor Andrés Belaunde, <u>Meditaciones Peruanas</u> (Lima: Talleres Gráficos Villanueva, 1963), pp. 99-105.

3. Gino Germani, <u>Política y Sociedad en una Época de Transición</u> (Buenos Aires, Editorial Paidos, 1962) pp. 171-176, deals with the type of mentalities turned out by the traditional system.

4. Harry Kantor, <u>The Ideology and the Program of the Peruvian Aprista Movement</u> (Berkeley: University of California Press, 1953), pp. 60-73. The Apristas see Peru as a class state whereby a dominating class oppresses the rest of the population.

5. Bert F. Hoselitz, <u>Sociological Aspects of Economic Growth</u> (New York: The Free Press, 1960) deals with family influences as does Thomas C. Cochran, "Cultural Factors in Economic Growth," <u>Journal of Economic History,</u> 20 (1960), pp. 515-530.

6. Francois Bourricaud, <u>La oligarchía peruana,</u> ECO-Revista de la cultura de occidente, Bogota, Colombia (November and December, 1965) stresses this inability of the middle class to develop and maintain an ideology and set of values distinctly its own.

7. Nelly Festini, "Women in Public Life in Peru," The Annals Vol. 375 (January, 1968), pp. 58-60.

8. R. J. Owens, Peru (London: Oxford University Press, 1963), p. 70.

9. Author's visit to the hacienda of Patricio Lasso in 1965, cited in Appendix II, which brings together examples of subjective, as distinct from statistical, historical or other objective, data on the perspectives of the landed elite. This chapter further refines my model of that elite, viewing it as a political class. A model "performs a selective function in guiding scarce intellectual resources toward deliberate consideration of social and political consequences." In this case, the consequences are those to Peru of that class. The "rules of the game," presented with due reservations in this chapter as throughout, are designed to illustrate the importance of subjective phenomena, such as its preferences, perceptions, volitions, expectations and identities, in the analysis of landed elite political behavior. The "rules" seek to show how members of the Peruvian landed elite approach politics. That elite is viewed as an aggregation of individuals with wants (for prestige, wealth, etc.) and powers (over their peasants) into a collective or macrocosmic want or power (e.g., the desire and power of the group of landowners as a class to defend and promote their interests). This study presents a model of a political man (the landowner) and a political class (the landed elite). In isolating this political man, focus was kept on two values: wealth and power. Of each was asked: Of what does it consist in Peru? Who has it? How did they get it? How do they keep it? Land and the labor to use it along with products of the land figured prominently in the answers to each of these questions. This explains the rural focus in this study. Rural zones are where the land is and where these prime values abide in Peru. Too often in the past, it seems, have explanations of Peru's political life been sought in what happens in Lima. The quotation above is from Harold D. Lasswell, in C. L. Taylor (ed.), Aggregate Data Analysis: Social and Political Indicators in Cross-National Research (Paris: Mouton and Co., 1968), p. 16.

Chapter VI

Political Practices of
Coastal Landowners

Important distinctions exist between the desert coastal regions of Peru and the mountainous interior ranging from the upper reaches of the Andes to the forested Selva or jungle in the east. The reader has noted the dismal aspect of retrogression and abandon in the Andean highlands. By contrast, one sees a relatively modern, commercialized plantation area along the coast. The terms Sierra and Costa used herein conform to most descriptions of Peru. However, a vital fact is that the two blend together in, as R. J. Owens notes, "forty or so oases as bright green stains on an otherwise endless strip of duncolored sand."[1] From an airplane, these patches of green stretch along the banks of perpetually swift-running rivers in jagged valleys that ascend eastward to altitudes of 6,000 feet or more. This 1,400 mile long coastal fringe, which includes the lower slopes of the Andes up to about 6,500 feet, varies in width from over 100 miles to less than fifty. With only thirteen percent of the area of the country, it contains about twenty-seven percent of the inhabitants. The interior highlands, by contrast, contain some sixty-five percent of the total population, explaining the Sierra's importance in this study.

Before the turn of the century, the center of gravity of the Peruvian economy rested in the mines of the interior. However, the great expansion of sugar and cotton production along the coast, beginning with World War I, completed what the earlier guano exploitation had begun.[2] A newly rich social class that had begun to emerge in the latter half of the 19th century solidified itself. Coastal plantations became the mainstay of the economy. Peruvian governments, always short of money, turned to members of this class for loans. Concessions and other favors were granted in return. The wealthy few, including many newly arrived foreigners, waxed richer.

Despite their electoral power and domination over the

bulk of the population, the gamonal and cacique of highland
Peru live outside the fashionable world of Lima.   Collectively, the wealth produced by their haciendas is small.   Crops,
when grown, yield meager harvests due to the backward
technology employed.   Latifundios of the country's vast
mountainous interior account for only five to ten percent of
farm output by value.   This is largely because of their self-
sufficient subsistence character.   Strong economic contrasts
exist with the biggest sugar and cotton plantations on the
coast.   There, one sees evidence of modern equipment and
methods.   Expenditures for tractors, well drilling equipment
and fertilizers are considerable.   The administrators are
trained engineers, a large number having been educated in
the U. S.   Returns on investment are quite high, being dis-
tributed among the beneficiaries in what is essentially a fam-
ily-controlled capitalist enterprise.   Besides the large coastal haciendas, smaller properties exist owned by individuals,
some of them newcomers to the ranks of the landowning
class.   The large scale producers, exporting sugar and cotton to world markets, exert a rigid control over the economic and financial policies of the nation.

Despite differences in wealth and life styles, there
are essential similarities in Peru's landowning class, whether
of the coast or the interior.   Larger properties on the coast
are, in fact, often both lowland and highland (Sierra) haciendas because of gradual expansion along river courses
(control of water resources in Peru being often as desirable
as control of land).   Appendix I identifies forty-six very
sizeable holdings (over 5, 000 hectares) in the so-called
coastal zone, many of which, if one verifies their locales
against a detailed map of the country, are found in Departments lying at the foot of and extending into the high Andes.
As will be shown in the following chapter, a prime defensive
tactic of the landed elite against threats of agrarian reform
has been to argue and write into the law that only the "backward, retrograde" Sierra haciendas should be affected whereas the "modern, progressive" coastal latifundios shall be declared "inafectables" (unaffected) under the law.   Distinctions
between Sierra and Costa become self-serving from a landed
elite viewpoint.

Clarifying the "Model" Being Presented

The "oneness" of the landed upper class, as has been
argued here, in terms of its political behavior bears empha-

sizing. Peru's landed elite seems to typify an earlier period where an elite has been formed under preindustrial conditions. This contrasts to the United States, for example,
where elites are drawn from a plurality of groups--industri-
al, military, labor, professional, to name a few. In the
model of a dominant landed elite which I present here, certain political types exercise an effective control over inhabitants and decisions within large sections of Peru. Their
power appears to be rooted in ownership of land. These political personages (chief of which is the large landowner)
function under the appearance of centralization but, in reality,
power rests with the rulers of component territories, i. e.,
the latifundios. Preceding chapters have dwelt at some
length with Peru's interior because the pattern of rule (expressed in "rules of the game, " in part) is most visible
there.

The model approximates in some respects that of a
feudal society where Central Government rule is not yet articulated with large contiguous territories within the nation.
In Peru, however, power relations within the various parts
of the whole are well developed. Such relations can be tentatively set forth as "rules. " What are these "rules of the
game" and what is their scientific status? In earlier chapters, in seeking to show how the landed elite maintain their
control, it was suggested that the political behavior of this
group reflects certain regularities or patterns that pass from
father to son through a political socialization process. I
present an analysis of political behavior that stresses underlying values and psycho-cultural aspects. The "rules" are
suppositions or generalizations following initial identification
of the phenomena by Peruvian writers or knowledgeable foreign observers. In offering them, it is not implied that the
landed upper class has an explicit "operational code. " Available evidence is low for these propositions. They can best
be understood as "unspoken perceptions" and "do's and
don'ts, " much as one can speak of the informal "rules" that
guide the conduct of, say, members of the U. S. Senate.

In 1948 Nathan Leites gave an explanation of the kind
of political analysis that consists of "codifying political behavior into rules. "[3] He called it the formulation of "psycho-
cultural hypotheses about political acts, " or the "psycho-cultural analysis of political acts. " American political behavior, for example, shows a high degree of internal homogeneity. So it is with Peru. A premise in this study has
been that the same kind of homogeneity exists in Peru's po-

litical life. What has been looked for, and reported herein,
are culturally typical political acts, e. g., the attitude of
master on the part of the landed elite member and of subservience on the part of middle and lower class persons. In
this chapter and the next, I turn to various types of political
acts representing concrete political phenomena. These include selection of Cabinet members, accretion of large landholdings and counter-elite efforts to break up these holdings
through agrarian reform. Attention centers on the coastal
landholders because ownership of one of these coastal plantations is generally equated with membership in the Peruvian
"oligarchy, " a common term in this country. [4]

Identifying Principal Landowners

        Sources of data on who belongs to this landowning
group are hard to come by. Peruvians are sensitive to in-
quiries in this regard. The only thorough study on the subject of who are the principal landholders was one initiated
by President Augusto Leguía in 1929. Results appeared in
a volume published by the Ministerio de Hacienda (Treasury
Department) in 1939. The book is exceedingly rare today.
It was intended for taxation purposes. No comparable data
have been collected since 1929. The government maintains
a Registro de la Propiedad Immueble (Register of Real Property), but this is incomplete as Peruvian laws on the recording of land titles and transfers are very lax. Two of
the better sources are the commercial publications, Guia
Vernal del Perú, issued by Andres Vernal Consultants in
1960, and the Vademecum del Inversionista, 1960-61, issued
by the Banco de Credito del Perú. Information on irrigation
water rights, obtained from the Dirección de Aguas de Rega-
dío (Office of Irrigation Waters), throws important light on
who are the owners of properties having water rights.

        Drawing on these sources, it has been possible to
draw up a list of the principal landowners in Peru (see Appendix I). This list of 343 Peruvian families with substantial landholdings enables one to compare, for example, power holders (defined as Cabinet ministers and top administrators or politicians) with the list of landowners. As will be
shown below, some interesting conclusions flow from these
data. There are other interesting hypotheses. Have the
aristocratic elements kept their power because they have regularly welcomed rising newcomers into their ranks? This
can be determined by finding out what proportion of these

landowning families (assuming that the aristocracy is to be
found within their numbers) represent new names in the
country's elite, i. e., do not figure in the 19th century or
earlier lists of distinguished Peruvian families. Does ownership of a hacienda or two constitute a sine qua non for membership in the aristocracy? A judgment on this can be arrived at by finding out, for example, what proportion of the
membership of the exclusive Club Nacional (considered the
stronghold of the elite, followed by the Country Club de Lima
and the Country Club El Bosque) appears on our list of landholders. Has there been an influx of "new rich, " based in
commerce, industry and banking rather than ownership of
land, into the upper reaches of Peruvian society? Our list
permits us to isolate the landholding families first and then
ascertain who in the exclusive ranks of society (taking the
membership lists of exclusive clubs as our best guide) derives his wealth and prestige from these other fields of activity. Source data cited above gives names of the directors
of leading firms and banks. It is feasible in this way to fix
criteria that, in practice, control recruitment of new members into the elite, e. g., whether it be landownership, commercial holdings or banking ties or a combination of all
three. It is not my purpose, however, to pursue these fas-
cinating byways. Instead, I shall focus on establishing the
relationship between landownership and political power.

The "Old Elite" as a Landholding Group

Two Peruvian writers, Mario Vasquez and Felipe
Cossío del Pomar, have provided a useful list of names of
the families comprising the Peruvian aristocracy as it stood
at the end of the 19th century. [5] These are shown below
following the arrangement adopted by these two individuals:

Peru's "Old Elite" Families

"Colonial" Elite (Pre-Independence)		"Republican" Elite (19th Century)
Aspillaga*	Olaechea*	Beltrán*
Althaus*	Montero*	Boza*
Alvarez*	Lavalle	Masías*
Barreda*	Osma	Solf y Muro
Candamo	Pardo*	Gamarra
Canseco	Prado*	Santa Cruz
Diez*	Romana*	Paz*
La Jara	Nieto	Soldán*
Ferreyros	Vivanco	
Fernandini*	Orbegoso*	

"Foreign Born" Elite	"Provincial" Elite
(Born Late 19th Century	(North Part of Country)

Berckemeyer*	Nicolini*	Bracamonte
Ferrand*	Olceste	Cardonez
Freundt	Patrón*	Herrera*
D'Onofrio	Rizo*	Pinillos*
Gibson	Rosell*	Urdapillete
Guimoye	Rossello	Valdemar
Lecca	Wiesse	Cárdenas
Gildemeister*		

* Name appears on list of landowning families (see Appendix I).

It will be seen that more than half (twenty-three out of forty-two names) of the above listed families are in the category of sizeable landowners as shown in Appendix I. What is more striking, however, is the great number of names of landholding families which do not appear in our lists of "old elite" members. This indicates that the Vasquez and Cossío del Pomar designations of who constitutes "old elite" may be highly subjective, drawing on family reputations mainly and omitting many important names. One notes immediately the absence from their lists of such well-known "aristocratic" families (in the eyes of outsiders) as the Miro Quesadas, the Paz Soldáns and the Moreyras. It is, therefore, prudent to inquire further into which families are wielders of political power. The holding of a Cabinet post in the two civilian administrations since 1956 shall be cited as evidence of a family or a family member being part of the politically powerful landed elite.

Cabinet Members as Landholders

If what has been said earlier about the important part played by landownership in Peru's political life is correct, a sizeable number of Cabinet ministers should be drawn from among the landed families. Lists were compiled from the record of Cabinet changes during the second Prado Administration--1956-1962, (the first being in 1939-1945) and the recent Belaunde Administration (1963-1968) to show to what extent landlords have constituted the main reference group of these Peruvian Presidents in making ministerial appointments.

A number of interesting facts were revealed. In selecting
Cabinet members, Peruvian Presidents recognize certain
norms governing this process, or so it would seem from the
nearly identical percentages of ministers drawn from the
landholding elite in both the Prado and Belaunde administrations.   Little is known about the methods of Cabinet selection in Peru. One may affirm however, that well over half
will represent the stable, conservative aristocracy which has
been interpreted as sharing a common denominator, namely,
ownership of large tracts of land.   The landlords as a class
do appear to be a principal reference group of Peru's Presidents in choosing members of their Cabinets.

A close look at Cabinet changes to fix the relation of
landownership to ministerial appointments was taken.   The
Cabinets of President Prado during his 1956-1962 administration underwent, in general, five transformations and those
of President Belaunde (through 1966) four with various individual Cabinet changes.   Under President Prado, landed elite
representatives held the critical Ministries of Agriculture,
Development, Finance, Government and the Prime Minister-
ship from eighty to one hundred percent of the time.   The
less important (from the viewpoint of an upper class bent on
countering challenges to its dominance) Ministries of Education, Justice, Health and Labor were held by landed elite
representatives from twenty to seventy-five percent of the
time.   Under President Belaunde, no clear pattern emerged.
The Ministers of Development and Education appear to have
been landed elite representatives from eighty to one hundred
percent of the time, followed by Government at sixty percent, Finance at two-thirds of the time and Agriculture and
Justice fifty percent.   The two Prime Ministers under Belaunde, both practicing physicians, do not figure on our lists
of important landowners in the country.

Life History Characteristics of Cabinet Members

A significant finding coming out of biographic data on
Cabinet ministers is the high proportion bearing the names
of families we have identified with the landed elite.   What
else do these data show?[6]   The upper class enjoys unusual
advantages, to obtain education, distinction, varied employ-
ments and high public posts.   When the biographies of Cabinet members are minutely examined, a number of them
group themselves immediately as "upper class. "   Under
President Prado, thirty-six of the thirty-seven ministers

fell into this class grouping, using the criteria of (1) unusual advantages, (2) connection to "old elite," and (3) appearance of name of landed elite list. Under President Belaunde, twenty-one of the thirty-one ministers shown seemed to be identifiable as "upper class." The remaining ten under Belaunde were in a somewhat lower social rank. Those falling in this group lacked (1) a family tie to either of our "old elite" or landed elite and (2) evidence of unusual advantages, as deduced from their life history data.

Prado's ministers took up their portfolios in his second administration at an average age well into their fifties, whereas Belaunde's ministers entered Cabinet office at an average age of forty-three. The Prado group were relatively well-experienced in high public office, mostly the appointive type. With few exceptions, the Belaundista ministers lacked experience in the higher posts. A high proportion, however, had been elected to Congress previously, eight of the nine ministers in this category having been elected as a Senator or Deputy in the 1963 elections. Ninety percent of the Belaundista ministers were drawn directly from the ranks of Acción Popular workers, the party which President Belaunde founded in 1956, and revived in 1962. Party activity thus became a prime criterion for Belaunde in making Cabinet appointments.

The continuity of rule by a politically active part of the aristocracy is best illustrated by the Prado administrations. Ten of Prado's ministers during his second administration (Alvarado, Alzamora, Belaunde, Cisneros, Carillo, Gallo, Hilbeck, Moreyra, Romero, Thorndike) had served as ministers during his earlier term in office, or had been appointed previously by Prado to other high government posts. A number of these individuals, according to biographic information, were active in commerce and banking, the latter a special concern to President Prado because of his heading the Banco Popular del Perú, owned by the Prado family (which also, incidentally, acquired during the second Prado administration a virtual monopoly of the country's cement industry).

Most commentaries on the Peruvian "oligarchy" speak of it as a "coastal plutocracy," e.g., Victor Andrés Belaunde. A study of the regional origins of Cabinet ministers since 1956 provides evidence to substantiate this assertion. Of the thirty-seven ministers under Prado, thirty-four persons or ninety-two percent came from the Lima-Callao area (twenty-

seven persons) or elsewhere along the coast (seven persons)
principally the town of Arequipa and vicinity. Of Belaunde's
thirty-one ministers, all but five persons (four from the
Sierra and one from the Selva or jungle) or eighty-four percent came from Lima-Callão or the Arequipa-coastal area.
It is clear that the politically active stratum in Peru, if one
is to judge from the evidence of Cabinet appointments, come
from the coastal zone, and specifically from the capital and
second city. [7]

Some Additional "Rules of the Game"

     For the most part, the coastal landowners are eco-
nomically powerful individuals, contrasted with the less well-
off <u>hacendados</u> and <u>gamonales</u> of the interior. The "ideal
type" within this coastal plutocracy is the man of many years
and honors, who has typically served as Cabinet minister,
banker, industrialist, diplomat or government adviser (or,
often as not, in a combination of all these in a rich and varied career). His "world-view" is at once modern and traditional. What, then, are some of the "rules" by which
and others like him work their will vis-à-vis bureaucracy,
legislature and state itself?

Rule No. 15--<u>Keep the Elite "Permeable" by Admitting to</u>
               <u>the Upper Class Anyone Acquiring Large Land-</u>
               <u>holdings or Attaining High Positions in Bank-</u>
               <u>ing, Industry, Commerce or, to a Lesser Ex-</u>
               <u>tent, Government</u>

     The data have shown that a close tie exists between
the holding of land and the holding of power positions (defined mainly as Cabinet posts). Of sixty-eight Cabinet Ministers examined, forty-two (or sixty-two percent) were a-
mong the nation's leading landowners. Of that forty-two, no
less than nineteen (or twenty-eight percent) of all ministers
under Presidents Prado and Belaunde were members of families holding 5,000 hectares or more. An additional eight
were in the "medium landholder" category (owning between
1,000 and 5,000 hectares), putting thirty-nine percent of all
ministers during the 1956-66 decade in the category of large
or medium landowners. When it is recalled that 0.4 percent of the country's landowners hold 77.7 percent of the
arable land, [8] the significance of this disproportion becomes
clear. The landed elite as a class is grossly over-repre-
sented in the Cabinets. Information on ownership of busi-

ness, banking and commercial enterprises is not available.
Thus, it is not possible to state whether business and banking interests are similarly disproportionately represented in
the Cabinets.   An examination of names of the principal officers and directors of leading firms shows that large landowning families are strongly represented. [9]   These include
such families as: Aspillaga Anderson, Beltrán Espantoso,
Bellido Espinoza, Miranda, Moreyra y Paz Soldán, Palacios,
Izaga, Picasso, Costa Élice, Fernandini, Dibos, Bercke-
meyer, Cillóniz, Fumagalli, Guimoye, Romana, Lopez, Gilde-
meister, Masías, Olaechea, Pardo, Prado, Pesquiera, de la
Piedra, Ramos Dammert, Hilbeck Seminario and Gallo
Porras.

By and large, Peru's powerful economic elite is not
split along rural-urban lines or even Sierra-coastal lines.
The largest landowners have large shares in many of the
country's most lucrative business and commercial enterprises,
including the leading banks and insurance companies, news-
papers and radio stations, fish meal and importing concerns,
wherever they are located.   The families tend to monopolize
the particularly lucrative fields.   The self-sufficiency ideal
(the "hacendado mentality") generally prevails: for financing,
establish one's own bank; if machinery is needed, establish
one's own importing firm; if insurance or lumber, open up
one's own insurance or timber concern.   These great families are restrictive as to marriage and formal alliances
with other clans.   They exercise varying degrees of control
over members, some being cohesive and others less so.   In
general, they are flexible, welcoming talented newcomers into their ranks (more often as employees or advisers than as
formal family members).   The constant aim of the landed
families is to get members into key positions, in Cabinets,
banks, the National Congress, higher echelons of government
and business concerns.   As strategically placed individuals,
they can do favors for other members of the clan, open up
opportunities for them, engage in protective or defensive
maneuvers when necessary.

Only twenty-three of the 343 names on our list of
landowners are on the list of "Old Elite" members, which
has been defined as families that were prominent during the
first quarter of the 20th century or earlier.   Furthermore,
only seven of the sixty-eight Cabinet ministers are on that
list (Section 2, Appendix I).   This would seem to indicate a
marked permeability, i. e., many newcomers, into the ranks
of the landed elite over a half century or more.   This per-

meability or access to the higher ranks in Peruvian politics
and society shows the upper class is "open to talent," it
would appear. Certainly, dynamic, hard-working immigrant
families figure prominently in our listing of landed families.
Perhaps reflecting the decline in immigration after World
War I compared to the last half of the 19th century, names
of German, Italian and French origin are less numerous in
the listing of 343 landholders (where they are twenty-two percent of the total) than in the listing of "Old Elite" members
(thirty-nine percent). Peru's upper class, it would appear,
is hetereogeneous, accessible to "new rich," constantly re-
cruiting new members from ascending middle strata, yet able
to preserve its power.

Rule No. 16--Direct Use of Force to Protect Elite Interests
                is Often Easier and More Effective than At-
                tempting Quieter Exercise of Power

        If elite predominance is so pronounced in the country's
political life and if the President is traditionally regarded by
the dominant upper class as "one of us," why the frequent
violent overthrows of Peruvian Chiefs of State? The answer
seems to lie in the kind of cultural conditioning or socialization process examined here. Many students of Latin American politics stress the recognition there of violence as an
accepted instrument of political action. To this might be
added its utility, in a ruling class view, as a means of ac-
complishing a task neatly and directly. James Payne's study,
cited above, revolves largely on Peruvian labor leaders' use
of strikes as a political tactic. Upper class use of violence
may be seen in repressions of the peasantry, in the frequent
exiling of opponents and in the apparent ready acceptance by
the landowning-commercial group of violent removals of Peruvian Presidents from office. There appears to be a tacit
recognition that such "direct action" is in order whenever
upper sector monetary interests, for example, are threatened. A case in point would seem to be President Fernando
Belaunde Terry's Executive Orders of June, 1968 designed
to cope with Peru's continuing fiscal deterioration. These
Orders (Nos. 202-68 and 287-68) placed a tax on income
from wages and capital, a tax on urban and rural real estate, a tax on net worth of corporations, and eliminated
bearer shares, all measures that struck directly at the mon-
eyed class. Some three months later, a military coup overthrew him as Chief of State. The pretext was his handling
of a petroleum dispute. If connected, the two events tend
to substantiate the existence of the above "rules" by the

group that retains its identity as a ruling class.   More will
be said of this in the concluding chapter.

Rule No. 17--Reject the "Idea of Peru" for the Peruvian
                    Nation Exists Only Marginally to the Interests
                    of the Clan which are First and Foremost Eco-
                    nomic and Financial

        Victor Andrés Belaunde uses the term "coastal plu-
tocracy" to point out the economic power of landowning families.   Their power is exercised more often in the economic
sphere than in the national parliament.   Upper class power
does not reside solely in ownership of property but in active
and effective control of the country's monetary resources.
Export earnings constitute the main portion.   Foreign exchange resources that do not remain abroad are controlled
by the exporters through their control of the country's system of marketing and credit.   A close student of Peru,
François Bourricaud, stresses the "capitalist mentality" of
the oligarchy.   Commercial and economic policy is its special preserve, he says, the objective being to win for the
exporters "every last penny of gains from sales abroad."
In keeping with the desire to maximize profits and returns,
the families limit their political aims.

        What have these limited aims usually consisted of?
First, historically, has been the desire to wrest favors
from pliant governments.   Most often, this has been accomplished through the "good offices" of a strategically-placed
clan member.   (For example, in 1956 as Minister of Finance
to President Prado, Juan Pardo Heeren, a scion of landed
families on both sides, arranged for customs exemptions for
the clan's textile business.)   Winning absolute exemptions
from taxation has been highest among these aims.   The object is to make sure taxes gravitate onto the middle class
and popular masses.   Second, keeping the Presidency in
hands friendly to the landed elite, either through a pliant civilian leader or military junta, remains a constant objective.
The important thing is that the upper class never be con-
fronted as a group.   It must not be attacked in what it considers its essential interests.   Thus, the premium is on
maneuver, on indirect exercise of influence (vis-à-vis the
President, the bureaucracy or the Congress).   Stress is
placed on manipulation and negotiation.   The processes are
seldom overt or public.   They are, however, frequently al-
luded to by knowledgeable Peruvians.   The watchwords among
the upper class appear to be: do not participate directly in

politics, for reasons of prudence; do not be too visible, in
order to avoid being a target; the essential is to get "solutions" that favor one's clan, or at least conform to its preferences and interests.   The result is that the nation, that
is, something beyond the family or clan, does not exist for
the typical elite member, other than as a geographical designation.

Peru as a Private Preserve

        The upper class, to summarize the above, regards
Peru as its private preserve.   I am speaking here, it should
be emphasized, not about a closed, caste-like structure
called the upper class but rather about a mentality.   This
mentality about what is appropriate to the ruling class is
shared by contenders to that class no less than by those already in it.   One does not find in Peru any idea of or feeling for the "aristocratic republic," in Aristotle's or Tocqueville's or Edmund Burke's sense.   There is no concept of
"noblesse oblige," or of "rule by the best."   A succession
of Peruvian writers are vehement in condemning the supposed
moral and personal deficiencies of the upper class.   Simon
G. Hanson has this upper class in mind when he writes that
they are content "to exploit and exploit and exploit while en-
gaging in a riot of conspicuous consumption and in a skilled
movement of their assets to Switzerland."   He is speaking
both of individuals and of a point of view, the latter deeply
rooted in white and mestizo segments of the population and
tracing back to the time of the Conquest.

        When saying that, for the elite, the nation as such
"does not exist," it is meant that the elite refuses to treat
reciprocally with the rest of the population.   It does not consider them as the other partakers of the national patrimony.
The ruling class does not admit the right of other classes
to participate in or to share power.   Individuals of talent
are admitted to the upper ranks, but not whole social classes,
such as the dependent middle class or the lower class mestizos, cholos and Indians.   Being above the laws, the elements
we are examining get around them as a class.   Blocking attempts to carry out vigorous action programs such as those
embarked upon by President Belaunde, the upper class tends
to view these as illusory and romantic.   As will be treated
below, the better elements favor gradual change, because
they sense the growing power of the urban masses and the
dangers of continued rural unrest and exodus.   Those with

effective power, as has been pointed out, do not see this
larger picture. The Peruvian nation exists only marginally
to the interests of a particular clan, in the typical Peruvian
"oligarch's" mind. New government programs and activities
represent simply new sectors for their family to penetrate,
for the favors, jobs and contracts that are offered. The
dominant sectors participate in and support the larger concerns of the Peruvian nation only to the extent necessary to
assure sizeable advantages flowing to the various clans.

Notes

1.   R. J. Owens, Peru (London: Oxford University Press,
     1963), p. 2.

2.   Emilio Romero, Historia Económica del Perú (Buenos
     Aires, Editorial Sudamerica, 1949) is a prime source
     of information on Peru's economic history, as is Jorge
     Basadre whose Historia de la republica del Perú, 10
     vols. (Lima, 1961-1964) is the standard reference
     work. Victor Andrés Belaunde, La Realidad Nacional
     (Lima, 1945) also treats the economic picture in some
     detail. Jonathan Levin, The Export Economies: Their
     Pattern of Development in Historical Perspective (Cam-
     bridge, Mass., 1960) depicts the growth of the coastal
     plantations following the guano boom.

3.   Nathan Leites, "Psycho-Cultural Hypotheses About Pol-
     itical Acts," World Politics, Vol. I (October, 1948),
     pp. 102-119. Among social scientists, anthropologists
     were the earliest to try to describe and explain an
     entire way of life of a primitive people. Lasswell has
     led political scientists to seek this kind of knowledge.
     What Leites sought for was akin to the study of national
     character traits, on which a large body of literature
     has accumulated. Because of the impressionistic na-
     ture of most national character studies, the kind of
     analysis recommended by Lasswell and Leites searches
     for "psychological regularities in large groups" but on
     the basis of observations systematically made and re-
     corded. "Rules" have been set down in order to make
     clear what is believed to be typical behavior patterns
     of the landed elite. Some may object to writing down
     "rules of the game" for which only very insufficient
     evidence is at hand. The value in asserting them lies
     in thus fostering their disproof or approval, as the case

may be. At minimum, they will promote the inventing
of useful hypotheses. What does one look for in seeking to fix the "rules of the game" of a particular type
of political behavior? The "rules" simply say that certain acts are likely to occur. They need not always
occur or recur. One asks whether a behavior pattern
is so, why it is, and what does it signify? The hypotheses set forth herein deal with a limited set of
acts, principally the relations between the landholding
class and the large mass of the population. When it
is asserted that certain behavior is typical, differences
have not been overlooked, for example, the fact that
many landowners are apolitical while others enjoy un-
questioned political pre-eminence.

4. In general, the term "oligarchy" has been avoided because of the perjorative nature of the word. James L.
Payne, Labor and Politics in Peru: The System of Political Bargaining (New Haven: Yale University Press,
1965), pp. 272-275, says: "The exact nature and extent of this group is never stated clearly" and adds:
"The suggestion that, on issues of political bargaining,
large numbers of citizens have a voice in decision making goes against the popular notion that Peru is controlled by a small oligarchy" (p. 272). To Payne, the
distribution of political power in Peru seems like that
of the U.S. democratic system. To him, the decision
maker (the President) is made responsible to the Peruvian citizen by the latter's skillful use of violence and
threats of violence. In Payne's "descriptive model of
political interaction," civilian violence and military intervention are the dependent variables whereas the independent variables are the varied reasons that lead the
workers to select political bargaining as their major
strategy (p. 268). Payne omits any mention of the conservative class or the landholding element, but does
cite their organizations in commerce and industry as
power factors.

For a contrary view, clearly identifying the banking-
commercial-coastal landowning group as the "oligarchy,"
see François Bourricaud, Pouvoir et Societé dans le
Perou Contemporain (Paris: Librairie Armand Colin,
1967). (Excerpts from Bourricaud have been cited
previously in these notes.) Another useful work dealing with the methodological problem involved in determining power positions in a political system is W. Polsby,

Community Power and Political Theory (New Haven:
Yale University Press, 1963.

5. Mario C. Vasquez, "The Peruvian Elite," lecture given
    at Cornell University in 1964 (mimeograph). During
    the author's visits to Peru in 1964-1966, information
    was sought on which families were considered "old
    elite" by asking knowledgeable Peruvians to name them.

6. Biographic data on leading Peruvians were forthcoming
    from: Manuel Beltroy, Peruanos Notables (1957);
    Pequeño Diccionario Biografico del Perú (Lima: Field
    Ediciones, 1961); "Who's Who in Latin America, " Vol.
    4 (Palo Alto: Stanford University Press, 1947); Carlos
    Malpica, Los Duenos del Perú (Lima: Fondo de Cultura
    Popular, 1963) pp. 9-61.

7. As an indication of being "politically active, " a family
    was thus categorized by its: (1) having a family mem-
    ber in the Cabinet during the 1955-65 decade; (2) being
    listed by knowledgeable Peruvians as being part of
    Peru's "Old Elite"; or (3) having a family member ac-
    tive in two principal "defensive" organizations during
    the crucial 1963-64 year when agrarian reform legisla-
    tion was in process of being passed, i. e., Sociedad
    Nacional Agraria (National Agrarian Society) or Aso-
    ciación de Criadores de Laneres del Perú (Peruvian
    Woolgrowers Association). Appendix I (Section II, A-
    B-C) lists fifty-six names of Peruvian families (called
    therein "oligarchs") who, besides owning land, appear
    to meet one or more of these three "tests. "

    Section II, (D) provides 110 names of large landowners
    who might be called "non-political" (really "politically
    inactive") because they meet none of these three cri-
    teria. From the "rules of the game" cited immediately
    after, I conclude that they remain inactive because
    they are able to protect and advance their interests
    fully without becoming too visible through Cabinet mem-
    bership and the like. Moreover, the tradition of their
    family may be in the direction of banking, industry and
    commerce rather than active political service. Many
    names in Section II (D) are immediately recognizable
    as being prominent of commercial and banking circles,
    if not in Cabinet posts. Some persons, however, may
    question the "non-political" designation. Robert E.
    Scott calls Peru's powerful economic groups Fuerzas

Económicas Vivas in Elites in Latin America, edited
by Seymour M. Lipset and Aldo Solari (London: Oxford University Press, 1967), p. 138.   Some ten organizations of the elite constitute, in the eyes of some
Peruvians, the visible manifestation of "private government. "

8.   Ministry of Agriculture figures published by National
     Planning Institute, 1963.   This 0. 4 percent of the land-
     owners includes all those holding 500 hectares or more.

9.   Vademecum del Inversionista, published by Banco de
     Credito, 1962-1963 gives a number of names of officers
     and directors of leading firms.

Chapter VII

Peru's Counter-Elite and the Problem of
Agrarian Reform

This chapter proposes to portray the critics of the
social system that has, before and during the 20th century,
shown an enormous and successful resistance.   Above all,
the Peruvian ruling class has resisted the demands of less
privileged middle and lower classes for a share in the national patrimony.   On the surface, during these recent decades
Peruvian society has changed.   It has become more varied
than the rigid two-class model implies.   It is worth taking a
look at these differences within classes before proceeding.

Peru's upper class contains at the top a layer of
bankers, financiers, the largest importers and exporters,
the coastal and larger Sierra hacendados.   These men are
rich and cosmopolitan.   They personify the "oligarchy."   A
lower layer is composed of ranking politicians, owners of
companies, military officers and clergymen of high rank,
holders of urban real estate, economically secure intellectuals and the lesser hacendados of the coast and the interior.
This upper class is relatively homogeneous.   It shares an
elite viewpoint and demonstrates social and psychological cohesion.

Peru's middle class, too, is marked by upper and
lower levels.   On the former are lower ranking military officers and clergymen, government officials, professional men,
self-employed businessmen, proprietors of small haciendas
and farms, owners of transport agencies and large retailers.
The lower level of the middle class includes the national police and non-commissioned army officers, teachers, less
well-paid functionaries, the regular clergy, renters of smaller
urban housing and the like.   The lower class in the country
similarly is composed of varied segments: salaried workers
and persons with technical skills living in the larger cities;
peasants of the cholo type who are drivers or small landholders in rural areas; finally, the Indian and mestizo peasants who live on haciendas or in indigenous communities un-

116

der a system of peonage or servitude. This variety of social groupings is misleading, however. Peru continues to be,
in Disraeli's phrase, "two nations," the "haves and the have
nots," with the "haves" limited to the strata at the very top.

Values and Aspirations of Peru's Counter-Elite

Peru's landed elite fits by and large the description
of conservative oligarchies given by Gaetano Mosca, Roberto
Michels and by modern writers like Milton Esman.[1] With
the exception of Victor Raúl Haya de la Torre, the country's
upper class has produced no ideologues, articulating a view
of the future. As has been seen, the top men are traditional in their style of rule. They distrust mass movements and
mass agitation. They oppose whatever might disrupt the
complex interclan relationships they have built up. Taking
few political risks, they focus on the problem of the moment,
e. g., eliminating a José Luis Bustamante from the Presidency in 1947-48 or preventing Haya de la Torre from acquiring it in 1962. The problems of tomorrow can only be
imagined. Therefore, they are not their concern. Protecting and conserving the power base that supports their rule
(mainly ownership of land and control of economic resources)
is the "oligarchy's" constant preoccupation. Reliance on
precedents and established "rules of the game," such as
those examined here, predisposes everyone to caution and
passive routine, thus perpetuating the status quo. When
threatened, the upper class regime readily resorts to repression, turning over the reins of government to military
strongmen.

Appearance of Social Critics on the Scene

Not all of Peru's leaders (virtually all drawn from
the upper class or upper middle class) fit this pattern.
Three successive waves of critics and opponents to the existing rule have emerged since the early 1900's. Frederick B.
Pike, an historian of the present state of affairs, singles
out a group of indigenista reformers in the first decade of
the 20th century.[2] Under the influence of positivism and
Spencerian ideas, three reformers dominated this early reform movement in the political sphere: Mariano Cornejo,
Javier Prado y Ugarteche and Manuel Vicente Villarán. Another writer of this period, Gabriel González Prada, threw
diatribes at the Church and the status quo, but politically re-

mained on the sidelines. Cornejo, a capable orator who
held important positions and in 1919 served as Prime Minister and Minister of Interior, emphasized gradual reform a-
long the pathways of freedom, democracy and anti-dictator-
ship. Javier Prado, scion of one of the country's richest
families, served many years in the National Congress. He
argued for massive immigration from Europe and for an educational system that would produce farmers, agronomists,
manufacturers, businessmen and other "practical and sensi-
ble" men. Villarán, Peru's greatest educator, strived to
instill a sense of nationality in the Peruvian upper and middle classes. He characterized the Peruvian's chief qualities
as "a disdain for work, a love for the acquisition of money
without any personal effort, a fondness for personal idleness,
a taste for fiestas and a tendency toward extravagance. " He
declared "we have acquired an ignorance of industrial and
commercial professions and a fondness for literature, rhetoric and poetry. "[3]

      A second group of dissident elite members came to
prominence during the 1920's. Luis E. Valcarcel, Hildebrando Castro Pozo, José Carlos Mariátegui, Manuel J.
Gamarra and Haya de la Torre made their voices heard during the eleven year rule of Augusto B. Leguía (1919-1930). [4]
Valcarcel, a close student of the Indians, advocated the violent suppression of Spanish institutions. He called for the
physical elimination of many of the members of white and
mestizo Peru. The unjust and exploitative capitalism of the
"coastal plutocracy, " Castro Pozo argued, must be replaced
by a socialism patterned after ancient Inca practices. Gamarra, the principal voice for moderation among the indi-
genistas, asked only for greater autonomy for the Sierra,
to stop the exploitation of the interior for the benefit of the
people of the coast and the capital. Haya de la Torre's
mystical case for an alliance of all the indigenous peoples
of the Americas centered, insofar as the program of the
Aprista Party was concerned, on winning over the urban
population to an immediate socialist revolution.

      The third or modern wave of reform-minded Peru-
vians flowed during the 1950's and the early 1960's. Fernando Belaúnde's La conquista del Perú por los Peruanos,
published in 1958, led the way to creation of a politically
effective reform movement, Acción Popular. Other social
critics in this epoch include: Leonidas Castro Bastos,
Edgardo Seoane Corales, Jorge Bravo Bresani, José María
Arguedas, Felipe Cossío del Pomar, Victor Andrés Belaunde,

José de la Riva Aguëro, José Matos Mar, Mario C. Vasquez,
Oscar Nunez del Prado, Grabriel Escobar M., Anibal Quijano Obregón, Ciro Alegría, Enrique Chirinos Soto, Hector
Chirinos Lorentzen, José Mejía Valera, Anibal Ismodes
Cairo, Carlos Malpica and Hugo Neira.[5] Ranging from defenders of a moderate policy of social reform to outright rev-
olutionists, this group reflects greater hetereogeneity than
either the 1900-1910 or 1920-1930 opposition to the existing
order. What does the mentality of this modern "counter
elite" consist of? How do they view the present situation in
Peru? What changes would they make in it?

Peru as Seen by Present-Day Peruvians

The most moderate of the reformers, Fernando Be-
laundo Terry and the No. 2 man in Acción Popular, Edgardo
Seoane, see the long-neglected interior as the key to the
country's future. They elaborated as their party's platform
in the early 1960's a program of co-existence and cooperation between the coast and the Sierra to replace the old one
of indifference or exploitation. In their books, these statesmen argue for collaboration between capitalism and western-
ized ways on the one hand and socialism and traditions of
communal labor of ancient Inca Peru on the other. Belaunde
has called on the native communities (which he as Presidential candidate was the first to visit extensively) to advance
themselves through the same methods employed by their ancient ancestors. He wants to see the Indians migrate toward the jungle and not toward the coast. Seoane, an able
and humanitarian man, was Acción Popular's theorist on
agrarian matters. He proposed as a remedy to long-standing
injustices in rural Peru widespread redistribution of land
coupled with efforts at increased productivity, especially in
the coastal haciendas. A middle way was thus sought to the
pressing problem of landless masses. Seoane's goal was a
solution that would not menace the interests of the power-
wielding groups in Lima, largely identified with the coastal
landholders.[6]

Other modern exponents of indigenismo (affection for
the Indian and ancient Inca ways) like Alegría, Arguedas,
Riva Aguëro, Nuñez del Prado and Vasquez document the
need for drastic agrarian reforms. They argue eloquently
that the masses must have not simply an access to landownership but agricultural credit, less onerous leases, improved
marketing arrangements and better rural living conditions

generally.   They see little hope in such a program being
realized through the Aprista Party.   Besides disassociating
itself with indigenismo during the 1950's, Haya de la Torre's
party lost its zeal for reform somewhere along the way, in
their view.   They recall that during the 1963 campaign, the
Aprista leader called for patience and maintained that Peru's
rural problems were not really terribly pressing.   The attitude of younger Peruvians who see that no progress has
been made by these critics toward solving or ameliorating
Peru's social problems is somewhat ambivalent.   Typical is
the remark of one of them, with reference to the Communist-
led guerrillas fighting in the mountains in 1966:   "Sometimes
I feel like condemning them.   At other times I feel like going out and joining them. "

        A reasoned criticism of Peru's socio-economic struc-
ture has been articulated by a few Peruvians of the current
generation.   Influenced by Marxist ideas acquired during university years and from José Carlos Mariátegui's works,
among others, they present a picture of a "prerevolutionary"
state of affairs in Peru. [7]   It is a view shared by many foreign observers.   Central to their thinking is the search for
an "autonomous" Peru, one that is not at the mercy of either
foreign or domestic "colonialists. "   These latter they identify
with the large businesses, the grandes empresas, that appear
to be above the state.   Most of these firms got underway in
the latter half of the 19th century as a result of the inflow
of English capital and the guano boom.   These critics recall
that export of mineral products continued until World War I
as almost the sole source of wealth.   This trade was largely
in the hands of European, and later, American firms.   The
advent of President Leguía in 1919 brought to the fore a new
class of Peruvians and immigrants who obtained wealth
through government concessions, commissions and contracts.
Sugar and cotton became principal exports.   The locus of
wealth shifted toward individuals and companies acquiring
coastal and interior lands and irrigation rights.

        Peruvian governments were and are always in need
of money.   Since the wealthy were adept in avoiding any kind
of taxation, the rising class of monied interests assumed
increasing power "behind the throne. "   To get monetary support for government programs and the large public payroll,
Peruvian governments traditionally rely more on accommoda-
tion with these interests than on appropriations of the National Congress.   Jorge Bravo Bresani and José Matos Mar are
among the critics who point to the network of inter-relations

between foreign firms and foreign capital and Peruvian enterprises, between the hacendados and gamonales of the interior
with their cohorts in the capital, between the coastal plutocracy and the banks, import and export houses and government offices in Lima.   They state that this network has
placed effective power in the hands of "a chain of intermediaries. "   These are the top political men; the financiers,
bankers, industrialists and businessmen; the landowners, the
caciques and the higher public authorities; the "international-
minded Peruvians" with homes and financial ties outside the
country as well as those who work for or advise the foreign-
owned firms in the country.   (One of these latter, the British-
owned Backus & Johnson's Brewery del Peru, ranked among
the 200 largest non-U. S. firms in the world, the only South
American company appearing on this 1967 Fortune magazine
list.)   These "intermediaries" and the public corporations
and private Peruvian and foreign enterprises they represent
are the true "oligarchy" in the country, in the eyes of these
Peruvian critics.

Up-Dating Mariátegui's "Siete Ensayos"

The overall impression conveyed by Peru, in their
view, is that of "an archipelago of islands, " these being
small, self-contained hacienda plantations and isolated towns
with vast spaces of emptiness in between.   The towns have
no relations with one another.   Only infrequently do they have
intercourse with the capital.   The "rosary" of coastal valleys, all perpendicular to the sea, cast tentacles toward the
interior to get manpower and foodstuffs, but have no relations with similar "islands" to the north or south.   Production from the coastal valleys goes directly overseas from
several ports.   Contacts and communications maintained
among these "constellations" within Peru are far inferior to
the degree of contact with the outer world beyond Peru.

The picture painted is one of "internal colonization"
which, in the views of these social critics, characterizes
present-day Peru.   By this term they mean that the grandes
empresas are not developing the interior but rather exploiting
it and then depositing the bulk of the proceeds overseas.   Not
merely a "dual" society in Lambert's sense, Peru's reality
is that of a disarticulated, "plural, compartmented land, socially, economically and culturally. "   The great task, as seen
by these Peruvian observers, is to "integrate" the country,
to achieve its unification and establish its capacity for inde-

pendent, autonomous action. [8]

Depending for much of its validity on Marxist interpretations, their analysis turns largely on questions of ownership of the instruments of production. The "economic
power," by which they mean control over the main wealth-
producing resources (mines and coastal valleys) is identified
as residing in American capital and in the wealthy Peruvian
clans. These latter, they argue, often are the creation of
dynamic English, German, French and Italian immigrants
who have intermarried with the Colonial and 19th century
"Old Elite" families. Peru's pressing needs are (1) to break
down the barriers between classes and blend the particles of
class and racial groupings into one Peruvian national culture;
(2) to raise the living standards of the rural and urban
masses as well as the precarious middle class; (3) to re-
arrange marketing of the nation's export production so that
the gains realized therefrom flow to national coffers and not
into private control; (4) to establish central government control over commercial, economic and investment decisions,
thus diminishing international and private domestic influences
at work in these arenas.

What this "counter-elite" offers amounts to an up-
dating of Mariátegui's Seven Essays of Interpretation of the
Peruvian Reality. Summarized in briefest compass above,
the new doctrines hold great appeal for engineers, architects,
economists, sociologists and other younger professionals
deeply committed to the future of Peru. These "technicians"
are mostly of upper class or upper middle class origin. In
essence, they want to apply Peruvian appreciations and techniques in a search for national solutions. How has the conservative, older landed elite responded to them? How the
traditional elite has twice "solved" the pressing question of
land redistribution will now be traced, taking Peru's over-
arching agrarian problems as the focus. It tells much about
the agility of the ruling class in disposing, at least tempo-
rarily, with this vexing issue.

Agitation During the 1930's for a Better Deal for the Peasants

The reform-minded leaders of the first decade of the
20th century, among them Cornejo, Villarán, González
Prada, preached a policy of "gradualism." They placed
their hopes in a gradual improvement of social and economic

conditions, although often in violent and colorful language. The men of the 1920's, like Haya de la Torre and Mariátegui, urged a path of violence. In their view, the Indians would sweep to the coast someday and vindicate their rights. The formation of the Peruvian Communist Party in 1930 by José Carlos Mariategui (who was a most unorthodox Marxist), Eudocio Ravines and Ricardo Martínez de la Torre signalized the changed climate. Haya de la Torre was the most vocal in pressing for the redemption of the Indian proletariat and calling for the overthrow of the ruling elite.[9] President Leguía, for his part, drew some conclusions from the radicalization of the educated opponents during the 1920's. A short, wily, intensely dynamic man, Leguía sought to counter the power of the old upper class with a "new class" of his creation. Welcoming foreign loans and embarking on public works in the interior, he played to the masses while spreading contracts, commissions and favors among his own retinue of followers in the capital. Leguía posed as the friend of the Indians without, however, doing anything for them.

The climax came in the years 1930-39, following the overthrow of Leguía and the collapse of world markets for Peru's exports. It is not the purpose of this study to recount the events of this dramatic decade in Peru's history. Rather, how Peru's ruling groups met the demand for sweeping reforms will be pointed out. They took fright. Frederick Pike and other historians have detailed the defensive maneuvers culminating in the lengthy dictatorship from 1933-39 of the caudillo General Oscar R. Benavides. Haya de la Torre was the generally acknowledged winner of the 1931 elections. The military, controlling the ballot boxes, declared that the "legal candidate" (i. e., the one supported by the established order), Col. Luis M. Sanchez Cerro, had won. In Trujillo, Haya de la Torre's home town, a spontaneous rebellion was put down by the Army with the killing of thousands of Apristas. To distract public attention, the Government formented a new border dispute with Colombia over Leticia. The Peruvian elite was, in truth, joining in defense of the existing state of affairs against any attempt whatsoever to modify it. In the ensuing oppression and stagnation, opposition voices were stilled. Any change was rejected as radical, untried, ominous-sounding expedients. During the 1930's and 1940's, Peru's traditional conservative rulers tended to become more intransigent in defense of the status quo. The view took hold that the cause of protecting and glorifying the Indian was really an attempt by alien forces-- Communism, Protestantism, International Capitalism--to alter

the life and culture of the Peruvian people. Frederick Pike
espouses, along with others, this Catholic-conservative viewpoint. One editorial typical of the late 1930's declared that
all indigenista movements in Peru were actually Communist
fronts. 10 Indigenismo and the case for agrarian reform
came thus to be identified by friends and foes alike with Communism and Marxian socialism.

Reopening the Agrarian Issue in the Late 1950's

The situation remained essentially unchanged into the
middle of the 1950's. A promise of democratic conciliation
under President Bustamante y Rivero in 1945-47 was frus-
trated by his overthrow by General Odría's and the latter's
ascent to power. Peru's social crisis continued unabated
beneath the surface during the generally prosperous 1950's.
Aprista leader Haya de la Torre's zeal for reform diminished.
New leadership was sought by those who felt that the country
could not sustain indefinitely an impoverished rural mass
living on the verge of starvation. Peruvians of all classes
looked down upon these Indian masses as inferior beings,
even as they recognized their cultural triumphs of the past. 11
The ending of Odría's repressive regime in 1956 signalized
a change in attitude. A mounting tide of migrants to Lima
created a growing ring of ugly barriadas encircling the city.
The influx showed that all was not well in the Sierra. For
twenty-five years, it had been a sign of radical ideas to talk
of agrarian reform. Under President Manuel Prado beginning in 1956, it became once again respectable. A "Commission on Agrarian Reform and Housing" was set up in that
year. Its report was published in 1960. 12 Prado, one of
Peru's wealthiest men, appointed members of his own class
to the Commission which was headed by Pedro Beltrán. The
report showed great optimism regarding the prospects of col-
onizing the eastern slopes of the Andes in the remote jungles.
(It said that over the years, numerous concessions of these
jungle lands had been granted by the Government, the total
for the years 1900-1960 being 3,260,655 hectares.)

The Commission minimized the importance of land
concentration in the coastal zone. Instead, it localized the
problem of agrarian reform as being in the Sierra. It said
the problem was one essentially of "minifundia" (too small
holdings) and charged the National Institute of Agrarian Reform, which it recommended be set up, to resolve the
"minifundia" problem before it attacked the question of con-

centration of holdings.   Suggestions to protect the Indians
occupied the bulk of the report and merely repeated guaran-
tees which were already part of Peru's legal code.   A variety of "escape clauses" were inserted in the Commission's
report, notably with regard to permissible size of holdings.
A variety of reasons were given why a given property was
to be deemed "inafectable, " i. e., not affected by the legislation.   It suggested permitting properties to be registered in
a variety of names (or in the names of individual stockholders
in a land corporation), each person being permitted the legal
maximum.   Even the limits fixed for size of holdings, e. g.,
on the coast 250 hectares of irrigated land and 5, 000 hectares
of non-irrigated pasture lands, were "not to affect those holdings acquired before the passage of the agrarian reform law. "
Thus, did Peru's landed elite deal with the problem of grossly inequitable distribution of land during 1958-60.

The Agrarian Reform Law of 1963 and its Aftermath

        The "reform Beltranista, " the 1960 report was called,
was denounced in Congress and in the leftist press in 1960-
62 as a farce, a "cunning slight of hand" ("escamoteo"), a
"pseudo-reform stage-managed by the latifundistas. "   The
agitation quickened.   Incoming President Belaúnde in 1963
presented his own Agrarian Reform Law.   It had been drafted
in its essentials by his First Vice President, Edgardo Seoane
Corales, a sizeable coastal landowner.   The two Acción
Popular leaders sought a middle course.   They aimed at neither deceiving the progressive elements in their party who
wanted real reform nor frightening the conservative upper
class from which both individuals stemmed (and drew much
of their support).   In essence, the 1963 law opted for the
"technical" reform argued during the early 1960's with great
skill by the apologists and economists of the National Agrarian
Society.   The view favors land reform, but argues that the
time-honored method of cutting up large estates only cuts
output.   Rather than wasting time trying to redistribute land
and to increase the productivity of illiterate peasant farmers,
the Peruvian state should concentrate on "technical" improvements.   The goal should be to increase production in the
short run, chiefly by concentrating on providing capital and
advice.   Thus, the argument runs, will large, rich farmers
be induced to adopt modern methods.   Pedro Beltrán's La
Prensa editorialized this viewpoint in these words:

        The extravagant majority dreams only of expropria-

tion and parceling out. Without putting in operation
a credit apparatus for low-cost loans--an enormous
and costly enterprise--without technical assistance
of an advanced degree, without the elaboration of
reasonable and equitable criteria for the division
of parcels, experience will lead unfailingly to ca-
tastrophe. Reform is necessary, but it must have
as its first objective: increase in production, improvement in productivity. It must avoid ruining
the climate of confidence without which capital, instead of flowing inward to transform the country,
will not hesitate to flee. [13]

Vice President Edgardo Seoane's plea for "agrarian
justice" (see Chapter I above) also sought the answer to injustice in the "technical" reform. Increasing production was
the important goal, he agreed. A contrary view, that of the
"political" reform, was little heard. Using Mexico's experience as a guide, it argues that justice flows from a certain equalizing of power relations, that breaking the power
of the landholding upper class and stripping the Church of its
lands were the necessary preconditions for agrarian justice.
"Liquidation of the remains of the colonial feudal order is
the first elemental condition for progress, " José Carlos
Mariátegui wrote. [14]

To Beltrán's production arguments, Seoane opposed a
humanitarian view of the condition of the peasants in the
highlands and the needs of a worker and his family. Priority
in the 1963 law was to be given "to the zones where feudal
forms of exploitation, property and production continue to
exist. " Expropriations were to be "regionalized, " that is,
be placed in the interior of the country. "Changes of structure" (a euphemism for "expropriation, " a word carefully
avoided in the law and the writing surrounding it) were to be
"echelonned through successive zones, " beginning where the
agrarian problem is most acute. The great families of
Lima, as has been seen, draw their principal revenues from
coastal plantations, from mines and from business enterprises in the capital. Everyone agreed that the sizeable
holdings in the Sierra were in an abysmal state of productivity. Thus, the law proposed that land redistribution, insofar as it was called for, would occur in those highland
properties. Technical aid and farm credit would be greatly
expanded. By skillful formulas, assurances were written
into the legislation that it would not affect the economic or
power position of the landed class. In this form, the Agrar-

ian Reform Law finally went on the books, promulgated as Law No. 15037 on May 21, 1964.

Most striking among the many exemptions in the new law were the "regimes of exception." These were properties not affected because of their specific exclusion under the terms of the legislation. A careful study of the law and its subsequent implementation by the Comité Interamericano de Desarrollo Agrícola (CIDA) was published in 1966.[15] It declares that, because exceptions are so numerous and the provisions for "afectabilidad," i. e., being affected, so conservative, on the entire coast of Peru only some 54, 000 hectares of cultivable land would be available for expropriation and the settling of new families. CIDA added "this could be reduced to nothing if one considers the further reductions in the "afectable" area that the law authorizes." In the Sierra, the prospect was only slightly more promising. The law authorized exemptions of all farms of 5, 000 hectares or less, a figure that may be increased to 20, 000 hectares in various circumstances, besides exclusions for reasons other than size. CIDA calculates that only some 224, 000 hectares of cultivable land were made available for expropriation and settlement in this region. (Total usable land in the Sierra is in the vicinity of 10. 7 million hectares.) In the Selva or jungle zone no land that is already cultivable can be taken over under the law. Pointing out that many of the concessions granted since 1900 in this jungle area have never been constituted as formal haciendas, CIDA said that under strict interpretation of the concessions the lands should revert to the state. CIDA figured that the Selva might offer some 1. 3 million hectares of land useful for cultivation and settlement, if this were done.

What the Legislation Reveals

The tortuous progress of agrarian reform laws shows clearly the tactics of the landowning upper class under the pressures to do something about the misery of the mass of rural inhabitants in Peru. Elite reactions can be summed up in these carefully devised measures to blunt and deflect the law's impact:

1. Reduce to a minimum the amount of land affected by the law (The 5, 000 hectare exemption might be compared with the 300 hectares of well-tended pastures that a similar New Zealand law held as exempt.)

2.   Exclude most of the principal haciendas throughout the country from the provisions of the law (This
is done by permitting farms, haciendas or land corporations to receive the maximum exemption for any
number of legal or natural persons.   CIDA cites that
the National Office of Agrarian Reform had to establish 4, 275 minimums of 5, 000 hectares each, for example, even though only 1, 327 properties were involved.)

3.   Avoid any real increase in the income flowing to
interior parts of the country (CIDA's study found no
evidence to support the supposed high efficiency and
productivity of the coastal plantations which the law
was carefully designed to protect and foster.   The
law's emphasis elsewhere on redistribution of income
in favor of the lower classes was clearly being frus-
trated, CIDA concluded.)

4.   Spin out the processes of selection of properties
to be affected, of the prices to be fixed for land and
improvements, of expropriation itself, of selection of
the new beneficiaries both in administrative and judicial channels and then, if expropriation unavoidable,
secure maximum economic gain (Peru's law is a
straight buyer-seller relationship and makes no reference to "restitution of the land. "   In this it is un-
like Mexico's and Bolivia's agrarian reform laws.
Prices to be paid by the government must take account of, besides declared tax value, the actual commercial value of the land and its "potential productivity" in the case of idle or uncultivated lands.   Pay-
ment must be in cash for livestock, installations and
improvements, with the land being compensated in
twenty to twenty-two year bonds paying four or five
percent.   Besides bearing the government's guarantee,
these bonds must be accepted in state banks as col-
lateral for loans (Articles 231, 235, 236).   Despite
the authorizing of $224 million worth of bonds plus
monies for administration and payments in cash since
1964, the result of these clauses has been that the
reform through 1966 had proved so costly as to force
its virtual cessation.)

"Rules of the Game" in Matters of Reform Efforts

This chapter has briefly recounted the handling by

Peru's ruling class of the inter-related problems summed
up as agrarian reform. Included among these are rural
stagnation, mass exodus to the cities, excessive concentration of landownership, low agricultural productivity and an
imbalance in wealth and power. It is worth exploring some
additional "rules" as revealed by this excursion into the
agitation for land reform which, as of 1967, has come to a
standstill.

Rule No. 18--When Some Action is Unavoidable, Confide in the "Incomplete Reform," with Numerous Loopholes

The numerical superiority of the Indians has, as we
have seen, been historically a source of preoccupation to the
Peruvian landed elite. Thoughtful members of the upper
class dwell on the dangers inherent in a sub-privileged rural
mass (now becoming urban as well) that may someday link
with disaffected or radicalized elements of the elite to produce revolutionary changes. To ward this off, periodic
concessions have been necessary. Within Peru's electoral
processes, there has been a gradual loosening of restrictions on the right to vote (184,000 registered voters in
1908, rising to 330,000 in 1930 and, with the granting of
suffrage to women, to 2,069,861 registered voters in 1963).
Electoral reform has been "incomplete," however. As Victor
Andrés Belaunde points out, the rural election result was
the same whether there was an exceedingly restricted or
widely extended number of voters. Effective control rested
with the gamonales, who told the voters how to vote. Mod-
ifications in the electoral law were gradually introduced.
Again, according to this author, the changes merely meant
that, instead of "buying a few tinterillos and sub-prefects,
pressures had to be exerted on a larger dependent population."16

The tactic was that of the "incomplete reform."
Agree to a reform in principle, but always leave an "out."
The essential power equation must remain the same, with
the dominant class remaining firmly in the saddle or with
their interests unaffected. The old Spanish principle of the
"fuero" (literally, privilege or exemption) has had frequent
application in Peruvian legislation. Make sure the reform
is incomplete, in the sense that it leaves plenty of loopholes, exemptions, "not-affecteds," and thus nullify its
stated purpose. According to Belaúnde, the gamonales
"who disposed of the Indian masses and therefore of elec-

tions" understood readily that incomplete or false reforms
would not harm them.

A similar strategy has been applied to demands for
changes in agrarian structure. The tactics have varied.
Heavy repression was the watchword in the 1930's. In the
1960's, it has been a skillful shifting of the demand from a
"political" reform to a "technical" reform. The law finally
adopted in 1964 preserves unchanged the system of agriculture and the holdings on the coast, placing the onus on the
more archaic sector in the interior. Vice President Seoane,
in a private interview, said he felt it was a pseudo-reform,
but nevertheless, has encouraged its execution. 17 The in-
genious compromises in the law mark it as the first step
only. A long series of legislative enactments followed by
rigorous execution will be necessary before Peruvian agrarian
reform becomes a reality, if a judgement can be made from
Mexico's experience.

Rule No. 19--Rely More on Administration as the Principal
            Vehicle of Action and Less on Legislative En-
            actment

As in most societies, the measure of one's power in
Peru is the influence one can bring to bear. In practice,
this means influencing the many functionaries, ranging from
the President of the Republic downwards, involved in the administration or the execution of laws. Public opinion barely
exists, reducing the importance of influence on the mass of
the population. What is valued most is the ability to work
one's will on central government authorities. There is, in
consequence, a constant corrupting of functionaries, if not
in money then in the promise of favors returned. Peru's
public administrators are conscious of weakness, for they
lack any formal legitimacy in the sense that no one expects
them to act impartially, objectively. A typical functionary
is put there by a powerful figure. The bureaucrat is expected to serve the interests of that figure or the larger clan
to which he belongs. Formal office holding assumes no great
importance in the eyes of many elite members, as long as
they can work their will indirectly.

A long line of Peruvians has pointed to the "vast and
submissive bureaucracy" as the place where both the "personalist regime" (the President) and the ruling class work their
wills. Acción Popular, in power from 1963 to 1968, represented the most recent effort to find a different base for the

exercise of power, namely, popular support and participation by ordinary people in governmental matters.   It did not succeed, being overthrown by the Peruvian Army in late 1968. Excessive spending took its toll in elite support, but the abortive nature of the 1964 agrarian reform may be said to have been its undoing with the people.   The legislation was defeated as much in its administration, in keeping with the "rule" above, as in its many loopholes and exemptions inserted into the law itself.

Notes

1.   Milton J. Esman, "Politics of Development Administration," Approaches to Development: Politics, Administration and Change, edited by John Montgomery and William Siffin (New York: McGraw-Hill, 1966), pp. 88-90.

2.   Frederick B. Pike, "The Old and the New APRA in Peru: Myth and Reality," Inter-American Economic Affairs, Vol. 18, No. 2 (Autumn, 1964).   Pike's position is that this promising reform movement had formulated a "program and set of values acceptable to divergent class interests" but was ended by APRA's "esoteric theories" that "sought to tear down the whole Peruvian social, economic and political structure" rather than build "on a concensus of national opinion." pp. 8-10.

3.   Manuel Vicente Villarán, Páginas escogidas, Forward by Jorge Basadre (Lima, 1962) p. 259.

4.   Luis E. Valcarcel, Tempestad en los Andes (Lima, 1927); Manuel J. Gamarra, Orientación y organización; población y descentralización; programa de reconstrución nacional (Cuzco, 1926); Hildebrando Castro Pozo, Nuestra comunidad indígena (Lima, 1924).

5.   The following works are worth noting: Leonidas Castro Baston, Geohistoria de Perú: ensayo económico-político-social (Lima, 1962); Hector Chirinos Lorentzen, Perú: Al bienestar o el caos (Lima, 1965); Carlos Malpica, Guerra a muerte al latifundio (Lima, Ediciones "Voz Rebelde," 1962); José Valera Mejía, Anibal Ismodes et. al., La Sociedad de Masas (Lima, Department of Sociology, University of San Marcos, 1965).

132 Wealth and Power in Peru

6. Edgardo Seoane, Surcos de la Paz (Lima, 1963).

7. Jorge Bravo Bresani, "Mito y Realidad de la Oligarquía Peruano," Revista de Sociología, Vol. 3, No. 4 (University of San Marcos, 1966), pp. 43-71, gives these views most clearly. He is supported by such authors as Milton C. Taylor, "Problems of Development in Peru," Journal of Inter-American Studies, Vol. IX, No. 1 (1967); Edmundo Flores, "El Problema Agrario del Perú," Trimestre Economico, Vol. XVII, Mexico and Thomas R. Ford, Man and Land in Peru (Gainesville: University of Florida Press, 1955). A contrary view is afforded by Frederick B. Pike, The Modern History of Peru (New York: Frederick A. Praeger, 1967), pp. 258-331. Pike views the 20th century Peruvian scene as being dominated by "reformist" elements within the conservative upper class who, under President Fernando Belaúnde Terry in the 1960's, were successful in creating a "mystique" of development. Pike cites evidence of the rise to prominence of a Peruvian middle class. He finds it to be especially visible in Arequipa, Trujillo and other smaller cities. Thus, he does not see a "pre-revolutionary" situation. A more profound view, in my judgment one shared by most acute Peruvian observers, holds that Peru is still "feudal," in the sense that under feudalism a power system (or "power domain" in Richard N. Adams' phrase) is such that it can act unilaterally. In Peru, the Army, the Church, the large landowning element can and do act independently of the Central Government. The latter's power (expressed in the President) consists of "being able to influence by inducing cooperation and, occasionally, compliance" from these power systems. The substance of the power wielded by President Belaúnde's bureaucrats and ministers would not seem to be nearly as great as Pike's reading of recent Peruvian history would indicate. To mirror reality, Pike's view would have to show that centralization has in fact taken place in Peru and that the power wielded by the independent "power domains" is now subject to direction and control from the center (that is, the Central Government). I do not believe this has yet come to pass.

8. Jorge Bravo Bresani, op. cit., pp. 59-63.

9. Victor Raúl Haya de la Torre, Pensamiento Político de Haya de la Torre, Vol. 1 (Lima, 1961).

10. Frederick B. Pike, "Peru and the Quest for Reform by Compromise," Inter-American Economic Affairs, Vol. 20, No. 4 (Spring, 1967), pp. 27-29.

11. Baltazar Caravedo, Humberto Rotundo and Javier Mariátegui, Estudios de psiquiatría social (Lima, 1963).

12. Cited in Alvin Cohen, "Societal Structure, Agrarian Reform and Economic Development in Peru," Inter-American Economic Affairs, Vol. 18, No. 1 (Spring, 1964), pp. 46-47.

13. "La Prensa," July 15, 1962.

14. José Carlos Mariátegui, Siete ensayos de interpretación de la realidad peruana, 2d ed. (Lima, Biblioteca Amauta, 1958), p. 252.

15. Pan American Union, Tenencia de la Tierra y Desarrollo Socio-Económico del Sector Agricola--PERÚ (Washington: Comité Interamericano de Desarrollo Agricola--CIDA, 1966), pp. 391-464.

16. Victor Andrés Belaúnde, Meditaciones Peruanas (Lima: Talleres Graficos Villanueva, 1963) p. 85.

17. Edgardo Seoane, conversation with author in Mexico City in January, 1966.

Chapter VIII

Peru and the "Ruling Elite Model"

The preceding pages depict Peruvian society as being characterized by an upper and a lower class with a barely visible middle class. Within the upper class there exists a landed elite which forms, it is argued, the principal locus of wealth and power in the country. Members of this ruling element come under mounting attacks from a "counter-elite" composed of younger technicians and intellectuals. In a concluding chapter, this conflict of goals and values will be summarized and certain barely discernable trends will be indicated. It is useful, however, to place this study in the discipline of political science, specifically elite studies. How, too, does it relate to the growing literature on political development and the politics of developing areas?

A paragraph above declared this to be a study of "elite politics." The concept warrants further clarifying. Where politics are held to be the preserve of a single segment of the population and the bulk of the people are effectively excluded from political processes, we have "elite politics." While definitions vary, "political development" generally means a gradual transition from elite to mass politics. By this is meant a change within a political system in favor of greater liberty, popular sovereignty and free institutions, for the benefit of the mass and not just an elite.[1] Political scientists, sociologists and economists have devised the word "modernization" and Karl W. Deutsch has used the term "social mobilization" to express this movement from traditional to modern ways.[2] Samuel P. Huntington's conception of political development as "the institutionalization of political organizations and procedures" bears striking relevance to Peru's polity which, as we have seen, is marked by reliance on informal ways of acting, i.e., getting things done.

In this, as in other areas, Lasswell is particularly helpful. He lays stress on the importance of "the contextual principle" and of configurative analysis of the type attempted here. He suggests that there is no single prescription or

panacea for the political and social ills of developing countries.   There is no "single solution," whether it be political
parties, the military, the charismatic leader, traditional institutions, broader electoral participation or informed public
opinion.   The problem is to find a model that leaves room
for varying patterns of political development.   The typology
of developing political systems should be one that suggests
the appropriateness of different prescriptions, each adapted
to the operation of a given system.

Configurative Analysis

My debt to Lasswell's guidelines for the making of an
elite study (more specifically, a psychological study of a
landed elite) has been acknowledged.   In his pioneering studies on political elites, Lasswell and his co-workers stress
quantifying data in order to uncover events that are often repeated.   He called for systemic analysis of such "configurative wholes" as an elite political culture.   Political scientists
tend to ignore individual behavior, concerning themselves instead with large-scale institutions and processes.   Psycho-
analytic studies of personality, fostered by Lasswell, represent an effort to alter this tendency.   They constitute micro-
analysis.   Studies of functional elites such as appear in
Lipset and Solari's Elites in Latin America similarly are
done at a micro level of analysis, in that they emphasize the
"parts" rather than the "whole."   Now, a "configuration" is
an emergent whole made up of parts.   A dominant elite may
be viewed as an "emergent whole" where the sum is greater
than the parts.   The "emergent" aspect resides in a property,
such as elite "solidarity" or "cohesion" or "political dexter-
ity," which may vary with varying threats to the group's
survival.   Group "solidarity" can only be seen at the macro
level.   It constitutes an example of a new "whole" appearing
(e. g., a landed elite) with characteristics that do not exist
if one views the constituent members of that elite as single
units.

Behavior at the macro level requires new descriptive
concepts and new empirical propositions, a process which
Lasswell has called "configurative analysis."   The generalizations offered in preceding pages as "rules of the game"
are efforts in this direction.   They must be seen as "empirical propositions independent of concepts relevant to the micro level of individual personalities or interacting groups."[3]
They differ markedly from old-style assertions about "nation-

al character. " These latter usually have been "extrapolated
observations of behavior on the micro level, " in Heinz
Eulau's words. In a sense, the "rules" are cultural traits,
as anthropologists use this term. Traits are acts which appear with a certain frequency in a culture. An interesting
example of such a "trait" is cited by Robert E. Scott when
he writes in Elites in Latin America that Peru's "established
Fuerzas Económicas Vivas"--a designation corresponding to
"landed elite":

> . . . have become so structured that the presi-
> dents of some ten functional associations hold reg-
> ular meetings where they discuss differences among
> member organizations, attempting to resolve dis-
> putes privately whenever possible. At these meet-
> ings, reactions of the several participating group-
> ings toward proposed governmental action also are
> considered and collective action is decided. Pub-
> licly this action may take the form of statements
> by the heads of individual organizations or even
> full-page newspaper advertisements signed by the
> presidents of all the member groups explaining
> their collective position and sometimes containing
> veiled hints at untoward consequences for the econ-
> omy of the country and the jobs of their employees
> if their advice is not heeded. These private gov-
> ernments acting in concert can generate a tremen-
> dous amount of covert pressure, for their members
> pay a very large share of all taxes collected in Pe-
> ru and have many other ways of making or break-
> ing a particular regime. [4]

Levels of Analysis

In what Eulau calls "the most significant methodological essay he ever published, " Lasswell set forth in the title
of his "General Framework: Person, Personality, Group,
Culture" four "levels" of analysis. [5] Each is dealt with by
one of the three basic behavioral sciences which study human
behavior from a particular level-relevant perspective: psychology dealing with behavior at the level of the individual
person; sociology with behavior at the level of the group (society); anthropology with behavior at the level of culture.
Political science, Eulau points out, "occupies an eminently
interstitial position between the three basic behavioral sciences, " as do such intermediate disciplines as social psy-

chology, political sociology or culture-and-personality. Social and political scientists "sense that behavior at the level
of a group, sub-culture or culture follows laws that are
quite independent of propositions about microscopic behavior"
(such as interest a psychologist or anthropologist, for example). 6

    In simpler words, one can say that the cultural con-
tent of behavior permeates otherwise non-patterned acts of
behavior. Lasswell brings into play the "contextual principle" (sometimes called the "principle of interdetermination")
to suggest the possibility of analyzing behavior on several
and diverse levels. "Value system" and "language of politics" are phenomena which constitute a distinct level in a society or culture and may be analyzed on their own macro
level. "Configurative analysis" as a method affirms that:

> . . . whatever phenomena are to be observed on
> whatever levels of analysis--political institutions,
> social structures, cultural patterns, norms of con-
> duct, symbolic systems, and so on--they are to
> be observed in relation to the total context in a
> given stage of human development. 7

    The total configuration or context varies greatly with
the stage of human development reached. Peru's stage would
seem to be that of 17th or 18th century Europe, still. It
thus requires a level of macroanalysis which takes as its
frame of reference or point of departure the postulated continued existence of a "ruling elite," as the term was understood by Aristotle or Machiavelli. In analyzing, as an example, the group interest of the Fuerzas Económicas Vivas
mentioned by Scott one would see that this is something quite
different from the private agendas noted at the level of the
family or the individual person. The delineation of "rules of
the game" represents a form of contextual analysis at the
level of the social group (in this case a dominant landowning
element). When, at times, it has been sought to make clear
certain phenomena by speaking of "ideal types," the level has
shifted to that of personality. The study, like political sociology, searches for principles that connect macro and micro characteristics (the latter becoming more visible as a
society develops, differentiates and adopts divisions of labor
within itself). Sound general analysis in these circumstances
demands interdisciplinary cooperation. It is for this reason
that this study sought to draw on the findings of psychologists,
anthropologists and sociologists. Political scientists, work-

ing as Eulau says in the interstices of these disciplines, may
then be more concerned with macro structures and the properties and processes they discern within them.

A brief treatment of different elite theories seeking
to explain countries like Peru will make clearer my effort
to view the landed elite as a "whole," following the methodological guides referred to.

The "Ruling Elite Model"

Is Peru a case where "they" run things? Is the line
of argument here that Peruvian politics are dominated by a
few families, an "oligarchy," a shadowy group of "wirepul-
lers" behind the scenes? This is one of the plausible elite
theories put forward by scholars. What is its applicability
to the Peruvian case? The idea of such a ruling elite
springs from a common belief, said to be "realistic," that
politics are run by a few overt or covert leaders. C. Wright
Mills' The Power Elite is typical of this approach. His kind
of analysis has a powerful appeal to many persons. The
theory argues that in all communities there is a ruling elite.
If it is not composed of the acknowledged leaders, then behind them stand the hidden rulers. More precisely, this
theory asserts that in a particular political system there exists a group of people who exercise a preponderant power
over other actors in the system. Robert A. Dahl points out
that what this means is that the preferences and desires of
the ruling group win out over these of persons outside the
narrow governing circle. [8] By the theory, the ruling elite
has a set of preferences that regularly prevail in all cases
of disagreement involving key political issues. They thus
come to constitute a "controlling group."

A majority in a democracy is a controlling group.
To be a ruling elite, the dominant group must be less than
a majority in size. The ruling elite, by definition, is a
controlling group that is not the result of the operation of
democratic rules. Its composition is fairly stable. The
members' preferences are closely akin to one another, especially on key issues.

How does one describe such an elite? One usually
specifies membership by name, position, socio-economic
class or some characteristic such as landownership. The
elite theorist may say that the elite rules or has high poten-

tial for control. He cites as his proof that if the members agree on a key political alternative and certain implementing actions, then that alternative will be chosen. C. Wright Mills, for example, gives high potential for control to the bureaucratic (governmental, industrial and military) element in U.S. society. Actual political effectiveness of a ruling elite, the theory states, depends on both high potential for control and potential for unity in exercising that control.

The proponent of the "ruling elite" view usually points out that there is a group of individuals with more influence than others in the system. The scope of influence of the ruling elite extends widely rather than being limited to specific concerns as in the case of functional elites (see below).

In the literature, the following test of the existence of a ruling elite is proposed:

> In a political system where there is disagreement on key political choices, if the 'ruling elite' prefers an alternative and other actors or groups prefer other alternatives, then in all or nearly all of these cases the alternative preferred by the ruling elite will be the one actually adopted. [9]

Examination of concrete actions is the key. Dahl emphasizes that no one can suppose that he has established the dominance of a specific group in a community or nation without basing his analysis on the careful reconstruction of a series of concrete cases. The decisions examined must also constitute a fair sample of the key political decisions taken in that system, to assure scientific validity to the test.

The "Functional Elites" Model

Another widely held view of "elite" refers to those positions in society which are the summits of key social structures. By this definition, the elite are those who occupy the higher positions in government, economic life, armed forces, politics, religion, professional and mass organizations. "Elite groups" is perhaps more descriptive of this concept. Mosca and Pareto, as we have seen, distinguish between the group that form a political or governing elite--those who participate more or less directly in political decisions--and the many groups that make up the nongoverning elite--those at the top in nonpolitical structures. Func-

tional elite analysis forms an alternative point of view to
class analysis.   Marxists reject elite concepts because of
Karl Marx's assumption that economic power relationships
offer the key to the character of a society.   The idea of diverse functional elites owes much to Lasswell.   Values of
those at the top in various segments of society affect the
rate and direction of economic and social change.   Lasswell
wrote "there are as many elites as there are values.   Besides the elite of power (the political elite) there are elites
of wealth, respect, knowledge (to name a few). "[10]

Robert E. Scott and other writers on functional elites
use as their starting point the specialized functions characteristic of modern social and economic life, each led by the
more able, alert or politically-minded of the traditional ruling classes.   Barrington Moore, Jr., writes that widespread
education, improved communications and transportation and
increased contacts between upper and lower classes broke the
long-established dominance of a single elite, the landed gen-
try.   Moore particularly signalizes the importance of close
scrutiny of rural patterns.   He finds in the differing relations between peasants and masters the crucial differences
in how modernity appears on the scene, whether as democracy in England or as totalitarian rule in Russia.[11]

Modernity is characterized by a shift of political power to a new breed of financiers, businessmen and bureaucrats.   New groupings further down the social scale appear.
Elites representing the new professions, industrial workers,
ethnic groups and small farmers begin to demand entry into
the political decision-making process.   Faced with technological and social changes, traditional elements slowly and
grudgingly accord political legitimacy to these new elites acting as spokesmen for the middle class and the masses.   This
pattern of change occurs over long periods.   It involves riots, civil wars and suppression of political movements.
Eventually, the political structure in such modernizing states
is reformed to meet new conditions.   Traditional values are
revised to fit new situations which, in turn, permit new social relationships to evolve.   Politics become the responsibility of full-time, professional politicians.   Acting as bro-
kers for their respective groups, functional elites develop
as new "rules of the political game" replace those of an earlier era.   These "rules" feature fair play, efficiency in organization and a premium on lobbying and other indirect
ways of influencing political decisions.

Proponents of the "functional elites" theory argue that in modernizing countries like Peru diversification of function is occurring. This process "produces new elites so fast that the persons controlling the political structure are quite unable to reorient their thinking and action to make room for the new elites." "In Latin America," they say, "political change takes place under conditions of forced draft speed."[12] Their political role thus occupies the center of attention in the Lipset and Solari book. The theory of functional elites portrays the politics of the region as essentially "challenging elites" versus "traditional elites." In the former category, one finds dissident Army and Church leaders recruited down the social scale. The "challengers" include middle-range bureaucrats, managers, teachers, labor leaders, small businessmen and some professional men. Weaknesses in the theory appear when its proponents affirm that the so-called "challenging elites" adopt the elitist norms and conservative tendencies of existing ruling groups. Often, they seek out their followers in popular organizations like labor unions. A sharp sense of hierarchy separates the leadership cadres at the top of these functional elites from the masses below. In most of these functional groupings, lack of effective interaction between leader and followers produces "a series of independent and often irresponsible elites." The traditional elite quickly co-opt leaders appearing in mechanized agriculture, finance, commerce and government. In the face of a united landed elite, the many individuals classed as functional elites remain disorganized in their political activities.

Inapplicability of the "Functional Elites" Model

In the extensive political science literature dealing with developing states, the present is viewed as a transitional stage in most areas. The writers see multiplication of interests and new functional elite groups. The research done for this study led to a doubt that this is an accurate description of the configuration of events in Peru. What seems to be happening there is a process of social disintegration and bipolarization rather than an increasing differentiation and aggregation of interests of the kind pictured in much of the recent literature. This will be discussed in more detail in the next chapter. Neither leading political parties like A. P. R. A. or Acción Popular nor the National Congress performs an aggregating or "nation-building" function. The parties, still mainly vehicles of one leader like Haya de la Torre or Fernando Belaúnde, adopt ideologies

that appeal only to small groups of dedicated followers. In
the Congress, particularistic or parochial interests abound,
making it unrepresentative of any general interest.   Peruvian
Presidents, in practice, ally themselves with segments of
the traditional elites.   All these elements are the products
of the particular political environment studied here.   Functional interest associations, other than those representing the
upper class, barely exist.   Members of that class alone have
the political competence, as was shown above, to operate
formally through governmental agencies or through informal
channels of influence.

The main "rapid change" observable in Peru consists
of the migration of rural dwellers to the cities.   Other than
that, the evidence assembled here points to a strengthening
of the landed upper class and of its own and its ally, the
Peruvian military's, role in politics.   The rural social structure built around the latifundio institution gave Peruvian society a certain cohesion in which Church teachings acted as
a strong cement.   That society was held together by its traditions and by institutions like the large estate and the self-
governing Indian community.   Peru's common people, moving to the cities in increasing numbers, become an agglom-
eration of atomized individuals, while the upper and middle
class sense a mounting insecurity.   The overall picture, as
we shall see below, is one of a disintegrating or "bipolariz-
ing" social order rather than a "differentiating and increasingly functional" society.

In this author's view, the "ruling class model" more
accurately describes Peruvian reality.   The "ruling class"
as an object of analysis appears infrequently in American
political science literature.   It has been left largely to sociologists.   Norton Long states that "the prime fact of politics is the struggle of classes."[13]   Most modern political
scientists avoid these issues.   In part, this results from
the belief that the phenomena of "class struggle" or a "ruling class" are simply not exemplified in the American scene.
The idea is that "no one rules," that power is always
"shared power."   The "functional elites" model is popular
with U.S. social scientists because they find it easier to
write about middle and lower classes.   There is also a cultural bias in favor of finding evidence of "rapid change" or
"progress" in other societies.   Evidence of "modernizing"
and "more democratic" political patterns is constantly sought
rather than proofs of stasis or retrogression and existence
of authoritarian patterns.

In Peru the political scientist is dealing with a distinctive political system. It is quite different from the modern "competitive politics" system most of them write about. Dahl, Lane, Easton and others describe systems where "key political issues" exist which involve actual disagreement in preferences among two or more groups and which are eventually resolved through the political system. Peru, on the contrary, is characterized by a traditional "elite politics" system where one group regularly gets its way in the face of mass indifference or impotence. The group, as Richard N. Adams shows, depends for its exercise of power largely on upper sector "ability to mobilize what is necessary for tactical advantage at a given point in time."[14] Along with Eric Wolf, Adams sees "power as the crucial feature of the upper sector . . . It would not be exaggerated to say that the entire internal structure of the upper sector may be seen as a series of relationships established and altered by virtue of a constant concern for gaining, retaining and using power." "Power-motivated behavior," he says, "might better be regarded as central features of the upper sector of Latin American society" rather than being "characterized as irregularities that the Latins will some day outgrow."[15]

The central issue arises from the fact that the still largely land-based upper sector "clearly has dominant control," a situation that can be reversed only "through the mobilization of the power latent in the lower sector." This can happen, Adams adds, "without some kind of violence only if the lower sector is provided with the organization, the skills and sufficient resources to permit survival through the inevitable period of conflict that would accompany the effort."[16] The likelihood, however, is that this will not happen. Rather than being a power structure that is necessarily transitional, the "ruling elite model" examined herein may well endure indefinitely. This and other eventualities are dealt with in the next chapter.

Notes

1. Noteworthy for students of the politics of underdeveloped countries are the following: David E. Apter, The Politics of Modernization (Chicago: University of Chicago Press, 1965); Gabriel Almond and James S. Coleman (eds.), The Politics of Developing Areas (Princeton: Princeton University Press, 1960); Daniel Lerner, The Passing of Traditional Society (New York: The

144   Wealth and Power in Peru

Free Press, 1958); Gabriel Almond and Sidney Verba,
The Civil Culture, Political Attitudes and Democracy
in Five Nations (Princeton University Press, 1963);
Robert E. Ward (ed.) Studying Politics Abroad, Field
Research in Developing Areas (Boston: Little-Brown,
1964); Robert E. Mitchell, "Barriers for Survey Research in Asia and Latin America, " American Behavioral Scientist, 9 (November, 1965).

2.   Karl W. Deutsch, "Social Mobilization and Political De-
velopment, " American Political Science Review, LX
(September, 1961); Samuel P. Huntington, "Political
Development and Political Decay, " World Politics, XVII
(April, 1965) pp. 386-430.

3.   Heinz Eulau, "The Maddening Methods of H. D. Lasswell, " The Journal of Politics, Vol. 30, No. 1 (February, 1968), pp. 20-24. Eulau begins this notable
exposition of Lasswell's methods by saying they are
"maddening, of course, only to those who do not want
to understand them in the first place. "

4.   Seymour M. Lipset and Aldo Solari (eds.) Elites in Latin America (London: Oxford University Press, 1967),
p. 138.

5.   Harold D. Lasswell, "General Framework: Person,
Personality, Group, Culture, " in The Analysis of Political Behavior (New York: Oxford University Press,
1948). This essay first appeared in Psychiatry, Vol.
2 (1939), pp. 533-561.

6.   Heinz Eulau, op. cit. , p. 18.

7.   Ibid. , pp. 20-21.

8.   Robert A. Dahl, "A Critique of the Ruling Elite Model, "
American Political Science Review, Vol. 52 (June,
1958), p. 466.

9.   Ibid. , pp. 466-467.

10. Harold D. Lasswell, et. al. , The Comparative Study of
Elites (Stanford, Calif.: Stanford University Press,
1952) pp. 6-7.

11. Barrington Moore, Jr. , Social Origins of Dictatorship

and Democracy, Lord and Peasant in the Making of the
Modern World (Boston: Beacon Press, 1966), pp. 415-
432. Moore's study of the historical pre-conditions
for the growth of democracy and authoritarianism,
while making little mention of Latin America, demonstrates the crucial significance of the kind of peasant-
landowner viewpoints and relationships analyzed in this
study. Moore states that the reason why so few studies
have been made of these phenomena is that "social in-
ertia" (or "social continuity") requires no explanation
and therefore has been largely ignored by social scientists (p. 486). He lays stress on the "social serving" role of the landed upper class in his Epilogue (pp.
484-490). A similar long-range view is presented in
Seymour Lipset's The First New Nation--The U.S. in
Historical Perspective (New York: Basic Books, 1963),
Lipset stresses the ever-present conflict between equality and inequality (Epilogue, pp. 340-343). To Lipset,
values such as these are the independent variable in
bringing on modernity. He investigates the effect of
values on the operation of social institutions. Moore
argues that values should be linked to historical social
situations and not viewed as causal factors.

12. Lipset and Solari, op. cit., pp. 130-136.

13. Norton Long, "Aristotle and Local Government, " Social
Research, Vol. 24 (Autumn, 1957), p. 303. Long
states that "Caciquism, the rule of local chieftains,
made a mockery of parliamentary democracy in eastern
Europe, parts of Italy, Spain and South America" (p.
297). For Aristotle as for Norton Long, "the key to
the constitution is the ruling class. . . ." "The governing class represents or appears to represent the
qualities that exemplify the conception of the good life
that informs the constitution. Its members are looked
up to and admired, since they most fully reflect the
ideal. Their position is felt to be just, to be legitimate, because in terms of the particular constitution it
is just that the richest, the most noble, the most
learned, should rule. " (p. 300). Long states that American political scientists have been reluctant to admit the
term "the ruling class" because of the "absence of class
consciousness in American society, " the unique American experience "in having a democratic revolution without the necessity of overthrowing a feudal order" and
because of the Marxist pre-emption of the concept of the

ruling class (pp. 308-309).

14. Richard N. Adams, The Second Sowing: Power and
     Secondary Development in Latin America (San Francis-
     co: Chandler Publishing Co., 1967), p. 59.

15. Ibid, p. 57. (For Wolf's views, see his particularly
     noteworthy article, "Types of Latin American Peas-
     antry: A Preliminary Discussion," American Anthro-
     pologist, Vol. 57, No. 3, June, 1955.)

16. Ibid., p. 269-270.

Chapter IX

Summary and Conclusions: Encouragement
of Basic Change

This study draws attention to large landholders as an
identifiable group in Peru. It postulates the existence of
certain recurring patterns which can be tentatively identified
as "rules of the political game." Several assumptions under-
lay the research, the chief one being that the landed elite
controls the principal source of power and wealth, land (and
its products), and thus the Peruvian political system. Another was that a cross-section of persons attaining the top
rungs of the country's educational structure might be said to
constitute a useful, even though unscientific, sample from
which worthwhile subjective data could be derived. During
many hours of structured discussion of three institutions (the
large estate, local government and the family), these individuals provided "eye witness" accounts, interpretations, personal experience and explanations to supplement factual knowledge and expert views. In the extensive literature consulted,
no explicit or overt "rules" were found. While an "operational code" may, in practice, exist, it has not been formulated by any theorist of Peru's conservative political order.
Instead, only hints appear. (Appendix II provides rare data).

What are the main conclusions that emerge from this
research effort? The principal finding is that the Peruvian
landed upper class (and, by implication, the large landholder
element in other Latin American countries) has survived into the last third of the 20th century because of its wants,
aspirations, values and tactics; in a word, its system of
rule, has been accepted, even emulated, by the rest of the
population. A second finding is that, despite the decline of
the latifundio institution economically, the power of the landed
upper sector is increasing along with its relative wealth and
its skill in playing the political game. In its political style,
its socializing practices and ways of preserving its sway,
the dominant upper class proves far superior to the disorganized middle class and the inert lower classes. The reader
will have gained an idea of the system of ideas of members

147

of the landed elite.   Chief among the values instilled in formative years is a strong conviction of the rightness and permanence of the status quo.   Identity of interest gives the
landed-commercial class a sense of shared feelings about
their own social role in relation to the rest of Peruvian society.   Their expectations regarding the future appear to exclude the possibility of revolution or violent change, owing
to their confidence in being able to keep things as they are.
Tentative conclusions about "rules of the game" of politics
show that this confidence may not be misplaced for Peru's
rulers have succeeded remarkably well in warding off change.
Yet, the political picture is modifying.   What are the out-
lines of the historical configuration toward which Peru is
heading?

        Singled out below are two major trends that appear
to be tending toward the slow death of an exclusively elite-
dominated society: disintegration and polarization.   What is
the evidence of the landed estate's slow disintegration?   According to the evidence assembled, the power of the central
government contests the authority of the cacique and increasingly competes with that of the gamonal.   The Indian masses
appear less willing to accept unquestioning obedience to the
patrón.   Sons of landowners seek business and professional
outlets for their talents, in the belief their families' rural
properties afford only arduous toil for meager returns.   Disintegration appears also in the form of mounting disorientation and anomie among the Peruvian peasantry.   Tides of
migration swell urban populations.   The wretchedness of the
Sierra Indians and mestizos appalls even the most callous
observer.

        Polarization takes the form of sharpening divisions
within the country's "dual society."   Neglected populations
barely exist in archaic, backward rural zones while Peru's
better off urban dwellers vie for government sinecures.   The
latter enjoy the comforts and amenities bought with whatever
public wealth is available.   Peruvian officials in top brackets
enjoy living standards equal to the best anywhere.   One finds
little evidence that they understand the needs or point of
view of the peasantry.   Squalor of the countryside spills over
into the city slums.   Meanwhile, the modern, educated,
landed upper class lives a life of exceptional ease and charm.
Its eyes are closed to the misery around it.   Bipolarization
is a drawing toward opposite poles.   According to Lasswell,
it usually occurs when there is an expectation of violence.
With upper and lower class drawing wider apart, does this

indicate that there are feelings that the danger of such violence is increasing? This is a point that merits further research. I foresee Peru, too, spinning toward violence.

Upper Class Sway Increasing

Among other salient conclusions, attention is drawn above to the continuing predominance of a system of rule rooted in ownership of land. Accented, too, are the inter-relationships and the inter-locking nature of three prime power elements--Church, Armed Forces and Landed Proprietors. Some indications point to the possibility that upper class control of resources may be increasing in Peru, judging from the fact that many large landholdings are of recent creation and the fact of continued dominance of Cabinets by elite representatives. This finding in the study runs contrary to books about emerging middle class rule in Latin America. Other evidence cited justifying tentative judgments about the continuing power of the elite comes from biographical and life history information, including sparse data on interlocking public and private positions held by Cabinet officials in the Prado and Belaúnde Administrations.

What are the chief features of the young elite members' essential pattern of thought regarding political happenings, particularly in rural zones? Political activities are reserved to the dominant groups, it is stated. The values that govern educational, economic and status relationships remain those of a landed aristocracy. Peruvian democracy, like that of Ecuador, Chile or Colombia, is accepted as hardly anything more than a privilege for the small elite. Political life is regarded largely as a series of transactions on a high level between one political leader, or a candidate and his party, and other leaders. Subordinate chiefs ("caciques" or bosses) more or less spontaneously place at the disposition of the politicians the votes of their friends, relatives, and followers. Popular will does not enter into consideration.

The landed elite feels it shares a common situation, a common interest, and common prerogatives. Politics have traditionally been used as a means to defend this shared interest, consisting of access to education and land ownership, among other advantages. Ascriptive norms are strong, determining what is accepted behavior. Politicians who violate their upper class views and positions are subject to sanctions,

a recent example being President Belaúnde's setbacks in the
eyes of the military and consequent removal from office in
November, 1968.

Absence of Participation by Middle Class

Powerful deprivations are imposed on those who seem
to challenge the existing order, including exile and confisca-
tion of one's property. These sanctions reside chiefly in the
values and beliefs of the population. On occasion, they may
be imposed by persons in power or by a form of ostracism
within the elite generally against actual or would-be deviants.
As a result of the absence of social criticism, Peru, in the
words of one of the leading counter-elite representatives, remains a "poor disarticulated country. " He refers not so
much to the fragmentation into isolated population clusters
as to the lack of any feeling of participation on the part of
the bulk of the Peruvian people.   The middle class no less
than the emerging cholo and peasant populations lack political
and worker organizations as the means to force their "entry
into politics. " They feel that only revolution will give them
access to power. The survival power of the elite, in fact,
seems to derive largely from the inability of the middle
class to adopt goals and values different from the upper
class.   The life goal of shopkeepers, businessmen, public
functionaries, small landowners, professional men and technicians is to serve or to be favored by the elite, rather than
to displace the oligarchic ruling group.   Nevertheless, there
is a feeling that the political base is being widened in the
sense that more people are rising to take some share in the
political process and at the same time the door is being o-
pened to the emergence of leaders without traditional elite
education and orientation.

From this study, it may be concluded that the upper
class does not form a permanent exploiting class on top that
is milking the poor. Co-opting of able newcomers into the
upper stratum instead keeps the system permeable.   Moreover, many Peruvians argue that the traditional hacienda
mode of production is deteriorating. What wealth exists is
largely appropriated by the landed class and comes mainly
from successful, modern commercial-type plantations and
from related banking and trading activities.   But the overall
production of wealth is scanty.

Mounting Polarity in the Social Order

The highly tentative "rules of the game" identified
above for the country's politics have a particular one-sided
quality.   Notably absent is anything in the political scene in-
suring equal chances for the masses as well as the elite,
or even the dissident elite against the entrenched interests.
The traditionalist ideology of the landed elite examined herein, judging from the views of the more free thinking younger
intellectuals, no longer corresponds with the vision of what
ought to be in the eyes of a majority of thoughtful Peruvians.
They believe that Peru, like other Latin American nations,
remains under the political and economic control of a small
segment of the population.   Strong family inter-relationships
and inherited wealth reinforce that minority's dominant position.   Even when one controlling group is overthrown, it is
merely replaced by another small clique from the same ruling elite.   Popular support is sought for the purpose of winning the election and getting into power.   Once there, the
new group denies any real say to the populace.   Jobs, a
main concern of the dissidents, are reserved for those with
close ties to the elite, without regard for technical qualifica-
tions.

Rejection of the existing political order extends to the
members of the National Congress.   Parliamentarians are
unable to make headway in bringing about changes because
they cannot control key factors of power like electoral machinery.   They feel that time is wasted in putting together
lists, in discussions with caciques, in propaganda, supplica-
tions, etc.   Why do this, when this time could be used to
preach revolution?   Overriding all is the distrust of the oligarchy.   There is a constant fear of their annuling elections
and causing a coup, if the opposition happens to be cast into
a majority position through a fair election.   In their infrequent political writings, the more vocal among the counter-
elite castigate the old-line leaders.   They are "politically
imprisoned, " it is said, citing Haya de la Torre as an example.   The old elite's frequent compromises, the dated political styles they learned in the thirties and forties, their
limited popular appeal cut them off from any support apart
from that of their own national and local henchmen.   Even
those who automatically vote Aprista are dwindling.   The
present "rules of the game, " which these leaders themselves
drew up, prevent any fresh and invigorating appeal to the
country's electorate on the part of the younger, dissident e-
lite elements.

A phrase frequently on the lips of participants in the
seminars was "tomar conciencia" or "crear conciencia, "
meaning a searching of one's conscience.   What is passing
through the minds of young Latin Americans seems to be a
rejection of democratic electoral mechanisms.   The twin en-
emies to many are the oligarchy and United States.   "Revolution" is the watchword.   It is conceived of as a fundamental reorganization of the state and society through the application of technique and science to bring about reforms in
favor of the masses.   These young thinkers show little concern for political tactics as a way of taking power.   They
do not think in terms of how to win elections.   Instead they
talk of "taking any road that the oligarchy leaves open to us. "
Democratically-inclined individuals exist but are in a strict
minority.   They are caught between two extremes visible in
the Peruvian political spectrum.   Outsiders working in the
country become aware of closed cliques in government ministries, Congress, universities, professional associations and
in the political parties.   Recognition of the profound division
between extreme right and left is vital for practical political
purposes to both insiders and outsiders working in Peru (and
elsewhere in Latin America).   It tells one with whom to col-
laborate for certain purposes.

While Peruvian traditionalists on the right are virtually medieval in outlook, with the familiar biases of landowning and patriarchal ruling groups, the anti-democratic, reactionary left is equally evident.   It is composed of an increasingly influential group of intellectuals who double as university teachers and lesser government officials.   Their goal
is social justice.   In their view, this is derived through a
centralizing of decisions into the hands of a central planning
body, through some industrialization, but mainly through the
control of society by a few reigning institutions.   Their af-
finity is toward planning as the chief instrument to bring
about an industrialized, urbanized society in which everyone
knows his place in the occupational and power hierarchy.
Absent from their thinking is the idea of politics as a struggle for power between elements representing a renewed, vigorously democratic Peru and the older traditional order.

Strikingly rare in the Peruvian political system are
"intermediary organizations, " that is, non-governmental associations that respond to group interests and link the people
with the government.   Intermediary organizations act as
sources of countervailing power.   They recruit participants
into the political process.   Peru is a society with few organ-

izations independent of the elite or the government.   It is
felt that this lack is one explanation for the frequency of dic-
tatorial governments.   Such democratic associations serve a
number of functions, chiefly as channels to the seats of power.   They lessen the likelihood of resort to violence and in-
hibit single powerful private bodies like the Sociedad Nacional
Agraria, representing the landed elite, from dominating all
political resources or monopolizing the allocation of benefits
flowing from the public treasury, e. g., agricultural credit.
They act as a source of new opinions.   Private associations
provide means of communicating ideas, particularly opposition
ideas, to a large section of the citizenry.   They serve to
train men in the skills of politics.   They help increase the
level of interest and participation in politics.   For all these
reasons, as was pointed out in discussions of intermediary
organizations, all such associations outside the control of the
landed elite have been suspect.

Changing Conception of Politics

Members of the new middle class and of the younger
elite, judging from the evidence, are experimenting with a
new conception of politics.   As currently viewed, politics is
a means for the upper class or the vested interests to dis-
tribute rewards and to fight off attacks against their position.
Challenges to this state of affairs are necessarily made to
appear as an attack upon the social order.   Those Peruvians
who derive privileges from the present system of allocation
of status, wealth and power perceive an attack on them as an
attack against the system itself.   Younger counter-elite members view this mentality as a prime block in the way of progress.

As they see it, the problem of the Peruvian middle
and lower class masses is to gather itself together.   In a
manner long familiar to the landed elite they should constitute
many interest groups or "a class for itself, " struggling and
contending in the political marketplace.   This demands a
sense of "group belongingness, " on the part of the middle
class initially.   By experiencing this sense of shared interests, becoming aware of it and by acting it out, a group begins to establish its identity.   A sense of common purpose
arises.   Individuals become an interest group, or association
or a political party, animated by their own set of values and
aims.   A healthy political system is one where, as Alexis de
Tocqueville wrote, the emergence of such new groupings and

the strengthening of old ones is a constant affair. Self-con-
fidence and self-esteem on the part of the participants increases. This is turn leads to changes within the system.

Democratizing Family and Education Influences

The reluctance of the landed elite to assume social
responsibilities stems from numerous factors, centering on
some of the attitudes instilled in youth mentioned in this
study.   Chief among these is the young elite members concept of family obligation.   Changing from a familistic society, where the good of one's extended family is the highest
virtue, to one where a man's primary loyalties are to himself and to numerous associations represents a major advance.   Peru, and most of Latin America, has yet to take
this step.   Social innovation and reconstruction in Western
Europe is historically identified with the emergence of the
middle class, "individually-founded" family.   The first signs
of such a momentous development, if it does occur, will be
within the family, because of its influence in shaping human
personality.   Discussions with young elite members brought
out the vast differences between the conceptions of life of
"patriarchal, " typically Peruvian upper class, Catholic families and the lower and middle class families in that country.
Constituting one role of the social world, the patriarchal or
"community" type of family provides education, employment,
social intercourse and security through the family.   The
male member relies primarily on the clan group in a passive
way.

The priest or father confessor plays a dynamic role
in such a family.   The alternative is the "personally founded"
or individual type of family.   Here, one's education is obtained through school and work, the labor union or trade association, the local community, by contact between the different social classes and through the action of public opinion.
Nepotism is held in low esteem rather than looked up to as
a virtue.   This excludes all personal consideration in the allocation of jobs or productive resources.   It means assigning
posts in government and in business enterprises to the most
competent people rather than to those who need them most or
are most thankful for them.   This "personally founded" type
is the one that is taking shape in middle and lower strata of
Latin American society.   In such a family, the individual asserts his personality.   In effect, he "makes his own education. "   The absense of any instruction in the young elite mem-

ber's civic duties came through repeatedly in the course of this research.

What can one say, in summary, of elite education? In Peru as in neighboring countries, as was shown in Chapter IV, the Church retains a monopoly on education of the young. As in colonial times, it remains "the true fountain of life, nourishing the activities, the passions, the virtue and even the sins of both lords and servants, functionaries and priests, merchants and soldiers." The elite member is drilled in the belief that all human actions must be judged simultaneously for their religious as well as secular meaning. By this is meant that the sacred and secular are inter-mixed. The Church presumption to regard all matters, e.g., politics and public policy, as falling within its sphere is accepted by him. Rejecting this concept profoundly wrenches his belief system. The elite member has been instilled with a conviction that human actions should be doubly sanctioned, by the civil authorities on the one hand but by the religious authorities on the other. This is called the "Doctrine of the Two Swords." This teaching has justified Church intervention in political and governmental matters. In his family and religious upbringing the young elitist acquires his preference for a rigid status system and for hierarchy. This is expressed in the feeling that loyalties must be vertically ordered and that lower class persons should "keep their place." They must accord with authority. This idea fixes the authoritarian principle deep in the elite members bosom.

In his personal advance from the sacred to the secular world, the upper class representative must himself reject many of these teachings, for example, that loyalty to one's family takes precedence over secondary loyalties (to one's neighbor, to the community, or the nation). Profound readjustment in his thinking is called for. One may cite the belief instilled in the elite member that class position and status relationships are given and are unchangeable. He must come to accept social mobility for those below him as both right and desirable. Few members of the Peruvian (or Latin American) elite succeed in making these revolutionary changes in their fundamental belief systems.

Motivations of the Elite

Latifundio society is declining. But does this mean that Peru's landed elite-controlled political system is weak-

ening? The prestige and social security attractions of landownership appeal to the middle class. The businessman,
artisan or official who has acquired wealth regards the acquisition of a hacienda as the top rung in the social climb.
Peru's cultural ideal, as we have seen, embraces the values
of a landed elite. The ideal reinforces the system.

In terms of political behavior, evidence of change is
less easy to come by. The social and educational advance
of the lower class as a requirement for effective sharing of
power remains incomprehensible to Peru's governing class.
Local chiefs (caciques and gamonales) exercise a lessened
but still strong personal authority. Their power to make
law only a "declaration of intention," in Jacques Lambert's
phrase, manifests itself often, the most recent example being
the abortive Agrarian Reform Law enacted in 1964. Peru
suffers both from extreme centralization and decentralization.
Decisions on the minutest matters are made still in Lima,
and often by the President himself. Despite its weakening
as a political force, the feudal domain known as the latifundio
continues to be a power in its own right. Elected officials
must constantly assess the votes it controls and its ability
to thwart the central administration. Caciquismo--which has
been defined as the actual economic, social and political authority wielded by one person over a village, a piece of land
or a clan--has declined in Peru as elsewhere since the last
century. But it is still the single most powerful force to be
reckoned with by a President or a Ministry in dealing with a
given locality. The threat remains of caudillismo, the dictatorship or dominance of a man with a strong personal following over the nation as a whole, with or without benefit of
election. Military juntas, in Peru, have tended to take the
place of the old style, 19th century caudillo. Nevertheless,
the door is open for other authoritarian regimes, both of the
caudillo and junta type, including those with leftist backing.

Research Tasks Ahead

This has been a study of the ethos of a ruling class.
It serves to open some fruitful avenues for future research
efforts, notably in terms of political process. Americans
are not accustomed to think in terms of class, or even of
the concept of a ruling class. From Aristotle onwards, political scientists have recognized that a central problem of
government is the ruling elite. Americans, believing in a
theory of social harmony rather than one of struggle, rarely

take a realistic view of the politics of other countries where
status differences are great and class conflict the rule.   Un-
wittingly, we strengthen an archaic ruling group without re-
alizing, or admitting, that we do so.   This study represents
a modest attempt to correct the balance.   Other questions
have been left for later research, among them the dynamics
of the Peruvian political structure.   This is dealt with only
in passing in this effort to focus on ethos, or guiding attitudes and values.   Another fruitful field for future study is
the methods by which participation of lower and middle class
elements is achieved through the device of their co-option into the dominant class through their success in military, business or bureaucratic hierarchies.   A description of the ac-
tualities of political power in Peru, or of the ways by which
influence is exercised by the wealthy and the powerful, should
prove of value to the discipline of political science.

Summing up, one may say that, in the broadest sense,
Peruvian social structure and politics are the way the aristocracy wants them to be.   The continuing predominance of
the landed elite (which it should be reaffirmed, is a changing, flexible group of individuals and families) springs from
the fact that they share a common value system and a monopoly over power and wealth coupled with the absence of equal
chances for the masses.   This gives them a common goal,
namely, to preserve this state of affairs as long as possible.   There is a rejection of democratic beliefs, such as
the ideas of equality and majority rule, and electoral processes except when the result favors the established order.
Church direction of education and, ultimately, of politics figures in the upper class ideal.   Strong repression of dissidents, with occasional lapses into military rule, are accepted
practices.   Nonetheless, the underlying trend is toward
greater democratization, unless dramatic measures are taken
to avert the victory of the Peruvian masses.

Within this picture, one may place counter-elite ex-
perimentation with new concepts of politics.   The Peruvian
elite's feeling has been that politics are for the purpose of
protecting vested interests and fighting off attacks against the
status quo.   An elaborate set of tactics (taken as hypotheses
herein and called "rules of the game") has unconsciously
evolved with this end in mind.   The counter-elite, young
technicians mostly, experiment with the idea of creating a
sense of "group belongingness" within the middle class, or
at least a technocratic elite within that class.   Their desire
to "search their consciences" reflects a subconscious effort

to revolutionize themselves. This is seen as preliminary to effecting a revolution within their society. There we have a probable future course of events--a gradual weakening of the existing state of Peruvian society as its injustices and backwardness are attacked from top and bottom.

Appendix I

Principle Landowning Families
in Peru

Section 1
General List of Landholding Families

(Asterisks indicate the relative size of the holdings
reported under a given family name. Those over 5,000
hectares have three asterisks; those between 1,000 and 5,000
hectares have two, and those between 500 and 1,000 hectares
are marked by one asterisk. Those under 500 hectares have
no asterisk. Names have been arranged alphabetically for
convenience in making correlations.)

A. Owning Properties in the Coastal Zone
   (All shown by family surname)

Abril	Barua	Cafferatta***
Acuña**	Barredo(a)***	Calvo
Aguëro**	Basombrío	del Campo*
Alayza*	Bellido**	Calderón
Alcázar	Benítes	Cardenas
Althaus	Bentín	Capurro
Alvarez*	Berckemeyer*	Canessa*
Alzamora	Bertello	Carpena***
Anderson***	Benavides*	Carillo**
Angosto	Bernadis	Cassinelli**
Aparicio	Beltrán**	Carrion
Arrese**	Boggio	de las Casas
Aspiazu*	Bell*	Cillóniz***
Asín	Bolognesi	Castanino
Aspillaga***	de la Borda***	Castañeda
Aurich***	Bortessi*	Cauvi
Baca***	Boza	Cepeda
Balmaceda*	Brescia***	Checa***
Bardelli*	Burga*	Chopitea***
Barducci*	Cacho	Cisneros
Barragán	Cabrera	Clotet***

Concha*	Gomez*	de Montori
Conetta*	González	Montero*
Cooper	Gotuzzo*	Moreyra***
Corbetto**	Graco***	Muelle
Correa	Graña	Muñoz***
Corrochano**	Grau	Mujica***
Costa	Guerra	Navarro
Cuglievan***	Guimoye	Najar***
Cuenca	Gutiérrez*	Nepena**
Dall'Orso***	Harten	Nicolini*
Dammert**	Helguero**	Neuhaus*
Dapelo*	Herrera	Noriega
Darquea*	Heros**	Nosiglia
Dasso	Heeren	Olaechea***
Delgado	von der Heyden***	Orbegoso
Diez*	Hernández**	Orlandini
Drago	Hilbeck***	los Ostendorf***
DuBois**	Hildalgo*	Pacora*
Echecopar*	Houghton*	Palacios***
Echenique	Irvine***	Pardo***
Eguiguren	Isola**	Pazos*
Elias	Iturregui	Patrón**
Eguren	Izaga	Paz
Elice*	Jayanca	Peratta
Espinoza**	Jiskra**	Peña
Espá	Kawa*	Persico
Espantoso**	Lecca	Peschiera**
Evangelista*	Leguía	Pinillos*
Febres	de Kats	del Pino
Fernández	Leight*	Piaggio
Fernandini***	Letts*	Picasso***
Ferrand*	León***	de la Piedra***
Ferrero*	Lopez***	Plana*
Flores*	Larco***	Prado
de Fracchia	Lau	Quesada
Fumagalli**	Loredo	Saavedra
Galleno*	Lamotte	Salazar
Gallo***	Larrabure	Salina
Gamboa	Larizbeascoa**	Salinas**
Ganoza	Masías***	Santisteban**
García**	Marrou***	Schaefer**
Gereda**	MacMullen*	Seminario***
Gastaneta	Malatesta*	Seoane**
Gerbolini**	Miró**	Skinner*
Genit*	Malpartida**	Solar**
Gildemeister***	Miranda***	Soldán**
Gillóniz	Molero	Sousa***

Rachitoff   Rospigliosi**   Valle
Ramos**   Romoli   Vargas
Razzetto**   Romana***   Vanini
Rebagliati*   Roncagholo*   Verdeguer
Remy**   Rosell   Vizquerra
Retto**   Rubini   Wiese***
Reusche**   Tealdo*   Wicks*
Rey***   Thorne**   Woodman**
Roca   Thiermann***   Yama*
Ricketts**   Trujillo   Yarleque*
Romero**   Tremouille*   Yrigoyen***
Rizo***   Truele**   Zarak***
Roesch*   Ugarteche*   Zoeger***
Rosa*   Urrutia**   Zuluaga
Rosas**   Valdiviezo*

(NOTE: The foregoing does not include all owners.)

B. Owning Properties in the Sierra
    (Since all haciendas in the Sierra are generally large,
    i. e., over 5, 000 hectares, the asterisk indicates that
    the name also appears on the list of property-owners on
    the Coast.)

Acuña*   Goicochea   Pancorvo
Alva   La Fuente   Pardo*
Alvarez*   Larrauri   Pastor
de Amat   León*   Pestana
Aranzabal   Lercari   Pinillos*
Arredondo   Luglio   del Pont
Barten   Luna   Porturas
Bazo   Maldonado   Puga
Bueno   Manchego   Rivera
Boza*   Miranda   Rodríguez
Casafranca   Muñoz*   Romana*
Cacho*   Marin   Romero
Cartland   Mejía   Santa María
Cuba (Cubas)   Marquez   Saravia
Danemberg   Miranda*   Schreiber
Durand   Molina   Sifuentes
de Duque   Moncada   Sousa*
Estrada   Monteagudo   Turpaud
Galjuf   Morales   Tupayachi
Gamarra   Oblitas   Wieland
Gibson   Olivieri   Wong
Gonzales*   Orbegoso*   Zignago

(NOTE: The foregoing does not represent a complete
listing of Sierra landholders.)

C. Owning Properties in the Selva
(All these holdings are very large, ranging from the
smallest shown, 20,346 hectares, to the largest, 320,000
hectares.   The asterisk indicates that the name also appears on the list of property-owners on the Coast.)

Arevalo	de los Heros*	Porras
Do Amaral	Lambarri	Prado*
Barreda*	La Torre	Rengifo
Chavez	Laos	Rodríguez
Chocano	Le Tourneau	Romainville
Cuglievan*	Mendoza	Roldan
Durand	Montero*	Sanchez
Forga	Morey	Soldan
Garland	Pacaya	Umuto
Gomal	Pardo*	Villalba
Gomales	Pastor	Wesche
Gomera	Perez	Yrigoyen*
Izquierdo	Peixoto	Zaballaxoa

(NOTE: The foregoing does not represent a complete
listing of Selva landholders.)

Section 2
Families Making Up the Peruvian "Oligarchy"
(Partial Listing)

(This section gives the identities of families making up the "oligarchy," insofar as the limited data permits one to make this judgment.)

A. Top Oligarchs--Families whose names appear on land-holder lists, Cabinet Minister lists and "Old Elite" lists

Beltran	Masias	Rizo
Espantoso	Pardo	Romana
Fernandini	Patron	Ugarteche
Lecca	Prado	

B. Landed Oligarchs--Families whose names appear on landholder lists, Cabinet lists, but not on "Old Elite" lists

Alzamora	Gomez	Orlandini
Aparicio	Gonzalez	Pestana
Correa	Guerra	Porras
Cubas	Gutierrez	Quesada
Concha	Grau	Ricketts
Carrillo	Hilbeck	Romero
Dammert	Heeren	Salazar
Dibos	Lopez	Sanchez
Cisneros	Mendoza	Seminario
Fernandez	Miro	Seoane
Gallo	Morales	Zarak
Ganoza	Muelle	
Garland	Munoz	

C. Top Oligarchs, II--Families whose names appear on landholder lists, on "Old Elite" lists, on Boards of SNA and ACLP, but not in Cabinets

Anderson	Barreda	Olaechea
Alvarez	Berckemeyer	Rosell
Aspillaga	Gibson	

163

(NOTE: SNA and ACLP Boards examined were for 1963-64 year only.)

D. <u>Landed Oligarchs</u>, II--Families whose names appear on landholder lists marked by one, two or three asterisks (meaning large holder) but do not appear on "Old Elite" lists nor on Cabinet or SNA and ACLP lists. (Coastal zone only) One asterisk here signifies ownership of more than 5,000 hectares of land.

Acuna	Evangelista	Pacora
Aguero	Ferrero	Palacios*
Alayza	Flores	Pazos
Arrese	Fumagalli	Peschiera
Aspiazu	Galleno	Picasso*
Aurich*	García	de la Piedra*
Baca*	Gereda	Plana
Balmaceda	Gerbolini	Salinas
Bardelli	Genit	Santiesteban
Barducci	Grace	Schaefer
Bellido	Helguero	Skinner
Benavides	de los Heros	Solar
Bell	von der Heyden*	Soldán
de la Borda*	Hernández	Sousa*
Brescia*	Hildalgo	Ramos
Burga	Houghton	Razzetto
Cafferatta*	Irvine*	Rebagliati
de Campo	Isola	Remy
Canessa	Jiskra	Retto
Carpena	Kawa	Reusche
Cassinelli	Leight	Rey*
Cillóniz*	Letts	Rosa
Checa*	León*	Rosas
Chopitea*	Larco*	Rospigliosi
Clotet*	Larizbeascoa	Roncagholo
Conetta	Marrou*	Tealdo
Corbetto	MacMullen	Thorne
Corrochano	Malatesta	Thiermann*
Cuglievan*	Malpartida	Tremouille
Dall'Orso*	Miranda*	Truele
Dapelo	Moreyra*	Urritia
Darquea	Mujica*	Valdiviezo
Du Bois	Najar*	Wicks
Echecopar	Nepena	Woodman
Elice	Neuhaus	Yama
Espinoza	los Ostendorf*	Yarleque

Yrigoyen*   Zoeger*

NOTE: Sources of above data appear in the text.

Appendix II

Some "Clinical Notes" on Attitudes and
Typical Behavior Patterns as
Witnessed by Younger
Elite Members

The crucial experiences in one's life are a vital part of the socialization process. This research cast light on significant memories and episodes in the lives of the 115 Latin Americans who took part in the seminars described in the text. Applying Lasswell's "configurative principle" (the act of perceiving and naming a social pattern, identifying a configuration or context), I made a point of noting down the participants' descriptions of significant events, particularly when these were labeled as indicating something salient in their culture. A cross-section of some fifty-five of these observations by foreign nationals of their own environment or growing-up process is presented below. The "identity" (in Lasswell's sense of the way the inner lives of people gradually gain intelligibility) assumed by most participants was that of a defender of the landed elite position vis-à-vis the masses. The "outcomes" or the values or goals toward which events in the Peruvian political process seem to be moving in the eyes of these representative youthful elite members were the familiar ones of respect, well being, wealth, power, skill. Copied verbatim from my notes, the following are organized on the basis of underlying attitudes and perceptions which they seem to reveal. Individuals are not identified in order to protect their anonymity.

A. Indicating the Life-Style of the Landed Upper Class, Its Shared Common Situation, Interests and Prerogatives, Along with the Absence of Equal Life Chances for the Masses

    1.   Sr. X (member of Seminar I) invited me to spend the day and evening on his hacienda, one of the largest in this part of the country. The buildings were unchanged from the 17th century when they were

built.   The gardens, redone by his father, were laid
out in the style of a French chateau.   The main house
was comfortable inside, but one had the feeling of being thrust back into a style of life of a by-gone era.
There were some dozen servants about the house.   A
chapel had fallen into disrepair and Sr. X said that
no regular church service or school was conducted on
the property, which was but one of two that he had
inherited (the other was immensely larger and extended
beyond the snowline in the mountains).   After lunch,
we walked to the milking shed (this was mainly a dairy
farm) and the two dozen or so milking girls stood at
attention and touched their caps when Sr. X and I approached, remaining thus until we left.   Later, walk-
ing about the nearby town to look at the colorful market, Sr. X was greeted in the same respectful manner on all sides.   He was certainly 'known' in the
vicinity.   In the course of our conversation about many
subjects, including the probable permanence of the existing dispensation in his country, Sr. X pointed to a
knot of Indians in ragged but warm dress and said:
'See, how these people smile at me.   They do not
hate me.   These people are content with their lot and
ask for nothing more. '

> (Notes made following visit to
> a hacienda some months after
> Seminar I)

2.   The immensely rich owner of a large hacienda
never married.   Instead, he lived with a succession
of 'wives' in the big manor house, meanwhile maintaining liaisons with numerous other women.   Exercising the 'droit du seigneur' as it pleased him, he
accumulated in his lifetime many offspring.   He never
indicated a preference for any one of his many
amantes (mistresses) and more than fifty hijos natu-
rales (illegitimate children).

> (Note made during Seminars I-
> VI)

3.   The hacendado rose to greet me.   He was a hand-
some man with fine features.   'Years ago, ' he began
in soft tones, 'the colonos at Hacienda A declared themselves "on strike" and refused to pay rent for their
parcels of land or to work for the hacienda.   They
petitioned the government to recognize their rightful
ownership of the land they occupied on the hacienda.

The government refused this recognition and instead
issued a decree reaffirming their rent and labor obligations.   The peasants revolted along with some of
the mestizo population of Polanca.   They killed a
priest who owned land adjacent to Hacienda A and who
had forced the colonos to sell their produce and livestock to him at prices the priest decided upon.   Since
then, I have tried to see the peasants' point of view.
I do not believe all the right is on the hacendado's
side. '

(Note made in Seminar I)

4.   The patrón entertained often.   Many caballeros
came to the hacienda.   We would play our musical instruments and serve them roasted lamb under the eu-
calyptus trees.   Our hacendado was a good man.   He
heard of my intentions and gave me jugs of aguardiente
to present to Y's parents when I paid my three visits
to them to ask for their fifteen year old daughter.
On my third call, her parents became very drunk and
I escaped with Y.   This is our customary way of beginning a trial marriage.

(Note made in Seminar I)

5.   Friendships within the elite are linked to one's
conformity with regard to the existing order.   Even
bishops must conform.   A new one is only elected if
he receives unanimous approval of all the bishoprics
in the country.   You may rise through the ranks from
seminarista to capitán and parroco rural or parroco
urbano.   But the ranks of monseñor and higher will
be closed to you.   In short, the campesinos have been
barred from all possibility of influence on the government or in the upper hierarchy of the Church.

(Note made in Seminar I)

6.   He said he thought often about Peru's political and
social structure.   Its main characteristic, he felt,
was a reluctance to accept change, however slight.
There was a powerful cultural and intellectual opposition to new ideas and leaders.   The governing class
applied the economic criteria of the upper class in
making their decisions.   The interests of the nation
were thus subordinated to the interests of groups and
families.   Peru's elite seemed to be a fusion of the
upper class descending from the 19th century and the
new rich.   It was closely allied with the Church which

drew its hierarchy from the elite. The strategic importance of the Peruvian military lay in its readiness
to step in 'in situations of political and social indeci-
sion. '

(Note made in Seminar III)

7.   Don Z died. His oldest son, a thin faced man in
his thirties, was the new patrón. He only seemed to
like two things, to ride furiously and to beat his colonos. Even when we worked an extra day a week
for him, he beat us. 'Patrón, why do you beat us
so?' I would ask him. 'Ill-bred huasipunguero,' he
would answer, 'better to keep quiet or I will give you
100 lashes.' One day, my six year old son lost one
of the hacienda's sheep in the hills. A fox, he said,
had eaten it. When the son learned of this, he flew
into a rage. He grabbed a knife and cut off my son's
ear and put it in his pouch. I went to the curandera
with my boy but the medicine women did not want to
treat him. When I came back to the hacienda, the
other colonos told me the son had thrown my wife and
other child off the property. He had thought I had
gone to the authorities to complain. While we were
talking, the patrón appeared, whip in hand. Striking
me on the head and feet, he made me run from the
hacienda. My wife's relatives told us to go to another hacienda some eighty miles away. There we have
lived until the present day.

(Note made in Seminar I)

8.   He described his decision, at age twenty-five, to
renounce the law profession, in which he had obtained
the doctor's degree, and devote himself entirely to
religious work. Brought up in a devout Catholic home,
he had early developed an interest in religion. The
decisive event changing his career had been the sum-
mer spent on an uncle's hacienda in the mountains of
Peru. The Catholicism of the hacienda was under the
stewardship of several priests of the Capuchin order
who were economically maintained by the hacienda itself. He noted that the priests objected vehemently
to the mestizo peasants ritual singing and dancing before the saints' images, and also to the ancient custom of offering food and drink to the images. The
Capuchins voiced objections so strongly that they lost
their influence over the natives who remained attached
to their traditional methods of exhibiting devotion.

The peasants were suspicious of the hacienda priests
because they felt that they acted as 'whisperers' to
the hacendado.   The priests had begun by saying mass
without charge, but later asked as much as 100 pesos.
The poorer villages' inability to afford the number of
masses to which they were accustomed further solidified their resentment against the priests.
(Note made in Seminar I)

9.   When I was twelve, I accompanied my father and
other colonos to the capital.   They were being taken
there on the hacendado's orders to take part in political demonstrations.   Some colonos stayed on in the
city on that occasion and did not return to Acashi.
(Note made in Seminar I)

10.   He repeated the statistic that only four out of
10,000 Latin Americans possess a university degree.
These persons form the dominant group who alone can
aspire to position, prosperity and power.
(Note made in Seminar I)

11.   The hacendado again won his case.   The court
voided the countersuit and ordered the peasants turned
out.   'It is a clear case of invasion of private property,' the judge declared unequivocally.   'The rights
of property must be respected.   There are plenty of
unoccupied land which can be colonized further in the
interior.'   The court left to the government the duty
of enforcing the decision.
(Note made in Seminar I)

B.   Indicating Prevailing Characteristics of Small Towns and
Interior Regions Generally (Drawn in Part from Papers
Presented by Seminar Members on the Institution of the
"Municipio" or Local Government)

12.   The municipio was the only town of any size that
had been created in the late 19th century when several
long-established haciendas in the region petitioned the
central government to send them a Prefect.   The municipio covered 1,200 square miles of semi-arid land.
Only small dispersed patches were under cultivation
due to the harshness of nature.   Dirt roads connected
the town with outlying haciendas.   Twice weekly bus
service linked the town with the national capital, 170

miles away.   For lack of transportation, even mules,
there was little communication among rural dwellers.
Only the women folk came to town on market days.
(Note made in Seminar III)

13.   There was no enterprise that could be called an
industry.   Virtually all productive activity was family-
oriented.   There was no bank, no food processing activity, no wholesale house or retail store of any consequence.   Nor had there been any effort to utilize
potential hydroelectric energy for small industries to
transform locally available raw materials like cotton
into finished goods.   Apart from the small number of
shopkeepers and skilled or unskilled craftsmen, jobs
were to be found only in public agencies or in subsistence agriculture.
(Note made in Seminar III)

14.   The local government consisted of the Prefect who
represented the central government, the mayor and
five aldermen or concejales.   Neither he as mayor
nor the aldermen received any remuneration.   These
officials were elected simultaneously for four-year
terms.   The Prefect enjoyed indefinite tenure depending on his good relations with the central government
authorities.   While the national constitution provided
for local government with considerable authority, in
practice the powers were very limited.   This was
due, in part, to the political pattern of the community
and the fact that real power was concentrated elsewhere.
(Note made in Seminar IV)

15.   Most of the mestizo peasants want what the
wealthy want: to be baptized by a priest, to go to
mass, to take part in politico--religious processions,
to wear good clothes, to drink and eat, to be respected and accepted as civilized.
(Note made in Seminar I)

16.   Everything the government had done had been paternalistic.   Frequently, it seemed to do more harm
than good.   The alcalde's father recalled the case of
an irrigation project nearby that helped the wrong
people (the hacienda owner on whose property it was
built).   The new production was exported.   The condition of the mass of the population in the area did

not really change at all.
(Note made in Seminar III)

17.   What the people felt most strongly about were local educational deficiencies.   'Schools' were of extremely low quality.   In one wreck of a house, one
noticed a score of anemic children monotonously par-
roting the alphabet.   Vocational schools were non-existent nor was any provision made for an adult literacy effort, kindergarten or a public library.   None of
the some twenty primary school teachers in the municipio had a teaching diploma.
(Note made in Seminar III)

18.   The cabildo abierto is a meeting of the citizenry
called by the Prefect.   The Prefect, a stout, glower-
ing man in his early fifties, conducted the rarely con-
vened town meeting.   As often happened, he was
flanked by two or three hangers-on.   The two hour
meeting was given over to the Prefect's laudatory account of the government's plans for the town.
(Note made in Seminar III)

19.   The Administrator of the hacienda was a mestizo
about fifty years old.   He had a reputation for running his hacienda efficiently if imperiously.   One day
he told me that a government commission would visit
the property soon to seek some arrangement by which
land could be given to the colonos while reserving a
part for the elite family.   On that occasion, I asked
the Administrator what was the total extent of the hacienda.   He was vague, but he stood near the casa
grande and pointed to the peaks in the distance.   'The
B family owns the land as far as the eye can see, '
he declared.   The family head wished to make peace
with the colonos resident on the land.   His son was
adamantly opposed to this and was all for throwing
the campesinos off the land.
(Note made in Seminar I)

20.   In this country, there are three problems: politicians, landlords and the Church.
(Note made in Seminar III)

21.   The Prefect firmly believes that within this structure, social benefits flow from the top down, from the
patrón in the form of the landlord or the central gov-

ernment to the campesino. If the benefits did not
flow, the campesino simply waits. The Prefect once
praised the headman of a village of fifty families for
refusing to try to raise thirty pesos (about $2.50) to
buy a log to improve a bridge. 'It is the Ministry of
Works responsibility. They will take care of it,' he
told them. But they never did.

(Note made in Seminar III)

22.   The relationship of the gamonal with these followers is intensely personal, mixed with sentiments of
loyalty and the expectation of favors on their part in
return for unquestioning obedience to the boss, especially at election time. What the caciques sought
most was a similar relationship with a Municipal
Councillor or a Deputy higher up the line. In return
for the cacique's loyalty, favors and concessions
could be obtained.

(Note made in Seminar III)

23.   In small towns here, the population is forced to
align itself with one of two factions. The antagonisms
may have political overtones, but they are secondary
to personal interrelationships. Differences center
around who married whom and agreed to be a godfa-
ther with whom in the last century.

(Note made in Seminar I)

24.   Canete (name fictitious) is in a mountainous area
isolated from the mainstream of national life. We
have two social classes--the gamonales (public officials, hacienda owners and overseers) and the lower
class. Divided by lines of social class, family ties
and wealth, Canete lacks the strong esprit de corps
of Indian peasant communities.

(Note made in Seminar III)

25.   Eighty families have lived on the hacienda as ten-
ants for generations. They were clustered in one
corner as most of the outlying portion of the property
had been evacuated and abandoned. Two hundred or
more families lived in thatched cottages, in those a-
reas. All the latter group were squatters, with no
legal right to remain.

(Note made in Seminar I)

C. Conveying Criticisms of the Existing Order, Including Disintegrative Tendencies at Work in Rural Zones

26.   He added there was only a dim awareness among Peru's elite of the abysmal conditions in suburban zones. Promises of action were made. Occasionally, there were attempts at fulfillment. One never knew what a thing would end up being. A one room school half way up the hill, for lack of a teacher willing to climb up twice a day, became an improvised meat market. A partly finished sewer line was one day filled in and became a roadway. Things that got built either took forever or were finished overnight, reflecting the country's hidden store of static and dynamic impulses.

(Note made in Seminar IV)

27.   The catedrático's position is very powerful. He is the 'big boss,' but is badly paid. His powerful position in the community and his great distance from the students are compensations for his low economic status. Outside their university duties, most catedraticos are lawyers, physicians, politicians or high officials. Senators and Deputies are among those who enjoy personal advantages under the present system, being often holders of catedras themselves or with a close relative who is a catedrático. These legislators form part of the problem on which they are asked to legislate. It is not likely that changes will be converted into law--not, at least, if they can help it.

(Note made in Seminar I)

28.   One of the most discouraging things about Peru is the cynical view everyone has about politics and public affairs. The capital is full of people who are offering bets, with no takers, that the new agrarian reform law will not be carried out. Experience lent support to the cynic's view.

(Note made in Seminar I)

29.   Among the deficiencies he saw in the present system he listed nine: (1) Tremendous and lacerating disproportions in wealth between the two percent who absorb forty-five percent of the national income and the ninety-eight percent who receive fifty-five percent; (2) The misuse of land due to its inadequate distribu-

tion and exploitation; (3) The export of capital and
other abuses by the rich against the community; (4)
The unjust, inhuman and cruel tax system that encourages fraud; (5) Non-application of laws resulting in a
characteristic inefficiency, weakness and impunity in
the judicial system; (6) Laxness and disorganization
in the public service; (7) Unworkability and discredit
of the political mechanisms; (8) Failures and confusion in education at all levels; (9) Foreign imitations
and lack of authenticity in the cultural life coupled
with a breaking of moral values.

                              (Note made in Seminar I)

30.   Naturally I am concerned about the grave problems
Peru is facing: stagnation in the countryside; closed
systems that keep the campesinos and small landholders on the margin of existence; grave dietary deficiencies among the urban and rural population; the
crowding of people into the cities; the unhealthy conditions in the 'suburban zones.' But these things will
not be resolved overnight.

                             (Note made in Seminar III)

31.   In underdeveloped countries, culturally backward,
exhausted by tremendous economic problems and social injustice, with a vast burden of backwardness,
political disorganization and instability on their shoul-
ders, youth acts in accordance with the powerful stim-
uli of the environment. The organizations of social
action are few. They agitate and at times replace
each other. But they do not exert a powerful influence.

                              (Note made in Seminar I)

32.   He remarked on the marked conservative bias at
higher levels of the Church hierarchy. Among the
clergy, as well as the European clergy working in the
country, there was a strong tendency to preserve the
status quo, a feeling also very common among the
economically powerful Catholic groups outside the
Church. In the past, the Church had had an unfavor-
able influence on the economic situation because investment tended to be channeled into economically un-
productive projects, principally large expensive buildings for exclusively religious purposes. There has
been a growing rigidity and immobility of capital as
the power of the religious institutions to acquire the

ownership of land and real estate grew continously.
(Note made in Seminar I)

33.   Doubt was expressed that existing grievances could
be remedied simply by institutional changes.   The conclusion was drawn that Peru's elites needed most of
all a proper political education that would communicate
to them the nuances and intimations of a national tradition based on the peasantry.
(Note made in Seminar I)

34.   I believe that the University ought to be an instrument to bring about changes in the established social
order.   That order does not and will not serve the
needs of the people.   Under present structures, it is
impossible for anyone who thinks to be other than a
revolutionary.
(Note made in Seminar III)

35.   He said one 'revolutionary' was a tall, fine-fea-
tured man of thirty-five, the son of one of the country's leading doctors.   Intelligent, widely read, he had
been the target of attack from his country's ruling
elite before because of his readiness to speak out.
His father, a kindly man with a feeling for the under-
dog, encouraged his son's rebelliousness.   Expressing
deep concern over the country's 'social disintegration'
as he called it, the father had insisted that his son
attend the National University for the very reason that
most students there came from families of modest circumstances.
(Notes made in Seminars I and
III)

D. Showing Socializing Experiences that Mold the Viewpoints
and Condition Elite Members Toward Conformity with the
Existing Order or that Make Them Reject It

36.   With some companions, he said he founded a literary circle and for two years directed the literary page
of a small weekly newspaper owned by a friend of his
father, representative in Congress from his district.
Besides being a landowner, his father had been Municipal Councillor, Controller General of the province,
manager of the local liquor factory and owner of the
principal newspaper in the region.
(Note made in Seminar I)

37.   There are great differences between the ideal and
the actual, between what people say and how they really behave.   One of the younger boys who lived in
the upper class section near the plaza in my town was
praised by his father for making some trowels with
my help.   But when we took them to the market to
sell them, he was stopped on the way and severely
beaten by his father for 'putting the family's name to
shame. '

(Note made in Seminar III)

38.   In the Church normal schools, boys and girls remain four to six years.   Some become nuns and
priests; others become schoolmasters.   We were subjected to strict monastic discipline.   This was presented to us as 'virtue' or 'self-discipline. '   It seemed
to me simply an enforced conformity.   Several of the
older students were obliged to vote, even though un-
der-age, for the Church-supported party in a national
election.

(Note made in Seminar I)

39.   To us the word empírico (empirical) conveys not
its scientific meaning of 'knowledge of reality acquired
through systematic observations. '   Here, they use it
in its 17th century, Church-inspired, Spanish meaning of quackery, charlatanry, imposture.

(Note made in Seminar I)

40.   The Bishop asked me if I felt the solution of the
apparent contradiction between the Church and science
was a conscious separation of the two worlds.   I said
I could not answer.   I replied instead: 'Experience
shows that the clergy can play an important part in
directing social and economic progress if they recognize this fact and also if they receive help and en-
couragement in secular fields.   This is all I ask:
That I be permitted to announce a "self-help campaign" calling on the men of the city's abandoned areas to work for their own betterment. '   'More of your
novelería, ' the Bishop muttered.

(Note made in Seminar I)

41.   He said that as a student he earned a modest livelihood carrying papers for a small fee in a shabby
leather case from downtown office to downtown office.
He would wait endlessly in dark splintery offices of

lawyers and bureaucrats for the necessary stamped
approval, meanwhile reading from one or another law
text which he carried with him. Sometimes, a conversation like this would ensue when he entered an office and asked the secretary: 'Is "Y" in?' 'No,' she
would reply. 'Do you know where he has gone?'
'No,' she answered. 'Do you know when he will be
back?' 'No,' she said. The student would sit for a
few minutes and then something occurred to him.
'Does "Y" work here?' he asked. 'No,' the secretary
said. 'His office is down the hall.' Students shared
much in common, notably a deep psychic need to
throw bricks at the existing order.

(Note made in Seminar IV)

E. Depicting Characteristics of and Political Practices in
Urban Zones, Especially Those Aimed at Winning Votes
or Thwarting the Opposition

42.   The patrón visited the caciques of each of the
barrios. More or less spontaneously, these jefecillos
placed at the disposition of the councilman the votes
of their friends, relatives, compadres and all adult
members of each individual's family. The barriada
leaders did not join in political parties. They pre-
ferred that candidates 'dispute for the blocs of votes
before very delicate and often unspoken alternatives.'
The caciques' main weapon, it appeared, besides the
solidarity of the primary group was the threat of
leaving the politicians at the mercy of the indifference
and apathy of the slum dwellers. They showed no
awareness of ideological differences among the country's political parties. The cacique viewed politics
as a game to give votes to him who offers the most
services and concrete advantages.

(Note made in Seminar I)

43.   These slum neighborhoods lack every kind of civic
convenience: water, sewage, transport, schools,
churches. Once a day, the city sends in a water
truck to supply household needs. In many visits, I
am always struck by their utterly abandoned look.
Yet, these very suburbs were the ones that elected
the political leaders of the city and, to a large extent,
of the country in the last election. Their electoral
strength is enormous. Of 200,000 slum dwellers,

over 100,000 met requirements and had the vote.   Only in recent elections have political parties begun to
discover the considerable political capital that these
forlorn masses of men and women represent.

(Note made in Seminar I)

44.   President Belaunde, when a youthful forty-eight and
an engineer without political experience, won a seat
in the Congress four years before reaching the Presidency.   His success was due to a government blun-
der and his ability to take advantage of it.   One of
his early meetings was held in front of the church on
the Plaza de la Independencia.   As his harangue rose
to fiery pitch, up rolled an army fire truck.   It
doused Belaúnde and the crowd with water.   The next
day, the newspaper carried a picture: a valiant Belaunde Presidential aspirant suffering indignities at
the hand of the dictator Odria.   After that, Belaunde
never lacked a crowd and listeners.

(Report of a published account
noted in Seminar VI)

45.   His work in directing the Christian Father's Movement brought him in daily contact with the misery of
the hillside slums.   What struck him most was the
tremendous apathy of the men there.   This marginal
population flowed in at such a rate from the countryside that it more than doubled the city's population in
ten years.   The growth occurred not through organized invasions, but almost spontaneously.   Each dwelling, however crowded, was always willing to absorb
the new arrivals--"los allegados" as they were called.
In addition to the permanent population, there were
the "monudos," the temporary residents of the slums
who came from the hills nearby and returned there
when work gave out in city construction jobs.

(Note made in Seminar I)

46.   A main task of the Church should consist in civi-
lizing these savage, dispairing human masses in the
urban slums.   But how to get the Church hierarchy
to accept this point of view?   The older generation of
Church leaders seems too interested in maintaining
the Church's connections with political power, derived
from the colonial past.   'These ties only prejudice its
spiritual mission and the part it could play in the pro-
motion of basic reforms.   The Church should criticize

governments when they failed to supply urgent human
wants, not enter into a "conspiracy of silence" with
the politicians.'
(Note made in Seminar I)

47.   The old theater was packed an hour before the
scheduled rally.   Situated midway between a maze of
street markets at the edge of town and a recently
created 'suburban zone,' the building had often been
used for political meetings.   No sooner had the program begun when it was broken up by police using
tear gas bombs.
(Notes made in Seminar III)

F.   Indications of Rejection of Democratic Beliefs and Elec-
toral Practices, both because Local Aristocrats Win the
Majority of Rural Votes Thanks to Their Following and
because Political Parties Constantly Make Deals with
These Economically and Politically Powerful Individuals,
Frustrating the Popular Will

48.   Anyone can run for any number of offices.   People
don't really know whom they are voting for.   The
system is a perfect way for party leaders to protect
themselves.   They can run in any number of Provinces, being reasonably sure to win in at least one.
It is harder for an outsider to crash the system, because he has got to provide for his own organization,
his own lists, and pay for printing his own ballots.
(Notes made in Seminar I)

49.   The vote is a way of showing your solidarity with
the directing class.   In our society, any person who
rises depends on another person and not on objective
and impersonal requirements that would assure him
occupational stability.   Any rise depends fundamentally
on conformity with respect to the directing class.
Elections are carried out like this one by centralized
political directorates, acting through the 'gamonales.'
Electoral fraud and economic, religious and social
pressures seek to support the existing structures.
(Notes made in Seminar I)

50.   The leading political party is really two parties.
One wing looks elderly.   Its leaders, although not all
old, have all been prominent for a long time.   They

would rather be thought of as rich men performing duties to which their station in life has called them.
They are politicians, nonetheless. Their style may
be seignorial in public, but their power comes from
raking together the dying embers of the traditional loyalties of Peru's elite. They can never hope for popularity outside the party, but they control it inside.
You only have to talk with any of them for a few minutes before they state their fear of a total revolution.

The other wing might be called the new nationalists.
They believe our government style has long since
passed out of existence among modern nations. Their
sympathies are with those of a government like Mexico's which decisively abandoned the feudalistic system
three decades ago, along with the economic and social
institutions which supported it.
                              (Notes made in Seminars I and
                              IV)

51.   The traditional way is for agreement always to be
reached by a show of power. Political groups appeal
to the students to take action and to hold demonstrations in order to give them a basis for carrying out
their policies. This pattern of operation reflects the
very texture of our societies, where the individual is
expected to use authority, in whatever form it is
available to him, to achieve his immediate ends.
                              (Notes made in Seminar I)

G. Indications of Bureaucratic Practices Frustrating the Designs of Reform-Minded Political Leaders

52.   Of all the advantages to be thus acquired, government jobs are the most prized. He noted the rules
for this important aspect of local politics:
--The public service is the purely personal prerogative of the patrón.
--In his exercise of power, the patrón is guided and
  controlled by established traditional norms.
--The way one performs his administrative duties is
  left to the individual tastes of each functionary.

Elections become, as a consequence of these deeply rooted attitudes, mainly a scramble for public
posts, with the newcomer turning out the old crowd,

at districtal, provincial and national levels.

(Notes made in Seminar I)

53.   Not one of the persons sitting on the council, myself included, is a technician, professionally qualified
to deal with the matters we discuss.   No one knows
how to build a road, or locate a viaduct, or read a
map, or fix the boundaries of a property, or run a
classroom.   Seven of the members are lawyers, four
are licenciados in philosophy.   More than half are
permanent 'interministerial committee' sitters for
their respective departments.   I sit on three of these
committees and I see the same faces on each one.
We are obliged to make speeches on matters we know
nothing about in order to pass the time.

(Note made in Seminar III)

54.   In the months that followed, the Mayor through his
visits to the capital nursed his Memorial through the
congested bureaucratic world.   From the Interior Ministry it went to the Treasury and Labor Ministries.
It remained for two months in these.   The Ministry
of Works, the Government Development Bank and the
Regional Development Committee had to pass on the
scheme.   In most of these Ministries, it has been
said, 'the Minister's secretary is his brother-in-law
and the porter is a third cousin of his wife. '   All
dealings with people are personalized either by family
or friendship affiliations.   'In a Ministry, you go first
to a relative whatever his rank, if you have one.   If
he is unable to expedite your problem personally, he
will know who can; in default of a relative a close
friend will do. '   This approach to the Ministry made
a theoretically impersonal organization into something
comprehensible for it was one's cousin or friend who
got things done.   Confusion, inefficiency and a rarely
'objective' civil servant also resulted, but this was
part of the bureaucratic system.

(Note made in Seminar IV)

55.   This understaffed Department of Audits is the target of requests and petitions from all over the land.
Senators and Deputies bombard it with urgent appeals,
reflecting the situation in many provinces and muni-
cipios.   The Government approves or rejects these
according to the degree of loyalty of the deputy or
representative, his personal simpatía, or, it seemed,

depending on the eloquent and flowery language of the petition. A well-reasoned, logical argument backed by facts has much less change than one couched in adulatory, wheedling terms.

(Note made in Seminar III)

Appendix III

A Note on Methodology

The uses of observed regularities in political behavior are numerous, both for the political practitioner as well as the academic student of politics. Regularities, once verified, have high predictive value. There has been much specialized literature purporting to explain Latin American politics. Its weakness is that the works are over generalized, lacking in specific data on political processes in particular countries. They rarely deal with the day-to-day, real world of politicians, nor in any systematic way with behavior patterns, but instead concentrate on historical events, formal procedures and surface aspects of local institutions.

To overcome this lack of specificity, I concentrate on one "context, " the Peruvian polity, and within it the landed elite. My desire has been to throw light on intra-cultural, informal political behavior, particularly on patterns of political action insofar as these are discernible. Presented as a series of tentative conclusions, these "rules of the game" seek to throw light on political behavior within a system of elite politics. I single out two kinds of political acts for intensive treatment to see what they reveal: (1) the choosing of Cabinet members by Presidents Manuel Prado and Fernando Belaúnde, Peru's two most recent civilian Presidents; (2) the actions of the large landholders vis-à-vis pressures for agrarian reform during the period 1960-1965. I ask how were the landed proprietors as a class in the country involved in these events?

Empirical evidence was drawn from a number of life histories supplied by participants, mostly Peruvians, in a series of six seminars which took place in the U.S. and Peru in 1964-1967. Primary data sources include observations and notes made during those seminars, plus interviews and field observations carried out in the course of seven short trips to Peru while the seminar series was in progress. Lasting from three days to three weeks, these visits permitted me to travel on three occasions through interior regions

185

to conduct interviews with Peruvians conversant with political
life in that country. Throughout the research effort, I delved
deeper into the literature in Spanish and English in the belief
that the results of the endeavor would prove of interest to
practitioners and students of politics alike.

Method and Research Design

My object has been to study political behavior in Peru.
The way I chose to do this was to look at the attitudes but
more particularly the political behavior of the landholding upper class. This is the element in Peruvian society that
largely determines the "rules of the game." The remarkable
political power shown by landowners in Latin America has
long been noted by observers. The equally noteworthy survival capacity of the landed elite figures in writings by natives and foreigners alike. My research thus aims to cast
light on the tactics of elite rule by which upper class dominance has been maintained. My method called for a careful
look through the literature for evidence of these tactics coupled with a search for psychological regularities, i. e., recurring value orientations, among a cross-section of young
elite members. Starting in 1964, systematic recording of
data supplied by participants in the series of seminars was
begun. The seminars concentrated on three major institutions
in Latin American society: the large landed estate (the hacienda), the system of local government (the municipio), and
the family, especially in rural areas (the familia). Of the
115 participants, sixty-seven were Peruvian; all but twenty-
four of the remainder were nationals of other Andean Zone
countries sharing common historical and cultural characteristics with Peru.[1] In order to take part, individuals had to
be college graduates or have the equivalent in educational
background. Such students of Peru as David Chaplin and William F. Whyte support the view that meeting a high educational requirement is presumptive evidence of closeness to
the elite.[2] Only four out of every 10,000 Latin Americans
manage to graduate from a university. Wealth is largely
concentrated in the hands of the landowning and commercial
classes in these predominantly agricultural countries. It is
thus possible to conclude that most of these individuals had
close ties to the landowning sector.

Difficulties of carrying on social science research in
Peru limited the on-the-spot effort largely to interviewing
former seminar participants who were aware of my research

interests. It was one best adapted to the political reality of
this country's tenuously democratic system, where memories
of military take-overs and subsequent repressions are strong.
A critical proposition or postulate guiding much of the research is the statement of Nathan Leites that culturally typical acts are related to the past life experiences of those
who perform them. Among political scientists, Robert Lane
dwells on how parental behavior conditions children's political attitudes. He cites that if children adopt a certain reaction in emotionally important, usually family situations,
then they are apt later on to adopt a similar reaction in
structurally analagous political situations. [3] Intimate, "psychological" childhood events do later determine adult behavior.
It is not argued that these experiences determine such behavior to the exclusion of various wider influences, such as economic, political, social and psychological aspects of the adult
environment. It is simply presumed that any adult act is
related to the mental predispositions of the individual which
in turn are connected with his previous experiences from
birth to the present time.

    Initial impetus for the entire effort came from Harold
D. Lasswell. This political scientist writes that "all men
loosen the bonds of the culture into which they are born by
becoming aware of it."[4] Participants in the seminars were
asked to look critically at the institutions of the landed estate, local government and the family. Each had to write
a "case study" of his experience with some aspect, however
modest, of one of the institutions prior to taking part in a
seminar. Later, as a member of a study group, the participant did field-trip, on-the-spot interviewing of Americans or
nationals of his own country who were knowledgeable about
the institution.

    These gatherings were useful as a basis for drawing
some conclusions about elite political socialization and behavior because they forced the participants to, in Lasswell's
phrase, "equip themselves with identity cards." Am I to
conceive of myself as a conservative or a radical? A Castro-
ite or a socialist? A traditional Latin American or a cosmopolitan, scientifically-minded modernist? The seminars
tended to bring out the "traditional self" within each Latin
American participant, in the course of extended discussions
of problems and social reality in their homelands. The
question each had to answer was: Who am I? Or rather,
as whom shall I identify myself? What the seminars gave
that could not be had from published sources was "subjective

data" (experiences and expectations, for example) to supplement information about political practices and the system of rule in the country.

Nature of Evidence Being Marshalled

In seeking to cast light on the political behavior of Peru's landed elite, I chose, in part, to explore the "received ideas" or habits of thought that are instilled into the members of the elite.   Veblen writes in his Theory of the Leisure Class:[5]

> Institutions are, in substance, prevalent habits of thought with respect to particular relations and particular functions of the individual and of the community; and the scheme of life, which is made up of the aggregate of institutions in force at a given time . . . may be broadly characterized as a prevalent spiritual attitude or a prevalent theory of life. . . . This spiritual attitude or theory of life is in the last analysis reducible to terms of a prevalent type of character.

To Veblen, institutions exist as "habits of thought." In Latin America, for example, these habits reflect a feudal-religious theory of life.   Readjusting an accepted institution is initially, and perhaps primarily, a mental effort.   Veblen called the process of institutional change "a more or less protracted and laborious effort to find and keep one's bearings under the altered circumstances."   The characteristic attitude of the elite or "leisure class" is one of "substantial and consistent resistance to innovation," a view borne out here.   Applying these ideas to the task at hand meant giving first priority to getting at what was in the minds of our modest and highly imperfect sample of the Peruvian "leisure class."   How did they view "what is"?   A primary reliance was to be on eliciting their life histories.   This was done by biographic questionnaires and by personal interview.   Significantly, insights were gained from their own words as voiced during the discussions or in their papers.   These latter were responses to the request that each participant write about his intimate memories of or experiences with one of the three institutions mentioned above, the hacienda, the family, and local government.   He was asked to recall incidents or typical acts of adults within each.

How (Cleveland and New York: World Publishing Co.,
Meridian Books, 1958), p. 194.

5.   Thorstein Veblen, The Theory of the Leisure Class (London: Allen & Unwin, 1924), p. 190.

Selected Annotated Bibliography

General

Works which form a basis for a conception of Latin A-
merican social history and political behavior patterns, within
the larger field of comparative politics, include the following:

Adams, Mildred (ed.). Latin America: Evolution or Explo-
    sion? New York: Dodd, Mead and Co., 1963.
    The authors, leading citizens of the Americas, seek
    to define the critical tensions within and among
    their nations, but produce few new insights.

Adams, Richard N. Social Change in Latin America Today.
    New York: Random House, 1960.
    First-rate analyses of forces reshaping the socie-
    ties of Latin America. The chapter on Peru is
    limited, however, to an account of the Vicos ex-
    periment principally.

Almond, Gabriel and Coleman, James (eds.). The Politics
    of Developing Areas. Princeton: Princeton University
    Press, 1960.
    George Blanksten's chapter on the "Politics of Lat-
    in America" treats parties and interest groups
    (including landowners as an "associational interest
    group") within a broad panorama of how political
    functions are performed and how the process of
    political change operates. The result is excessive-
    ly general.

Anderson, Charles W. "Political Factors in Latin American
    Economic Development," Journal of International Af-
    fairs, Vol. 20, 1966.
    Analyzing the political obstacles to economic devel-
    opment, Anderson cites discrepancies between for-
    mal intentions and concrete realization, rigidities
    inherent in existing institutions (the class system,
    the latifundia), conventions of Hispanic society

which delimit a narrow legitimate role for government and excessive expectations of governments which lack policy instruments appropriate to advanced Western society.

Apter, David E. The Politics of Modernization. Chicago: Chicago University Press, 1965.
   Dealing mainly with Africa, the work contains many valuable conceptual guidelines, but has little relevance to Latin America.

Cosío Villegas, Daniel. American Extremes. Austin: University of Texas Press, 1964.
   A series of essays by an original mind, the book provides extraordinarily useful perceptions of the region's internal problems, among them the immense psychological gulf between rich and poor.

D'Antonio, William V. and Pike, Frederick B. (eds.). Religion, Revolution and Reform. South Bend: University of Notre Dame Press, 1965.
   This collection of essays contains sharp criticisms of the existing order while presenting viewpoints of liberal Catholic Churchmen.

Deutsch, Karl W. "Social Mobilization and Political Development," American Political Science Review, LX (September, 1961).
   This important article presented theoretical guidelines for this research. Like Lasswell, he urges study of "institutions, roles, and ways of acting, of experiences and expectations, and finally of personal memories, habits and needs."

DeVries, Egbert and Echavarría, Jose Medina (eds.). Social Aspects of Economic Development in Latin America, Vol. I. Paris: UNESCO 1963.
   The book offers viewpoints from economics, sociology and political science as to the prerequisites and strategy for rapid economic development. Stress is laid on education and research rather than political changes. (Vol. II, edited by Echavarría, José Medina and Higgins, Benjamin, treats these problems from an economist's and sociologist's viewpoint alone.)

Form, William H. and Blum, Albert A. (eds.). Industrial

Relations and Social Change in Latin America.
Gainesville: University of Florida Press, 1965.
Useful in singling out as the prime political actors
these groups: the politicians, the clergy, the landowners, the industrialists, the effective voters,
the intellectuals and university students. This book
asks where the trade unions fit in the picture.

Gerassi, John. The Great Fear: The Reconquest of Latin
America by Latin Americans. New York, 1963.
Gerassi adopts the point of view of Latin American
intellectuals, putting much blame on the U. S. for
Latin America's ills.

Germani, Gino. Política y Sociedad en una Epoca de Transi-
ción. Buenos Aires, Editorial Paidos, 1963.
The author seeks to present the sociological data
available on changes underway, at the same time
asking what their political implications will be,
giving special attention to the landowners as a social class.

Gordon, Wendell C. The Political Economy of Latin America. New York: Columbia University Press, 1965.
Gordon surveys the region's economic institutions
and their political consequences. His main conclusion is "the tendency of the privileged and their
cohorts to resist fanatically any minor abatement
of their privileges is a heavy hand stifling the
progress of Latin America. "

Heath, Dwight B. and Adams, Richard N. (eds.). Contem-
porary Cultures and Societies of Latin America. New
York, 1965.
Although compiled by anthropologists, the book contains valuable information on political matters, especially in its discussion of Indian populations in
Peru and Bolivia.

Hirschman, Albert O. Journeys Toward Progress: Studies
of Economic Policy-Making in Latin America. New
York: Twentieth Century Fund, 1963.
Concerned with the behavior of decision-makers in
tackling political problems, the author sets aside
"prerequisites" of development and says that a
country must develop because of and in spite of
what it is. He stresses that subjective factors
(understanding, motivation) are crucial.

197

_____ (ed.). Latin American Issues; Essay and Comments. New York: Twentieth Century Fund, 1961.
Seeking to throw light on the "Latin American Style," Hirschman and other authors range widely but too superficially over their themes.

Hoselitz, Bert F. and Moore, Wilbert E. (eds.). Industrialization and Society. Paris: Mouton, 1963.
Essays by George I. Blanksten and William J. Goode, among others, treat of the transference of political loyalties and family change in societies entering an industrialized stage of development.

Gomez, R. A. Government and Politics in Latin America. New York: Random House, 1963.
Among the many similar works on Latin America, Gomez is useful because of his effort to deal with actual behavior, such as political morality and tendencies toward violence.

Humphreys, Robert A. and Lynch, John. The Origins of the Latin American Revolution. New York, 1965.
Hispanic traits and cultural factors along with domestic and external influences are analyzed in this work.

Johnson, John J. (ed.). Continuity and Change in Latin America. Stanford: Stanford University Press, 1964.
Individual chapters treat political and social roles of various segments of the population, providing a commendable analysis of prospects for social change in the area.

_____. The Military and Society in Latin America. Stanford University Press, 1964.
Johnson presents the changing military establishment in a favorable light, showing it as imbibing democratic and modernizing tendencies in recent decades.

_____. Political Change in Latin America: The Emergence of the Middle Sector. Stanford, 1962.
The book "discovers" the middle sector as a new and potent force in political life, a thesis which is questioned by Claudio Veliz and others.

Kantor, Harry and Chang-Rodriguez, Eugenio. La América Latina de Hoy. New York: The Ronald Press, 1961.

198

A collection of speeches and essays commenting on a range of Latin American problems, valuable because of its presenting the Latin American view.

Kling, Merle. "Toward a Theory of Power and Political Instability in Latin America," Western Political Quarterly, Vol. 9 (March, 1956).
    Kling argues that political office offers a dynamic opportunity for the upwardly-mobile to acquire riches and power and that this alone perpetuates chronic political instability.

Lambert, Jacques. Latin American Social Structures and Political Institutions. Berkeley: University of California Press, 1967.
    An extraordinarily valuable work that delves deeply into the landed elite's strategic position in Latin American politics.

Lasswell, Harold D. The Political Writings of Harold D. Lasswell. New York: The Free Press, 1951.
    The basic compilation of Lasswell's many writings.

Leites, Nathan. "Psycho-Cultural Hypotheses About Political Acts," World Politics, Vol. 1 (October, 1948).
    Essential theory for this research effort was derived from this article.

Lerner, Daniel. The Passing of Traditional Society. New York: The Free Press, 1958.
    In what has become a standard work, Lerner dwelt on psychological changes induced by the modernization process, focussing on the Middle East.

Lipset, Seymour Martin. Political Man: The Social Bases of Politics. New York: Doubleday, 1960.
    Prominent in both sociology and political science, Lipset seeks to identify the conditions that sustain democracy, laying stress on the relationship between economic development and democratic values.

Mecham, J. Lloyd. Church and State in Latin America, A History of Politico-Ecclesiastical Relations. Chapel Hill: University of North Carolina Press, 1966.
    A classic inquiry into the historical evolution of politico-ecclesiastical relationships, with emphasis on the Church's strong political position.

199

Needler, Martin C. (ed.). Political Systems of Latin America. New York: D. Van Nostrand Co., Inc., 1964. Up-to-date but generally weak, especially the chapter by R. A. Gomez on Peru.

Pearse, Andrew. "Agrarian Change Trends in Latin America," Latin American Research Review, Vol. 1, No. 3 (1966).
A highly useful account of the social and political factors explaining the persistence of latifundios in Latin America as well as their present-day significance.

Picón-Salas, Mariano. A Cultural History of Spanish America. Berkeley: University of California Press, 1965. This work presents the "inner history" of Spanish America, offering a synthesis of the region's cultural heritage from Spain.

Pike, Frederick B. (ed.). The Conflict Between Church and State in Latin America. New York: Alfred A. Knopf, 1964.
A specialist on Peru, Pike has compiled a valuable historical record of Church-State relations.

Shils, Edward. "The Intellectuals and the Political Development of the New States," Political Change in Underdeveloped Countries. Edited by J. Kautsky. New York: John Wiley, 1962.
Although it makes little reference to Latin America, the Kautsky volume contains much of value. Shils' article demonstrates the critical role of the Latin American intellectuals in producing movement within their generally static societies.

Silvert, Kalman H. The Conflict Society: Reaction and Revolution in Latin America. New York, 1966.
This collection of essays presents the author's reflections on the change from a medieval traditionalism to a modern industrial society, its special focus being the Latin American's continued highly traditional behavior patterns.

Stark, Harry. Social and Economic Frontiers in Latin America. Dubuque, Iowa: William C. Brown Co., 1961. While emphasizing labor and social security programs, this work is valuable in that it portrays

200

Latin American family concepts, showing what can
be done to improve the lot of the working class
family particularly.

Tannenbaum, Frank. "Toward an Appreciation of Latin America," The United States and Latin America. Columbia
University, New York: The American Assembly, 1956.
A summary statement of Tannenbaum's views about
the internal dynamics of Latin American society,
drawn largely from his studies of the Mexican revolution.

Torres Restrepo, Camilo. Camilo Torres, por el padre
Camilo Torres Restrepo (1956-1966), Sondeos No. 5.
Cuernavaca: Centro Intercultural de Documentación,
1966.
A passionate and original mind, Torres offers sociological interpretations of the Church's position
as a reactionary ally of the dominant upper class.

Veliz, Claudio (ed.). Obstacles to Change in Latin America.
London: Oxford University Press, 1965.
The product of a London conference on social
change, the authors' papers range widely and are
of variable quality, but they single out the forces
impeding the transformation of Latin American society.

_____. "Obstacles to Reform in Latin America," The World
Today, XIX (January, 1963).
Veliz examines populist movements, anti-American-
ism and urban middle class. He finds the latter
conservative and sharing the values of the upper
class. He places his hopes in the peasants and
workers as forces that will aid the reform-minded
intelligentsia to bring about fundamental social
change.

Ward, Robert E. (ed.). Studying Politics Abroad. Boston:
Little, Brown, 1964.
A primer of techniques for political scientists, but
of limited application.

Zea, Leopoldo. The Latin American Mind. Translated by
James H. Abbott and Lowell Dunham. Norman: Uni-
versity of Oklahoma Press, 1963.
A highly significant book, Zea's work dwells mainly

on 19th century idealogies such as Positivism and Romanticism, summarizing the views of many intellectuals.

Zeitlin, Maurice and Petras, James (eds.). Latin America: Reform or Revolution? Greenwich: Fawcett, 1968.
Leftist viewpoints are presented in a series of essays that argue reform is possible only through conflict. The volume has special relevance to Peru.

Elites

Included in this section are methodological guides for the study of elites as well as works dealing with ways of analyzing developing political systems, a subject of growing importance within the field of comparative politics.

Adams, Richard N. "Power and Power Domains," The Second Sowing: Power and Secondary Development in Latin America. San Francisco: Howard Chandler, 1967.
Drawing on his researches in Guatemala, Adams explores power systems like the military or the Church which are able to act independently.

Almond, Gabriel and Verba, Sidney. The Civil Culture. Princeton: Princeton University Press, 1963.
This study of attitudes in five countries (Britain, U.S., Germany, Italy and Mexico) applies modern techniques of research, principally use of survey data, to ascertain political beliefs, aspirations and actual participation in politics.

Banfield, Edward C. The Moral Basis of a Backward Society. Glencoe, Illinois: The Free Press, 1958.
Examines the ethos of a peasant community in Italy, offering "amoral familism" as its hypothesis to explain human behavior there. The book contains many methodological hints as to how to conduct psychological studies in a backward peasant society.

Brookings Institution. Development of the Emerging Countries: An Agenda for Research. Washington, D.C.: Brookings Institution, 1962.

The volume sets forth a range of data required if political and social development are to proceed in tandem with economic growth.

Beck, Carl and McKechine, J. Thomas. Political Elites: a select computerized bibliography. Cambridge, Mass.: M. I. T. Press, 1968.
An exhaustive survey of available studies, only few of which deal with Latin America.

Bottomore, T. B. Elites and Society. New York: Basic Books, 1964.
Bottomore's concise work looks at the function of elites in present-day democratic society. It offers few guides for the study of elites in primitive or developing countries.

Dahl, Robert A. "A Critique of the Ruling Elite Model," American Political Science Review, Vol. 52 (June, 1958).
As an operational test of the existence of rule by a small group, Dahl proposes the critical study of outcomes (i. e., does the "ruling elite" get its way) in a number of concrete cases.

DeGrazia, Alfred. Elite Analysis, a manual of methods of discovering the leadership of a society and its vulnerabilities to propaganda. Stanford: Institute of Journalistic Studies, Stanford University, 1955.
A particularly useful book which relies heavily on content analysis and use of sample survey data, methods of limited applicability, however, in the study of ruling elements in more primitive societies.

Eulau, Heinz. "The Maddening Methods of H. D. Lasswell," The Journal of Politics. Vol. 30, No. 1 (February, 1968).
In the search for regularities and uniformities in political behavior, Lasswell's suggestions have been adopted by leading scholars like Heinz Eulau, Ralph Braibanti and Morton Kaplan. Eulau, in this brief article, explains Lasswell's stress on moving research from concern over individual attributes to macrocosmic events or aggregates, such as behavior of an electoral constituency or a social class.

Goodrich, Daniel. Sons of the Establishment: Elite Youth

in Panama and Costa Rica. Chicago: Rand McNally, 1966.
>One of the few studies on the upper class in Latin America. Considerable use is made of interview data.

Hagen, Everett. On the Theory of Social Change. New York: Dorsey, 1962.
>Psychological factors are given first place as motors of economic development in this pathbreaking study.

Hyman, Herbert. Political Socialization. Glencoe, Illinois: The Free Press, 1959.
>The author treats political behavior as the product of learning and socialization processes.

Lasswell, Harold D., Lerner, D. and Rothwell, C. E. The Comparative Study of Elites. Stanford, Calif.: Stanford University Press, 1952.
>A short work that introduced a series of studies of elites and counter-elites. Valuable for methodological guides.

Lasswell, Harold D. and Soreno, Renzo (eds.). The Analysis of Political Behavior, An Empirical Approach. London: Routledge and Kegan Paul, 1948.
>A basic work, providing many suggestions for empirical study of both individual and aggregate behavior.

Lasswell, Harold D. and Lerner, Daniel (eds.). World Revolutionary Elites. Cambridge: M. I. T. Press, 1966.
>This volume pulls together accounts of the elite studies that have flowed from the 1952 series initiated at the Hoover Institute of War and Peace Studies. Valuable guides on the conduct of elite studies appear throughout the book.

Lipset, Seymour M. and Solari, Aldo (eds.). Elites in Latin America. London and New York: Oxford University Press, 1967.
>A number of authors present accounts of functional elites, ranging from the military and religious elites to the businessmen and student elites. A sizeable portion of the book is devoted to education of the newer elite groups. There is no treatment

of the landholding segment as a functional elite, constituting a serious weakness in an otherwise first-rate volume.

Long, Norton. "Aristotle and Local Government," Social Research. Vol. 24 (Autumn, 1957).
Aristotle's Politics, although believed by many to be out-of-date, contains essential knowledge for anyone studying actual divisions of power, wealth and prestige within different polities, as Long lucidly demonstrates.

Machiavelli, Niccolo. The Prince and the Discourses. New York: Modern Library, 1950.
Another classic, the work is a masterly handbook for the ruling class of a small principality, presenting many "rules of the game" for their guidance.

Moore, Barrington, Jr. Social Origins of Dictatorship and Democracy: Lord and Peasant in the Making of the Modern World. Boston: Beacon Press, 1966.
Moore examines the political role of the landed upper class and of the peasantry in the early stages of industrialization in an effort to determine the roots from which democracy and modern dictatorship have sprung. The book emphasizes the vital need for penetrating studies of happenings in rural zones of feudal or semi-feudal societies.

Mosca, Gaetano. The Ruling Class. Edited and revised by Arthur Livingston. New York: McGraw Hill, 1939.
A work from which most modern studies of governing elites have flowed, although without the methodological refinements of present-day elite studies.

Pareto, Vilfredo. The Mind and Society. Edited by Arthur Livingston. New York: Harcourt Brace and Co., 1935. (For an excellent short version of Pareto, see L. J. Henderson's Pareto's General Sociology.)
Pareto's work is still a classic and well worth the effort to read in its complete version.

Taylor, C. L. (ed.). Aggregate Data Analysis: Political and Social Indicators in Cross-National Research. Paris: Mouton and Co., 1968.
A compilation of papers interpreting the Yale World Data Analysis Program, which is an effort to pre-

sent "quantitative history" through publication of
statistical data on some 133 nations, the Program
drawing on Karl W. Deutsch's theory of social
mobilization. This book is useful for pointing out
limitations and problems in this effort.

Peru

Out of the wealth of material, only those having relevance to the theme of this study are included in the listing
below. The volumes cast light on why Peru has had neither
a revolution from above nor a peasant revolution from below.

Alegría, Ciro. El Mundo es ancho y ajeno. Minerva, Mexico, 1952.
The story of an Indian community despoiled by ad-
joining landowners, Alegría's novel presents an
accurate picture of Peru's unresolved central problem.

Austin, Allan. Estudio Sobre El Gobierno Municipal Del Perú. Lima: Institute of Public Administration (Oficina
Nacional de Racionalización y Capacitacion de la Administración Publica), November, 1964.
The most up-to-date study of municipal government,
but one that suffers from over-reliance on the reality of formal structure.

Basadre, Jorge. Historia de la republica del Perú, 10 Vols.
Lima, 1961-1964.
Like Luis Alberto Sanchez and others, Basadre is
a prolific writer on Peru. This is the standard
historical reference work on the country. Basadre
holds that a "civil war" has long been waged by
writers of Peruvian history, centering on indigenismo versus hispanismo.

Baston, Leonidas Castro. Geohistoria de Perú: ensayo
economico-político-social. Lima, 1962.
Baston's work presents in literary style his view
of Peru's past growth.

Bazan, Mario F. El proceso economico del Perú. Buenos
Aires, 1954.
Mainly a study of Peru's export economy, with its
reliance on sugar, cotton and minerals.

Belaúnde, Victor Andres.   Meditaciones Peruanas.   Lima:
    Talleres Gráficos Villanueva, 1963.
        A collection of essays.   In this work Belaúnde
        traces Peru's ills to psychological and spiritual
        traits.   A highly suggestive work.

Belaúnde-Terry, Fernando.   Peru's Own Conquest.   Lima:
    American Studies Press, 1965.
        The recently deposed President of Peru offered
        these provacative reflections on Peru's deep-rooted
        problems and his plans for dealing with them.   He
        stressed recapturing the communal institutions and
        spirit of the ancient Incas.

Beltran, Pedro G.   "Foreign Loans and Politics in Latin
    America, " Foreign Affairs (January, 1956).
        A leading publisher and politician, Beltran reviews
        the place of foreign capital in his own country's
        and Latin America's development.

Benavides Correa, Alfonso.   Interpelación a la cancillería.
    Lima, 1958.
        Useful for its account of events during the second
        Prado administration.

Bourricaud, Francois.   Changement a Puno, etude de socio-
    logie andine.   Paris, 1962.
        A short work dealing with conditions in haciendas
        near Puno.

Bravo, Jorge Bresani.   "Mito y Realidad de la Oligarquía
    Peruano, " Revista de Sociología, Vol. 3, No. 4.
    University of San Marcos, 1966.
        One of the outstanding present-day critics of Peru's
        backward social system, Bravo Bresani analyzes
        the nature of the "oligarchy" (which he identifies
        largely as large commercial interests and their
        "intermediaries").   He presents a reasoned view
        of the path toward "economic independence" along
        which Peru should move.

Bustamante Rivero, José Luis.   Tres años de lucha por la
    democracia en el Perú.   Buenos Aires, 1949.
        Justification for his actions as President during
        1945-48.   Bustamante blames the Apristas for many
        ills confronting Peru.

Chang-Rodríguez, Eugenio. La literatura política de González Prada, Mariátegui and Haya de la Torre. Mexico: Ediciones de Andrea, 1957.
Much commentary on the impact of these thinkers
is interspersed with passages from their works.

Chaplin, David. "Peruvian Social Mobility: Revolutionary
and Development Potential," Journal of Inter-American Studies, Vol. X, No. 4 (October, 1968).
A sociologist's view of the permeability of the upper class to upward moving individuals: good especially for its commentary of what this process
means.

_____. "Peru's Postponed Revolution," World Politics, XX
(April, 1968).
A sociologist analyzes Peru's failure to have a basic
social revolution. Like Bourricaud, he sees the
upper class as a monopolistic collection of "clans"
that is based on the neutralization of the middle
classes and "a shoveling aside" of the forgotten
lower classes. High elite fertility, a small but
significant infusion of foreign immigrants at the
top of the elite structure, extensive familial, commercial and political competition among elite members, a failure of the urban lower class to radi-
calize are among the factors emphasized by Chaplin.

Cohen, Alvin. "Societal Structure, Agrarian Reform and
Economic Development in Peru," Inter-American Economic Affairs, Vol. 18, No. 1 (Spring, 1964).
A study mainly of attempts at agrarian reform during the late 1950's.

Delgado, Luis Humberto. Nuevo Perú? Lima, 1945
This book is a critical essay showing the legacies
of the past that hold back the country's progress.

del Pomar, F. Cossío. Haya de la Torre, el indoamericano.
Mexico: D. F., Editorial America, 1939.
A prominent artist and art historian, Cossio del
Pomar has produced a highly readable biography of
the Aprista leader.

Dennis, Lawrence. "What Overthrew Leguía," New Republic,
LXIV (September 17, 1930).
Useful primarily for its account of President

Leguia's policies and how these were received within the Peruvian armed forces.

Dobyns, Henry F. The Social Matrix of Peruvian Indigenous Communities. Cornell University: Cornell Peru Project Monograph, Dept. of Anthropology, 1964.
A summary of Peruvian community studies containing good material on peasant attitudes and social relations. Reports also results of a mail questionnaire to heads of Indian communities.

Escobar, Gabriel. "La Cultura: Sistema de Valores," Lima, Plan Regional para el Desarrollo del Sur del Perú, Vol. XXII, PS/F/50, 1959.
One of several volumes compiled by the Southern Peru Regional Development Plan.

_____. Organizacion Social Y Cultural Del Sur Del Perú. Mexico D. F. Instituto Indigenista Interamericano, 1967.
A faculty member in Andean Seminars II and III, Escobar has produced a penetrating account of institutional factors and values in the south of Peru. His is one of the few books that deals with religious structure and its interrelationships with religious and economic factors. The picture painted is a grim one. A changed Church is his main hope.

González Prada, Manuel. Anarquía. Santiago de Chile: Ediciones Ercilla, 1936.

_____. Horas de Lucha, 2d ed. Callao: Tipografía Lux, 1929.

_____. Páginas Libres. New edition edited by Luis Alberto Sanchez. Lima, Editorial P. T. C. M., 1946.

_____. Pensamientos. Buenos Aires: Arco Iris, 1941.

The above are the most prominent of the works of this critic and thinker whose ideas have influenced succeeding generations. Apristas consider him the intellectual father of their movement. Gonzalez Prada laid stress on wrestling control of education from the Church as a prime means of molding a new Peru.

Hammel, Eugene A. Wealth, Authority and Prestige in the
Ica Valley. Peru. Albuquerque: University of New
Mexico Press, 1962.
Hammel examines the structural features of society
in a Peruvian coastal valley from Inca times to the
present day. A growing independence of basic social features and increasing opportunities for social
mobility characterize the most recent period, he
finds.

Haya de la Torre, Victor Raúl. El anti-imperialismo y el
Apra, 2d ed. Santiago de Chile: Ediciones Ercilla,
1936.
The basic theoretical work of this author in which
he sets forth the general principles of the Aprista
movement.

_____. Teoría y Táctica del Aprismo. Lima: Editorial
Cahuide, 1931.
Despite its title, this is a collection simply of
Haya de la Torre's writings from 1924 to 1930.

_____. Pensamiento Político de Haya de la Torre, Vol.
1. Lima, 1961.
A reissue of a number of Haya de la Torre's earlier works.

Juan, Jorge and de Ulloa, Antonio. Voyage to South America. New York, 1964. (This work was first published
in 1735.)
Recently reissued, the important work, commis-
sioned by the King of Spain, presents a highly critical view of conditions in the Spanish colonies in
the early 18th century.

Kantor, Harry. The Ideology and Program of the Peruvian
Aprista Movement. Berkeley: University of California
Press, 1953.
Kantor examines Aprista's domestic and international
programs along with the reasons for the movement's
hold on the Peruvian people. An interesting section (pp. 129-131) analyzes the methods by which
power is wielded in Peru. The Apristas have
sought for half a century, with little success, to
transform Peru into a living democracy rather than
the exploitative class state which they believe it to
be. Kantor sees control of the armed forces as
the key to power in Peru.

210

Lopez, Jacinto. La caida del gobierno constitucional en el
 Perú. New York: Carranza and Co., 1927.
  Although an old book, this work is useful in that
  it depicts the day-by-day power play that brought
  into being one of Peru's many dictatorships (that
  of Leguía in 1919-1920).

Lorentzen, Hector Chirinos. Perú: Al bienestar of el caos.
 Lima, 1965.
  A severe analysis of Peru's social ills is offered
  by a thirty year old engineer with remedies that
  lay stress on new attitudes in the public sector and
  among the economically powerful few.

Malpica, Carlos. Guerra a muerte al latifundio. Lima:
 Ediciones "Voz Rebelde," 1962.

_____. Los duenos del Perú. Lima: Fondo de Cultura
 Popular, 1965.
  A leftist deputy, Malpica presents a direct attack
  on the landed elite as the prime obstacle to the
  transformation which the country needs. The second volume is extracted from the first and lists
  the principal landowners with their individual holdings.

Mariátegui, José Carlos. Siete ensayos de interpretation de
 la realidad peruana, 2d ed. Lima: Editorial Libreria
 Peruana, 1934.
  Mariategui's was among the first voices favoring
  the integration of the Indian masses into Peruvian
  society. Present-day Peruvian leftists draw much
  of their inspiration from Mariátegui.

Metraux, Alfred. "The Social and Economic Structure of the
 Indian Communities of the Andean Region," International Labour Review (March, 1959).
  Metraux' work presents a stark picture of the conditions of the Indians, exploited by all elements
  above them in the Peruvian social structure.

Miro Quesada Laos, Carlos. Autopsía de los partidos poli-
 ticos. Lima, 1961.
  A scion of one of the leading families surveys Peruvian political history since the turn of the century. He finds the political parties ineffective cre-
  ations of single individuals.

Neira, Hugo. Cuzco: Tierra y Muerte. Lima: Populibros
    Peruanos, 1964.
        A collection of articles about the "guerrillas" and
        peasant invasions of the early 1960's.

Obregon, Anibal Quijano. "El Movimiento Campesino del
    Perú y Sus Lideres," América Latina, Ano 8, No. 4
    (October-December, 1965).
        A young sociologist, currently exiled from Peru in
        Chile, Anibal Quijano was a particularly able mem-
        ber of Andean Seminar I. This article, expanded
        and republished in Lipset and Solari's Elites in
        Latin America, depicts a rapid spread of organiza-
        tion among the rural masses, although little hard
        evidence is brought forward to bear out his con-
        clusions.

Owens, R. J. Peru. London: Oxford University Press,
    1963.
        After outlining Peru's historical development, the
        book describes current political, economic and so-
        cial events through the elections of 1963.

Payne, Arnold. The Peruvian Coup d'Etat of 1962: The
    Overthrow of Manuel Prado. Washington: Institute
    for the Comparative Study of Political Systems, Polit-
    ical Studies Series No. 5, 1968.
        One of a series of monographs of Latin American
        coups d'etat, this publication contains useful data
        on maneuvers preceding and following the 1962 mil-
        itary intervention.

Payne, James L. Labor and Politics in Peru: The System
    of Political Bargaining. New Haven: Yale University
    Press, 1965.
        Payne examines Peru's labor movement to learn
        its method of political bargaining which relies on
        threat of violence (i. e., strikes, riots or appeals
        for military intervention against the civilian govern-
        ment) as a means of getting its way in employer-
        employee conflicts. The book is informative and
        factual. Its utility lies in its presenting a study
        of the Peruvian labor movement and its position in
        the country's political life. Its scope is too lim-
        ited, e. g., it is based largely on interviews with
        a cross-section of labor leaders, to justify its sub-
        title as a study of the system of political bargain-
        ing.

Pike, Frederick B. A History of Republican Peru. London: Weidenfield and Nicolson, 1967. (Published by Praeger in 1967 as The Modern History of Peru.)

_____. "The Old and the New APRA in Peru: Myth and Reality," Inter-American Economic Affairs, Vol. 18, No. 2 (Autumn, 1964).

_____. "Peru and the Quest for Reform by Compromise," Inter-American Economic Affairs, Vol. 20, No. 4 (Spring, 1967).
> The two articles are essentially extracts from Pike's important volume on Peru. He sees many revolutionary groups, a number led by dissident elite members, trying to introduce reforms into the outdated institutions. Their early successes, he writes, were largely undone by the disruptive influence of Aprismo. A new reform momentum got underway with the election of Belaúnde Terry in 1962 which, to Pike, marked the advent of the Peruvian middle class as a power element in its own right. His theory of sweeping changes under-way led by a "moderate faction of former oligarch-ies" does not accord with the interpretation put for-ward in this dissertation. My view is essentially that the game of politics in Peru continues to be played by tested, and as yet unchanged, "rules."

Poblete Troncoso, Moises. La economía agraria de Amér-ica latina y el campesino. Santiago, 1957.
> Peru is treated only incidentally in this discussion of agrarian problems.

De la Puente, Luis. La reforma del agro peruano. Lima: Ediciones Ensayos Sociales, 1966.
> Arguing that semi-feudal regimes persist, the au-thor presents a project for an agrarian law far more stringent than that enacted in 1964.

Sanchez, Luis Albert. Haya de la Torre y el Apra. Santiago, 1955.
> A prolific writer on modern-day Peru, Sanchez presents here an updated version of his Raúl Haya de la Torre o el político (Santiago de Chile, Biblio-teca América, 1934), the best biography of the Aprista leader.

Steward, Julian H. (ed.). The Handbook of South American
    Indians. Washington, D.C.: Smithsonian Institution,
    1946-1950.
        Volume 2, The Andean Civilization, constitutes a
        classic work on Peru's past.

Stuart, Graham H. The Governmental System of Peru.
    Washington, D.C.: Carnegie Institution of Washington,
    1925.
        Outdated but still useful, Stuart's study of Peru's
        formal governmental structure reflects the 1920
        Constitution introduced by Augusto Leguía. This
        was replaced by the Constitution of 1933 which is
        still in force.

Stanger, F. M. "Church and State in Peru," HAHR, VII.
    Hispanic American Historical Review, 1927.
        This is one of the rare examinations of the Church's
        political role in Peru. Stanger foresaw a decline
        in its influence, but this has not occurred.

Szulc, Tad. Twilight of the Tyrants. New York: Henry
    Holt, 1959.
        The chapter in General Odría is particularly note-
        worthy.

Taylor, Milton C. "Problems of Development in Peru,"
    Journal of Inter-American Studies, Vol. IX, No. 1
    (1967).
        Feudal relationships and the human exploitation im-
        plicit in Peru's economic life receive censure by
        the writer.

Urbina, Alfredo. Los partidos y las crises del Apra. Lima,
    1956.
        Urbina retraces the internal development of Aprismo
        as well as its place in Peruvian politics.

_____. Nueva política nacional. Trujillo, Peru, 1962.
        Reforms more sweeping than those proposed by
        President Belaunde are set forth in this critical ex-
        amination of Peru's general backwardness.

Villanueva, Victor. El militarismo en el Peru. Lima:
    Empresa Gráfica T. Scheuch, 1962.
        The author, a former officer, justifies the military
        intervention of 1962 as a way to keep the Apristas

from power, but sees many dangers from these coups d'etat. (He lists thirty-two military insurrections between 1914 and 1962 in Peru of which only seven, however, achieved Presidential power). Villanueva links the military closely to the oligarchy, viewing the Army as the means adopted by it to keep the lower classes down. Military coups tend to take on their own momentum, he finds.

INDEX

218